TWO OLD FOOLS IN SPAIN AGAIN

NEW YORK TIMES BESTSELLING AUTHOR

VICTORIA TWEAD

Ant Press
Large Print
Edition

LARGE PRINT EDITION

Copyright © 2010 Victoria Twead

Formatted and published by Ant Press - www.antpress.org

Paperback ISBN: 978-1-922476-10-4

Hardback ISBN: 978-1-922476-33-3

Paperback Large Print ISBN: 978-1-922476-20-3

Hardback Large Print ISBN: 978-1-922476-53-1

Also available in digital editions.

All rights reserved.

No part of this book may be reproduced in any form or by any electronic or mechanical means, including Artificial Intelligence "training", information storage and retrieval systems, without written permission from the author, except for the use of brief quotations in a book review.

ᚠᚠᚠ

This symbol represents the Rainbow Man, or Indalo, the symbol of the Province of Almería, Spain.

CONTENTS

The Old Fools Series — vi
FREE Photo Book — vii

1. FAMILIES — 1
   Churros — 13
2. PESTS — 15
   Sizzling Chicken Wings and Paprika — 28
3. CREATURES GREAT AND SMALL — 30
   Barbecued Garlic Bread — 43
4. THE GRAND OPENING — 45
   Tomato and Paprika Chutney — 56
5. MOTHS AND YESO — 58
   Roasted Mushrooms with Onions and Herbs — 70
6. BABYSITTING — 72
   Egg and Anchovy Toast Tapas — 83
7. GOLF — 85
   Andalucian Beef Wraps — 97
8. A VILLAGE SECRET — 99
   Wild Mushrooms with Eggs — 110
9. THE VICAR AND HIS WIFE — 112
   Roasted Peaches — 123
10. THE FIESTA AND COLD WATER — 125
    Frisco Omelette — 138
11. NEWS — 140
12. DEATHS — 142

Broad Beans with Ham	153
13. PRUNING	155
Mackerel Paté	166
14. ORANGES AND THE LAW	168
Oranges and Cinnamon	179
15. OWLS AND KITTENS	180
Judith's Easy Lemon Curd	191
16. A SANDWICH	193
Classic BLT Toasted Sandwich	204
17. BIRTHDAYS	206
Steak with Paprika and Herbs	216
18. LETTERS	218
Fig Jam	229
19. BEARS, SPIDERS AND PENGUINS	230
Roasted Tomato Soup with Paprika	240
20. SENIOR MOMENTS	242
21. ZOMBIES AND A FARM	252
Goat's Cheese on Toast	264
22. ALICE	265
23. THE CEMETERY	276
Butternut Squash with Garlic and Herbs	287
24. PLUCKERS AND WILDFIRES	289
Iberian Ham with Peaches and Olive Oil	300
25. NEWS AND A PLAN	301
Spanish Almond Cake	312
26. SORTING THINGS OUT	314
Stuffed Tomatoes	325

27. HIGHS AND LOWS	327
Luc's Italian Pasta with Fresh Tomato Sauce	336
28. PREPARATIONS	338
Ana's Lemon Leaves	350
29. WINTER	352
Lamb Steaks with Hazelnuts and Paprika	362
30. UPS AND DOWNS	364
Spanish Easter Biscuits	375
31. EPILOGUE	377
A request…	386
So what happened next?	387
The Old Fools series	399
The Sixpenny Cross series	403
More books by Victoria Twead…	405
About the Author	407
Contacts and Links	408
More Ant Press Books	413
Publish with Ant Press	417

THE OLD FOOLS SERIES
ALSO AVAILABLE IN PAPERBACK, HARDBACK AND EBOOK EDITIONS

Two Old Fools in Spain Again is the fourth book in the *Old Fools* series by New York Times and Wall Street Journal bestselling author, Victoria Twead.

Chickens, Mules and Two Old Fools

Two Old Fools ~ Olé!

Two Old Fools on a Camel

Two Old Fools in Spain Again

Two Old Fools in Turmoil

Two Old Fools Down Under

Two Old Fools Fair Dinkum (coming soon)

Prequels

One Young Fool in Dorset

One Young Fool in South Africa

Latest Release:

Dear Fran, Love Dulcie: Life and Death in the Hills and Hollows of Bygone Australia compiled by Victoria Twead

FREE PHOTO BOOK
TO BROWSE OR DOWNLOAD

⚘⚘⚘

For photographs and additional unpublished material to accompany this book, browse or download the

FREE PHOTO BOOK

from

www.victoriatwead.com / free-stuff

👥👥👥

For all the amazing people, particularly my wonderful Facebook friends and members of 'We Love Memoirs', who have supported and encouraged me to finish this, the fourth in the Old Fools series.

Thank you for making me laugh, even when things were going a little awry.

1

FAMILIES

There was mould on the walls. Green and white fluffy random blotches decorated the ceiling in most of the rooms. The mirror in the bathroom had begun to rust and the beds and curtains smelled musty, as did the clothes hanging in the wardrobes. Old Spanish houses need to be lived in, need to be aired, or the damp takes over.

Our home had missed us while we were away for a year working in the Middle East. When we flung open the shutters to let the fresh mountain air flow through, I could almost hear the house sigh with relief.

But living with mould and rust was far more attractive than living and working in Bahrain, a country in turmoil, rocked by the Arab revolution. Joe and I were home, back in El Hoyo and no clumps of mould or damp mattresses could spoil our joy at being in our own house and sleeping in our own bed again.

"Bleach," I said, more to myself than Joe. "That's what we need, gallons of it. That'll put a stop to the mould."

If the house was bad, the garden was worse. Very few of my plants had survived the heat of the Spanish sun without water. The grapevine thrived, its ancient roots buried deep in the soil, but my flowerbeds and pots contained nothing but crisp, dry, brown sticks marking the places where shrubs and flowers had once bloomed.

"Don't you worry," I said to Regalo.

She was the only chicken to have survived, in spite of Paco's care, while we'd been away. Now she was relishing the freedom to wander freely about our overgrown garden. She didn't reply.

"I'll get this garden sorted out in no time. And we're going to get you some new sisters to keep you company. You'll be the oldest, so you'll be Top Hen."

Regalo had been the youngest of the flock, pecked and bullied by the others. It was ironic that she would now have a flock of her own to rule. Regalo looked up at me, head cocked to one side, then resumed her task of tugging out the weeds that flourished between the paving stones.

"I'm just popping round next door to see if Carmen has any bleach," I said to Joe.

He grunted and scratched himself, deep in concentration as he flicked through the manuals, trying to figure out how to reactivate the TV, dishwasher and Internet, all of which had refused to work since our return.

A curtain of chains to keep out the flies hung across the open door of our neighbours' house. Passersby couldn't see in, but anyone inside had a clear view out.

"*Pasa*, Veeky!" called Carmen, inviting me in.

I pushed the jangling metal curtain aside and entered their neat little house, already sniffing the wonderful aroma of something cooking.

Bianca, dozing under the kitchen table, raised her head briefly, opened one brown eye, wagged her stump of a tail and sank back to sleep. I remembered that she'd had eight puppies while we'd been away. It didn't seem two minutes since she'd been a puppy herself.

Carmen wiped her chubby hands on a tea cloth and kissed me soundly on both cheeks. She looked flushed and hot.

"I have made *churros* and there is fresh coffee. Sit down and I will pour you a glass."

I was always impressed by the delicious edibles that Carmen could conjure up on her one gas-ring stove and open fire. Being summer, the fire in the kitchen was not alight, but the kitchen was still very warm from her cooking session.

Carmen looked well. She was a few years older than I, but her face was still unlined and her round cheeks were rosy with health. Although she carried too much weight, she was never clumsy, but worked quickly and efficiently in her tiny kitchen.

She poured coffee into two glasses and sat down opposite me.

"You have lost weight," she said, looking me up and down.

I nodded. Bahrain had had that effect on both Joe and me.

She pushed a plate of *churros* across the table towards me and I selected one, still warm, dropping sugar as I bit into it. A few plates of these and I'd soon be back to my old plump self.

Churros are the Spanish equivalent of doughnuts, similar in shape to the horns of the *churro* sheep found in Spain. They are completely lacking in any nutritional value, extremely fattening and deliciously irresistible. The villagers often served them for breakfast with milky coffee or hot chocolate.

"How are you enjoying being back in Spain?" asked Carmen.

"Oh, it's great to be home," I said, after a sip of coffee. "It'll take a little while for us to sort everything out, but we don't mind. Our boxes haven't arrived from Bahrain yet."

We'd sent the boxes on to Spain a week before we'd left ourselves. As soon as we had the Internet working, I meant to track them and find out where they were.

"Joe's trying to get the TV and other stuff working and I wondered if you have any bleach I could borrow? I'd like to attack the patches of mould that are all over the house."

"Ah, yes," she said, leaning sideways and pulling a yellow bottle from under the sink. The kitchen was so small, she didn't need to get up from the table.

"Thank you," I said. "Now, tell me about Sofía. Do you think this boyfriend is The One? How did they meet?"

"Yes," she nodded, beaming. "I think he might be The One. Paco, he does not believe it, because we all know how picky Sofía is. But me, I think Alejandro is The One." She paused, lost in thought, probably dreaming of future grandchildren.

"And how did they meet?"

"Sofía and young Alejandro have known each other since they were children. Can you believe it? He was right under her nose all the time. Paco went to school with Alejandro's father, who is also called Alejandro. Alejandro and Paco have known each other since they were boys. Of course Alejandro is a millionaire now, but we have always been friends."

"Sofía's boyfriend is a millionaire's son?" I asked, surprised.

"Yes, but he is also a solicitor. The family have machinery shops, a chain of them across Spain. Young Alejandro looks after the legal side of things. They have many houses, one in the city and some in the country. They have a house in El Hoyo."

"They do? Which one?"

"You know the house with high walls, below the square? The one with big gates?"

I knew the one. Most of the houses in the village were ancient cottages, like ours, but there were a few grand ones hidden behind walls, occupied only for a few brief weeks in summer. As one walked past, guard dogs barked a warning. I'd always thought it was unoccupied.

"They don't use the house much," said Carmen, reading my thoughts. "But they have workmen who feed the dogs and animals."

"Animals?"

"Yes, they breed rabbits for the pot and chickens. And the gardener grows vegetables. Now that young Alejandro and Sofía are together, we have a very good supply of rabbit, chicken and eggs."

"Sounds like Sofía has found an ideal husband!" I observed.

"You will meet Alejandro and his parents," she said. "They spend more time in El Hoyo now."

"And what about the Ufartes?" I asked. "Maribel is having another baby?"

Carmen nodded, then pursed her lips and lowered her voice. "Yes, she is... Between you and me, I do not think everything is going well with that family."

"Really? Why not? They were dancing in the street last night. And the twins seemed fine."

"Mark my words, I can see problems." She leaned forward and beckoned me closer, as though eavesdroppers might hear. I could feel her hot breath on my face. "Lola is back!" she hissed.

"Lola Ufarte?"

"Yes! Well, she isn't really a Ufarte, she's Maribel's sister. Did you know she has already been married twice?"

"Really? Has she?"

"Oh, yes. Mark my words, trouble follows that girl."

As I absorbed this information and opened my mouth to speak, the metal curtain swung aside, making me jump. Paco blustered in, a bunch of white rabbits dangling from one fist. He was not a large man, but he filled the room. A young dog bounded at his feet, rushed to sniff me then sat panting beside Bianca. Further discussion about the Ufartes was at an end.

"Veeky!" Paco roared, throwing the corpses on the table with a dull thud. "How are you? And Joe? Carmen, prepare the pot! I have been at the house of Alejandro and I have rabbits for you to cook. Veeky, would you like one? There is too much here for us."

I glanced at the limp, white bunnies and tried hard not to think of Snowy, my first pet at the age of seven.

"Thank you, no," I said. Then, fondling the spaniel's soft ears, "Is this Bianca's son?"

"Yes, I will teach him to fetch the birds when I shoot them next season. He is a good dog, like his mother."

"What's his name?"

"Yukky."

A curious name, I thought, then realised he was probably called 'Jacky', which would sound very much like 'Yukky' to my English ears.

"I just popped in to borrow some bleach," I said. "I must go. I have cleaning to do and Joe's trying to get all the appliances working again."

I grabbed the bottle, thanked Carmen, said my goodbyes and left.

Out in the street, the Ufarte twins were sitting on their doorstep like mirror images, heads together, brown legs stretched out. I remembered something.

"Girls!" I called. "Come with me, I believe I have something for you inside."

The twins jumped up and skipped over, following me into the house.

"What is it, *Tía* Veeky?"

"Is it something from Arabia?"

"TV's working," said Joe as we passed him in the living room.

In the kitchen I picked up a bag and handed it over to the girls. They wrestled it open and squeaked with delight at the set of five wooden camels, each one in a different pose, ending with a tiny baby camel. My mind briefly shot back to our visit to the King's camels in Bahrain and how we'd gazed with awe at 450 camels, all in one spot.

The twins scampered out and as I scoured at the mould with Carmen's bleach, I wondered again about Lola Ufarte. The last time we had seen Lola was just before we left for Bahrain. She'd been notorious for entertaining the males of the village and had finally run off with the foreman of a building gang. I guessed that hadn't worked out, but why did her return spell trouble for the Ufarte family?

That evening, we stood on our roof terrace watching the sun sink behind the mountain. The sky was stained pink, the distant sea shimmering with the sun's dying rays.

Poor, lonely Regalo had already put herself to bed. I'd watched her enter the coop and pace below the roosting perch, stopping at intervals to crane her head, eyeing the perch as though this was the first time she'd ever seen it.

She then returned to her feeder and ate some more, before standing below the perch again, trying to decide whether this was to be her roost tonight, or not. Still undecided, she checked out a few other places where she could sleep. Finally she climbed the ladder having decided the perch was best after all.

I never could understand this chicken ritual, because chickens are creatures of habit. They always sleep in exactly the same place every night. Why bother to check out alternative spots when they'll always end up in the same one? It would be like us trying out all the beds in the house before finally climbing into our own.

Because Regalo had been bullied, she always slept on the outside perch. Being the lowest in the pecking order, the others had never allowed her to roost inside. Even though she was the only remaining chicken, with the entire coop to herself, she still chose to sleep outside.

I sighed and shut the door of the coop. Next week we'd drive to the horrible chicken shop and get her some company. Following a last preening session, Regalo sank down, tucked her head under her wing and slept.

Joe and I leaned on the roof terrace wall. "Well, it's not been a bad day," Joe said. "At least I got the TV working and the dishwasher's fixed."

We watched the procession of villagers in the distance walking along the road, up the hill out of the village. This was a regular evening affair, a constitutional where neighbour would greet neighbour and dog would greet dog.

I squinted, trying to identify the individual villagers across the valley in the failing light.

Paco didn't normally bother with the evening constitutional, but I could see the round figure of Carmen and her daughter Sofía, walking arm in arm. I recognised Little Paco in a knot of teenagers.

FAMILIES

"I can see the Ufartes," I said. "Carmen told me today that Lola Ufarte is back. She seemed to think that was a problem."

"Why?"

"I'm not sure. I didn't get the chance to ask."

The older Ufarte boys were growing tall. They kicked a ball ahead, while the twins walked with another little girl of their age. The adult Ufartes walked in a line across the road. Maribel waddled a little, weighed down by her unborn baby, one hand clutching the hand of the little boy we'd nicknamed Snap-On more than a year ago. Snap-On had grown sturdy and was finally willing to walk by himself, which must have been a relief to his mother.

Maribel's husband and her sister, Lola, walked side by side, with the smallest Ufarte between them. Even from that distance, I could see that Lola's skirt was extremely short and her hips swayed as she walked. Every now and then, Papa Ufarte and Lola would swing the toddler into the air. It was an unremarkable family scene, but the shared act of swinging the baby between them was curiously intimate, and excluded Maribel, sending a little chill down my back.

I tore my eyes away and scanned the rest of the procession.

"Joe, can you see those two figures nearly at the top of the hill? One fat one and one thin one? With the two little dogs and a pram?"

Joe stared, screwing up his eyes.

"Yes... They look familiar, I recognise the big one's bald head. Isn't that Roberto and Federico?"

The Boys, as we called them, were a married couple, one of the first gay couples to marry after a law was passed in Spain legalising same-sex marriage. The Boys lived in the house slightly above us, on the land that used to be our orchard. They were a nice couple and none of the villagers seemed to object to them, which surprised me as our neighbours were staunchly Catholic.

I watched the two men crest the hill. I'd never seen them walking anywhere before. Their idea of exercising their dogs had always been to let them roam free in the village for half an hour in the evenings.

"I wonder what they're doing pushing a pram?" I wondered, swatting at a mosquito circling me hungrily. "Come on, let's go in, I'm being eaten alive."

CHURROS

Difficult to resist in spite of the calories. Just dollop the mix into a plastic bag, snip off a corner, then squirt into the hot oil.

Ingredients

- 250ml (½ pint) water
- 50ml (1.7fl oz) sunflower oil
- ½ tsp salt
- 200g (7oz) plain flour
- 115g (4oz) dark chocolate
- 1 litre (34 fl oz) milk
- 1 tbsp cornflour
- 4 tbsp sugar
- Caster sugar
- Oil for deep frying

Method

- Put the water, oil and salt in a heavy pan and bring to the boil.

- Turn the heat down and add the flour. Beat together until the mixture forms a ball, then remove from heat.

- Heat the oil for deep frying until very hot.

- Using an icing syringe (or snip off the corner of a plastic bag), pipe thick strips into the oil and fry until golden brown.

- Place on a plate and sprinkle with the caster sugar.

- For the chocolate sauce, place the chocolate and half the milk in a pan and heat.

- Add the cornflour to the rest of the milk and mix into the chocolate together with the sugar.

- Continue heating the mixture on a low heat stirring constantly.

- Once the mixture has thickened remove from the heat and whisk until really smooth and serve with the warm churros.

Kindly donated by reader, David Sutton-Rowe

2

PESTS

Summer nights in southern Spain are hot, even if one's bedroom is a cool cave-room, as ours was. In addition to the heat, mosquitoes adore me and are prepared to travel for miles just for a taste of my blood. They never touch Joe, much to my annoyance, but zoom straight to me. Unless I use gallons of insect repellent, they will happily feast on me all night.

After the first few uncomfortable nights with the high-pitched whine of mosquitoes ringing in my ears, I tried to remember to spray the bedroom before we went to bed.

Unfortunately, that night I forgot. Every mosquito in Andalucía celebrated and phoned its friends and relations.

"Come on!" they sang to each other, "It's

Veeky for supper tonight! She hasn't sprayed, let's feast!"

By morning, I was a mass of red, itchy bumps. Joe had not a single mosquito bite, but he hadn't entirely escaped.

"Have I got something on my neck?" he asked, craning his head this way and that in the bathroom mirror.

I stopped scratching my bites for a moment and examined him closely. To my astonishment, on his neck were two puncture wounds, side by side, perhaps an inch apart.

"What is it?" he asked. "Mosquito bites?"

"No, there aren't any lumps, just two holes..."

"Well, what are they like?"

"I know this sounds silly, but if I didn't know better, I'd say you've been bitten by a vampire."

"Don't be ridiculous!"

"I'm just saying that's what it looks like."

"Here, hand me that antiseptic cream. Vampires indeed!"

"Well, something's bitten you, that's for sure. Perhaps we should sleep with a crucifix in the bedroom in future."

"Very funny."

"Or pop into the church and get some holy water?"

"Enough!"

He applied the cream, which seemed to have a soothing effect as he stopped complaining after a while. We sat in the kitchen, deciding what jobs to tackle that day.

"The dishwasher is working now," said Joe, sipping his coffee. "And the Internet's back. I checked on our boxes' progress, by the way. According to UPS tracking, they're still in Bahrain."

"Not even left the country yet?"

"Nope. I think I'll give the chicken area a good cleaning out today, then we can go and get some new hens next week," he said, changing the subject.

"Good idea. Poor Regalo must be lonely. I'm still on mould and fungus duty today, I think."

I looked round the kitchen. So much to do! Everything needed cleaning and airing. Cobwebs needed removing. A lick of white paint wouldn't go amiss. Deep in thought, I was only distracted when I heard a faint buzzing noise. Mosquitoes during the day? Surely not! The buzzing grew louder and I concentrated on the sound.

"Joe, can you hear buzzing?"

Joe creased his brow, listening.

"Yes, I think I can..."

Now it was unmistakable, louder, more insistent. If it was a mosquito, it would have been the size of a goose.

"It sounds like a giant bee..."

We swung our heads this way and that, trying to locate the source of the maddening buzz.

"It's coming from the dishwasher!"

A monster bee trapped in the dishwasher? Joe jumped up and reached out to open it. Before he could pull the door open, we heard a fizzle, followed by a blue flash and a CRACK! The unmistakable smell of burning reached our noses and black smoke seeped from under the counter and round the sides of the dishwasher.

"Quick! Pull the whole thing out!" I shouted.

As Joe gripped the sides of the appliance and heaved it out, we could already see flames lapping up the wall. They flared from the electrical socket, lighting up the dark area. He snatched up the nearest available items: the apron I had won at one of El Hoyo's fiestas, then a new tea-towel with 'Welcome to Bahrain' splashed across it and finally my favourite cardigan. He smothered the flames and the crisis was averted.

"What on earth caused that?" I asked after we'd fanned the smoke outside and muted the smoke alarm.

Joe shook his head. "It wasn't me, I promise. I just fiddled with the controls, I didn't touch the plug *or* the socket."

"That was scary! What if we'd been asleep? Or out?"

"I agree, I'm going to check every socket in the house. The chicken coop will have to wait."

I was just adding 'more smoke alarms' and 'fire extinguisher' to my shopping list, under 'bleach' and 'chickens', when somebody hammered on our front door.

"English!"

It could only be Paco.

"Joe, let Paco in, will you?"

"English!" said Paco, crashing in. "I have brought you vegetables."

He dumped the heavy crate on the kitchen table and I crossed off 'vegetables' from my shopping list. Red, yellow and green shiny peppers vied with deep purple aubergines and prickly, fat, green, cucumbers. Enough to feed the Barcelona football team. I thanked him.

"I cannot stay," said Paco, as Joe reached for the brandy bottle. "We are going down the mountain for a few days." He stopped, sniffing the air. "What is that smell of burning?"

Joe explained and showed him the melted, burnt-out plug and pointed to the dishwasher, now back in its place.

"A bad business," said Paco. "Imagine if you had not been here and the fire had reached your gas bottle in the next cupboard! Whhomph! Your house, my house and El Hoyo would be gone!"

I blinked. Paco wasn't making me feel any better.

Paco roared with laughter. "I have forgotten one more vegetable that you must have. Wait, I will fetch it from my house."

He stamped out and returned a few minutes later.

"For you," he boomed, thrusting two heads of garlic joined by a long piece of twine into Joe's hands.

Joe stared at them, puzzled, then looked at Paco, waiting for enlightenment.

"Hang them round your neck when you go to bed!" roared Paco and thumped the wall with his fist, bending double with laughter. "I see you have been bitten by a vampire!"

Joe's hand flew to the wounds on his neck.

"Everybody knows I grow the best garlic!" bellowed Paco. "No vampire will bother you now!"

"I don't think that's very funny," said Joe as Paco stamped off, still guffawing, slamming the front door behind him.

We didn't solve the mystery of the neck bites, although Paco later guessed a spider may have been the attacker. I've never seen big spiders in Spain, not even in our log pile. I've seen far bigger, hairier spiders in Britain, and, of course, Australia.

I was reminded, however, of an incident many years ago when my sister-in-law and her partner had moored their boat in the local marina. Paul woke to find two punctures on his neck, just like Joe's and the Spanish doctor who examined him reckoned they were spider bites. So perhaps Paco was right.

Whatever the cause, Joe didn't take the garlic

to bed that night and I liberally sprayed our bedroom a few hours before bedtime. All vampires, spiders and mosquitoes stayed away but that didn't mean we had a peaceful night.

At around one o'clock, I woke to a tapping noise. It was muffled but regular and insistent. It sounded as though it was coming from next door but I thought it unlikely because I knew Paco's family had gone down the mountain for a few days.

Old Spanish cottages can have walls a metre thick and I was always surprised when any noise from next door penetrated through to us, but it did. I lay awake, listening.

"Joe!" I prodded him. "There's a funny noise coming from next door."

"Wah?"

"Can you hear that tapping noise?"

"Mm..."

"What do you think it is?"

"Dunno. Sounds like hammering, or something. Go to sleep."

Hammering? Even if Paco was in, he would never do any hammering at that time of night. The noises suddenly stopped and I drifted back to sleep. Later I was disturbed again by the same rhythmic noises. I checked the clock on my bedside table. Three.

"Joe!"

"Wah?"

"There's that noise again!"

"Go to sleep."

I lay still, trying to work out what it could be. Burglars? No. A woodpecker? Ridiculous. Deathwatch beetles? Unlikely. A nocturnal DIY project? Ludicrous.

Eventually it stopped and I slept again. Until 4.30am. The noise was back and I had a raging thirst. Ignoring the noise, I slipped out of bed and tried to find my slippers in the dark. I didn't want to turn on any lights and wake Joe again. I made my way to the kitchen barefooted and groped for the light switch.

To my absolute horror, I saw black shapes scuttling across the floor and into the shadows. Even to my bleary eyes they showed up in sharp contrast against the white floor tiles. Cockroaches!

I ran back to the bedroom and woke Joe.

"Joe! We've got cockroaches in the kitchen!"

"Wah? We got wah? Right…" and he resumed his snoring.

I gave up trying to rouse him and went back to the kitchen. No cockroaches to be seen, but I knew I hadn't imagined them. I drank a glass of water, staring at the floor the whole time, my bare toes curling in disgust. Then I added 'cockroach killer' to the shopping list before climbing back into bed to snatch a few more hours' sleep. The noise from next door had stopped.

In the morning, I let Joe sleep on while I

examined the kitchen again and checked 'cockroaches' on the Internet. The results didn't cheer me up at all.

When Joe arose, I reminded him about our little problem and, this time, he was much more attentive.

"How many did you see?"

"Loads!"

"How many is 'loads'?"

"Well, there must have been about … six."

"Hmm… Not exactly a plague then?"

"Don't be facetious. I've just Googled 'cockroaches'. I read that if you see a few, then it's likely there are dozens more around, just hidden."

I glanced round the kitchen floor, half-expecting to see eyes peering at me from every crevice.

In England, cockroaches rarely crossed my mind. I didn't know much about these resilient creatures then, but now I could probably answer questions about them on the TV show, *Mastermind*.

There are three main types of cockroach: the American, Oriental and German. Did you know that a cockroach can live for a week without its head, can run at three miles an hour and can hold its breath for forty minutes? Did you know cockroaches have eighteen knees and that their mouths work sideways?

All very interesting, but it didn't help with the

extermination of the wretched things in our kitchen.

"Would you mind doing the shopping on your own? I want to give the kitchen a really good clean and wash the floor. Here, I've made a list." I handed it to him.

Joe glanced at the list. "I'm going to need a trailer to bring that lot home."

"Well, don't go to the chicken shop. We can do that together later in the week. Regalo will just have to wait a few more days for some company."

Joe set off down the mountain and I washed and disinfected the kitchen floor. Then I swept the front doorstep, which always made me feel very Spanish. Further up the street, the Ufarte twins were playing with the wooden camels on their doorstep, while Granny Ufarte snoozed in her armchair in the shade.

I waved, but the twins were too immersed in their camel game to notice me. Their little Yorkshire terrier, Fifi, snuffled up to me and I was glad that Joe wasn't around. Fifi still nursed a deep hatred of Joe and the sight of him would have set her off on a yapping, snarling, nipping fest.

Roberto and Federico rounded the corner pushing the pram in front of them. As they approached, I leant on my broom and peered into the pram.

"What a lovely baby!" I said. "What's her

name?" Really I wanted to ask whose baby she was.

The baby was dressed all in pink, with a matching sunbonnet and little pink shoes embroidered with daisies. I cooed into the pram and she gurgled back.

"This is Emilia," said Roberto proudly, while Federico fussed with the baby's pillow and adjusted her toys.

"Is she staying with you?" I ventured.

"Emilia is ours."

"Oh, that's wonderful!" I knew that gay marriage was now legal and I'd heard that adoption by same-sex partners was also now permitted. Judging by little Emilia's sunny smile and her beautiful clothes and pram, she had fallen on her little pink feet. She was lucky to have found such devoted parents.

"I'm glad we saw you," said Roberto, always the more talkative of the two. "We were talking to Juan and Maribel Ufarte and they said you used to babysit for them, before you went to the Middle East."

"Er, yes..."

My hands tightened their grip on the broom. I could see where this was heading and I didn't know how to stop it.

"They said you love children."

"Yes, but..."

"Perfect!" said Roberto, clapping his hands and smiling at Federico beside him.

"In the winter, Federico and I want to take salsa classes down the mountain. You can look after Emilia!"

"I..."

"It will be just once a week, for an hour or two. We will tell you the times when we find out."

Federico nodded in agreement.

"We..." I started, but couldn't think of a response.

"That's good, then. We will see you at the grand opening. *Hasta luego!*" and they were already turning away, pushing the pram in front of them.

I groaned and rested my forehead on the broom handle. I was going to have to pick my moment to tell Joe about that. And what grand opening?

Just then, Paco's front door opened and Sofía skipped out, giggling, closely followed by a handsome young man. They didn't see me and the young man carried on pinching her bottom as she flapped his hand away half-heartedly.

"Stop it, Alejandro! Somebody will see!"

So Paco's house hadn't been empty last night! His daughter had stayed and so had Alejandro, her new boyfriend, the millionaire's son. Suddenly the nocturnal noises made sense. The pair were so wrapped up in each other they didn't notice me in my porch. They locked their door and swung off up the street, arms around each other.

PESTS

I looked across the valley and saw our car descending the twisting road into the village. Joe would be home in a few minutes. I wondered if he'd managed to purchase all the things on my list. Knowing Joe, he would have forgotten the most important items and come home with utterly random stuff instead.

SIZZLING CHICKEN WINGS AND PAPRIKA

Smoked Spanish paprika – a vital ingredient in Spanish cooking and a spice no kitchen should be without! This recipe for hot and spicy chicken wings takes on a flavoursome smoky twist with the addition of paprika in the marinade. Enjoy!

Ingredients

For the marinade:

- 24 chicken wings
- 200ml (7 fl oz) beer or Spanish lager
- 150ml (5½ fl oz) chicken stock
- 4 garlic cloves (crushed)
- 2 teaspoons hot pepper sauce
- Olive oil

To season:

- Splash of olive oil

- 1 teaspoon hot smoked paprika
- 1 teaspoon black pepper
- Pinch fresh oregano / thyme & rosemary
- Salt

Method

- Place the chicken wings in a large bowl or *cazuela* and mix well with the marinade ingredients, chill for two hours.
- Heat a little olive oil in a pan.
- Remove wings from marinade and add seasoning.
- Mix well and cook for 10 minutes on a medium to high heat.
- Transfer the chicken wings from the pan, place on a tray and bake in a medium oven for 10 – 15 minutes.

3

CREATURES GREAT AND SMALL

Joe lugged in the last of the shopping bags and dumped them on the kitchen floor. Spain is rather behind with recycling, but stores had just stopped issuing free plastic carrier-bags and our extra-strong re-usable Carrefour bags were lined up like a battalion of soldiers.

"Did you manage to get everything?" I asked.

"Yup. And before you ask, yes, I did get the cockroach killer."

Joe can read my mind like a psychic. He was still catching his breath from bringing in the shopping and I decided that now was not a good time to tell him about Emilia and our future babysitting task.

Instead, I busied myself putting things away and finally found it: a flat, red, plastic gadget with holes in the sides. It came with little insecticide blocks to be inserted in the holes.

"Cockroaches, are you watching?" I said, waving the contraption around. "Tonight you will be *dead!*"

"You know the building the council were working on when we left for Bahrain?" asked Joe.

"Um, yes. By the square?"

"Well, it's finished. They've finished painting it now. I drove past it and had a look."

"That's a surprise! Spain doesn't have any money."

"Not only is it finished, but there's going to be a grand opening in a couple of weeks. I passed Geronimo and he told me about it."

"Ah, that explains something the Boys said today."

"You saw the Boys?"

"Oh, only briefly, when I was sweeping the front doorstep. The baby is theirs, adopted I assume. She's gorgeous. What's the building going to be used for?" I asked, deftly changing the subject.

"The downstairs part is going to be a bar, according to Geronimo."

"Well, he'll like that! I bet he'll be their best customer."

"And the rooms upstairs will be a surgery for when the doctor visits. And offices."

"Gosh, no more going to Marcia's house to see the doctor then?"

"Nope, El Hoyo is getting very modern."

That night, we set the cockroach trap, baiting it according to the instructions. I slept easier, trusting that would be the end of our problem.

But cockroaches have been around since prehistoric times and they managed to survive much longer than any dinosaur. It would take more than a red, plastic gadget to end the cockroaches in our kitchen.

The following morning, I found two corpses on the floor. Well, it was a start. Shuddering, I swept them up, noticing that they were still alive, lying on their backs, their legs (and all 18 knees) still twitching.

"I'll stand on them," said Joe.

"No! You can't do that! I read on the Internet that they may be carrying eggs and you'll just spread their children all over the house."

Each morning produced a few more corpses, but I knew they were just the tip of the iceberg. I imagined the armies of cockroaches lurking in the shadows of my kitchen, looking at their watches, just waiting for us to go to bed.

The next time Joe went down the mountain, cockroach killer was still on the shopping list. But this time he returned with three cans of spray.

"Spray?" I asked. "Are we supposed to stay up all night in the dark and spray them as they appear?"

"Don't be ridiculous. Read the side of the can."

So I read the *modo de empleo* carefully and, that

night, followed the instructions to the letter. I sprayed at floor level, all around the edges of the room, paying particular attention to the gaps beside the cooker and fridge. The smell of it was diabolical, but it needed to be done.

Success! My labours bore fruit. Twenty black carcasses awaited me the next morning. Each morning produced more corpses, but the numbers were declining most satisfactorily. After a week, I'd used all three cans and disgusting black bodies no longer littered the kitchen floor. I disinfected all the kitchen cupboards (cockroaches can climb and fly) and heaved a huge sigh of relief.

However, I confess to having a sneaky admiration for the *cucaracha*. They've been around for millions of years and scientists maintain they are capable of surviving a nuclear blast. But that doesn't mean I would welcome them into my kitchen. Believe me, if one so much as pokes its head out from behind the cooker, it's history.

Perhaps we had a close shave because I was astonished to read the following cockroach story in the Olive Press, an excellent English language newspaper.

'A BRITISH man is lucky to be alive following an explosion that sent him flying through the wall of his Torrevieja flat.

Daran Cooper hit the pavement below his first-

floor apartment after a can of insecticide exploded in his hand.

He had been preparing a meal to celebrate his 48th birthday while his partner Carmen was trying to kill a cockroach with some bug spray.

Cooper took hold of the can, which then exploded, catapulting him out into the street.

Speaking from Torrevieja Hospital, Daran said: "I started spraying at the cockroach and some of the gas must have got into the washing machine.

"A moment later, there was the click of the wash cycle, followed by an almighty bang as I flew through where the wall used to be.

"There was glass and all kinds of stuff in the air, but miraculously I stayed conscious all the time and all I could think of was that I had to protect my head."

The explosion totally ripped out the wall of the flat, but Carmen escaped unharmed and the couple's five-year-old son Sebastian remained safely tucked up in bed.

Daran suffered a broken wrist, bruising and head wounds, as well as an elbow injury that required surgery.

Investigators initially believed the blast had been caused by a gas leak. However, fire crew sources have suggested the bug spray may have reacted in some way with nearby domestic appliances to spark the explosion.'

"I bet the cockroach survived," said Joe.

Poor Mr Cooper. Reading that article made us realise that we were lucky, things could have been a great deal worse.

Joe has a theory about the fire behind the dishwasher. He maintains it was caused by a cockroach crawling into the plug wiring, resulting in a short-circuit. We'll never know for sure. I wish I could say that the cockroach invasion was the last insect plague we suffered, but of course it wasn't.

Having conquered the mould and cockroaches, it was time to think about getting some more chickens to keep our poor lonesome hen, Regalo, company.

She wasn't entirely on her own, as the two village cats, Sylvia and Gravy, had reappeared. They had been born in our chicken coop years before and we sometimes fed them. The two sisters moved back into our garden and looked surprisingly fit and well considering that they'd been forced to fend for themselves for a year without help from us.

Once again we fed them scraps but were careful not to give too much, or too regularly. Had we done so, word would quickly have spread to the village cat community and we'd have been mobbed by the furry felines. Spain has a serious feral cat problem and we didn't want to add to it.

Sometimes I'd put out scraps, then stand back and watch. Sylvia, Gravy and Regalo the chicken would appear from nowhere and charge toward the treat. I hoped they'd share, but no, Regalo won the contest every time.

Chickens eat anything and she'd gobble the offerings while the cats crouched a little distance away, their eyes glued to the food, inching forward ever so slightly like lions stalking their prey. It wasn't until Regalo had eaten her fill, wiped her beak on the ground and strutted away, that the cats approached and devoured the leftovers.

Now that I had tidied the garden somewhat, it was time to put Regalo back in the coop permanently and get her some new sisters to live with. We hated the chicken shop, but it was the only place we knew where we could buy hens.

It was located on an industrial estate and was not small. Behind the building that housed the shop was a huge metal warehouse that stored a variety of items for sale: farm machinery, animal produce, bales of straw, plants, to name but a few. Alongside the warehouse was a smaller windowless brick building that housed the chickens and other poultry. On the ground and piled against walls, were mounds of onions, waiting to be shovelled into sacks.

"We'd like to buy some hens, please," said Joe to the assistant in the shop.

As usual, he led us outside and round the back of the shop. The smell of onions hung in the air.

We approached an outbuilding with no windows. He unlocked the big, wooden doors and pulled them open. From outside, you could barely hear the chickens, but now the noise hit our ears like an explosion. I don't know how many chickens were housed in that building, but I would hazard a guess at two or three hundred.

The chickens were kept in battery-style conditions, with row upon row of wire cages, stacked one above the other, each cage containing between one and five hens. They had no room to stretch their wings, no daylight and no solid ground to walk on. The smell was terrible and the sound of hundreds of hens, squawking and giving off alarm calls, was deafening.

"You choose," said Joe, as the assistant stood by.

How to choose? Today there were only brown ones and a few black ones and we had decided to buy six. I marched to an overcrowded cage and pointed.

"All these?" asked the assistant.

"No, just one."

The assistant opened the cage door and reached inside, grabbing the legs of the chicken I'd indicated. She shrieked and flapped as he dragged her out and her companions shrank, terrified, against the cage sides. The assistant awaited further instructions, the chicken dangling from his hand, upside-down and calm now. I stopped at the next blatantly overcrowded cage.

"All these?" asked the assistant hopefully.

"No, just one."

I wanted to make this operation as speedy as possible, but I also wanted to take one hen from the most crowded cages, leaving a little more space for the others. A futile attempt, as I knew the vacancies would soon be filled by more unfortunate chickens for sale.

Soon, four brown chickens and two black ones hung quietly from the assistant's fists. He strode out of the building with Joe and me close on his heels. Unceremoniously, he thrust the chickens headfirst into two waiting cardboard boxes and jabbed his penknife into the walls to make airholes. We were familiar with this procedure, having bought chickens several times before, but we never liked it.

On the journey home, the chickens were quiet, apart from one that coughed ominously. Regalo watched with interest as we entered the coop and opened the boxes.

Chickens occupying a coop will attack any newcomers and we had learned that the best time to introduce chickens to an existing group was at night, as hens can't see in the dark. However, we felt that as Regalo was totally outnumbered, we were safe to introduce them in daylight.

At first, the new chickens stood stock still in a group, beaks slightly open, panting a little, eyes blinking. How bright the light must have been for them! They'd never been outside before. Cramped in tiny cages, with a sky of corrugated iron over their heads and only artificial light, what must they have thought of the big, blue Spanish sky, the sun and the breezes? How strange the soil must have felt under their feet.

An hour later, the chickens had visibly relaxed. They still moved in a huddle, but they'd found the water and feeder and some were even scratching the ground a little and pecking the soil.

Regalo was beside herself with excitement. She ran at them, exerting her authority, trying to boss them about. But there were too many of them and the new girls were too confused to react, so she eventually gave up and simply accepted them.

We called the two beautiful black ones Serena and Venus and the one with the cough, Sick-Note. Hens bought from the chicken shop often had coughs but we weren't unduly worried as plenty of fresh air, good food and exercise usually cured them. Hopefully, Sick-Note would thrive in her new, healthy environment.

"What shall we call the others?" asked Joe.

The brown hens were identical, we couldn't tell them apart.

"How about calling them One, Two and Three?"

"How do we know which is which?"

"Doesn't really matter, does it? Perhaps when their characters develop a bit we'll know which is which."

"Okay and when Sick-Note loses her cough, she can be Four."

That night, when the shadows grew longer

and the sun sank out of sight behind the mountains, the newcomers piled on top of each other, pressed into one uncomfortable corner of the coop. Regalo peered down at them curiously from her high roosting perch, head on one side. I doubted that the new hens had the strength to climb up to join her.

As the summer days passed, the new girls gained in strength and confidence. First one hen, then another, followed Regalo's bedtime routine, until finally even Sick-Note began to spend her nights on the roosting perch. There was a better roost undercover, but Regalo, being Top Hen, led by example and they all slept outside. Each night they would all busily check out alternate roosting places, but always ended up with Regalo, outside, under the stars.

The new girls were settling well and their vocal range expanded. Before, they were either completely silent, or fired off alarm calls at the slightest sound or sight, even at a sparrow perching on the wire, eyeing their feeder longingly. Now they chatted and clucked and I knew we'd soon hear the raucous Egg Song, the triumphant announcement to the world that an egg had been laid. Following Regalo's example, they dust-bathed, purring with enjoyment as they flung dirt all over themselves, then stood and rattled their feathers clean.

No longer did they shriek in fright and run away when we fed them, but gradually learned to crowd around our feet, necks craning up to see what might be in the treat box. They even ignored Sylvia and Gravy, the two village cats that always hung around our garden. Sylvia and Gravy showed no interest in the chickens either.

One day, Gravy disappeared.

"What happened to your sister?" I asked Sylvia.

I never understood why village cats would sometimes vanish. Had they been poisoned? Shot? Or did they move to pastures new? Gravy was only three or four years old, so it wasn't old age that claimed her. The ruling tomcat of the time, a huge, battle-scarred Siamese with a face as wide as his body and almost flat ears, disappeared at the same time. I suspect they were culled, but I prefer to think that they eloped.

It was the chickens who alerted me to the new arrivals. Already well-used to Sylvia and Gravy, they didn't panic at the sight of them, but squawked alarm calls at the arrival of two new cats, jumping down from our wall into the garden.

I watched. They were just kittens and Sylvia was leading the way, encouraging them to sample the delights of our garden. We weren't sure if Sylvia had produced a litter this year, although we'd guessed. When she snatched a scrap of meat and bolted away with it over the garden wall, I suspected she was taking it to a litter of kittens stashed away somewhere.

The two new kittens soon made themselves at home. One was a tabby, like his missing Aunt Gravy and the other was black and white, complete with white face and comical black Hitler moustache. The black and white one turned out to be female, so we named her Felicity. Her tabby brother we named Snitch.

As more animals roamed our garden, unfortunately, more creepy crawlies were invading our house. We needed to wage war on strange insects that we had never encountered before.

BARBECUED GARLIC BREAD

Cooking garlic bread on the barbecue is very easy. There is only a small amount of preparation involved and you also have the opportunity to add a range of herbs to produce a variety of flavours and hints of the Mediterranean.

Ingredients

- 1 baguette
- 4 garlic cloves, finely chopped
- 150g (5oz) butter
- 1 sprig thyme
- Optional: chilli flakes, ½ teaspoon paprika, ground pepper

Method

- Take the bread and make deep cuts at half-inch intervals all the way along, making sure not to slice right through.

- Place the butter in a saucepan and gradually melt over a low heat.

- Meanwhile finely chop/dice the garlic cloves.

- When the butter has melted, add the garlic, stir well and leave for 10 minutes so the butter is left to cool.

- Using a teaspoon, spoon the garlic butter mixture into each cut in the bread (be generous). Sprinkle over with thyme.

- Wrap the bread securely in kitchen foil and cook over the barbecue for 15 – 20 minutes turning halfway through.

4

THE GRAND OPENING

Joe and I were looking forward to the opening of the new village bar, but a new problem was occupying our minds at the moment.

Moths.

Little brown moths fluttered all over the house and settled quietly on every available surface. They billowed in clouds from folds in towels and from clothes hanging in our wardrobes. They crawled up wall tiles and flitted irritatingly in front of our faces.

We simply couldn't understand where they were coming from. They weren't difficult to catch or exterminate, but for every two or three we disposed of, five more would take their place. I thought most moths were nocturnal, but these individuals seemed as active during the day as they were by night. Bright lights didn't particularly attract them, although they seemed drawn to the TV screen when it was switched on, crawling up slowly, obscuring our view.

The phone rang, taking our minds off moths momentarily. Joe, for some unknown reason, has an aversion to picking up the phone when it rings. He will find any excuse not to do so.

"I'm just going to fill the chicken feeder," he said.

I nodded and lifted the receiver. I could hear loud barking and I didn't need to guess who was on the other end.

"Good heavens, you wretched, flea-bitten critters! Dogs, be QUIET!"

"Judith, is that you?" I asked, smiling to myself.

Our English friend Judith still lived in the next village with her ancient mother and pack of rescue dogs. She was determined never to have more than nine. Having nine, she named the tenth, Half, so she could report having nine and a half when asked how many she had. When she adopted the eleventh dog, she called it Invisible.

"Bloody dogs! Pipe down! Yes, Vicky, it's me, you must be psychic!"

I let that one go.

"How's Mother?" I asked.

"Oh, you know, getting older but as badly behaved as ever, m'dear."

"Oh, good. And the dogs?"

"Taken on another one, dear girl!"

THE GRAND OPENING

"Really? Don't tell me... You now have nine and a half and one that's invisible. So what's the new one called?"

Judith chuckled. "It's a white one, dear thing. We've called him Ghost."

"Well, that's okay then, you still don't have ten dogs."

Judith chortled, breaking off to shout at the dogs again before resuming our conversation. Phone calls from Judith were always difficult with the hounds baying in the background.

"Just giving you a tinkle to find out if you're going to the bar opening next weekend."

"Yes, I think so."

"Jolly good! Haven't seen each other for yonks! We'll be able to do a spot of catching up!"

"That'll be..."

"God's teeth! Must go, dear," she said, cutting me short. "Looks like Half has found Mother's organic beef and mushroom pie..."

The phone was slammed down and the line went dead.

"Who was on the phone?" asked Joe, returning from outside.

"Oh, just Judith."

But he wasn't listening.

"We've got a problem," he said, scratching himself down below. "I know where those blasted moths are coming from. Come with me."

I followed him obediently into the workshop. We kept the chicken grain in a large plastic dustbin and Joe gingerly lifted the lid. A cloud of moths floated out.

"Look inside," he said.

I hardly needed to but I did. The seed was alive with moths. They crawled in waves over each other and up the sides of the bin.

"So, this is where they're hatching..." I said, nose wrinkled in disgust.

"Yep. What shall we do with it?"

"Well, chickens eat everything, insects, worms, I don't think it'll do them any harm. Probably add protein to their diet."

"What, we empty the whole lot into their coop?"

I considered. Looking around the workshop, I could see moths everywhere. Cobwebs were bowed down with their weight and moths crawled on the workbench and up the walls.

"No, I think we need to get rid of it."

Together, we heaved the dustbin onto the wheelbarrow. Joe wheeled it down the garden and out of the back gate, heading for a patch of waste ground beside the cemetery. Joe tipped it out and unsnapped the lid, allowing the seed to spill out into a big pile. Some moths took flight, whilst thousands of others began crawling away into the undergrowth.

Back in the garden, I hosed the dustbin out and sprayed the inside of the workshop liberally with pesticide. Sparrows were already flocking to the seed pile, chirruping with delight. I imagine

THE GRAND OPENING

the story of that free feast of moths and seed became a sparrow legend to be passed down to future generations. Within 24 hours, not a seed or moth remained.

Gradually, we stopped seeing moths in the house and hoped that was the end of the problem.

As the day of the Grand Opening drew near, the village prepared. Strings of coloured lights, normally reserved for the annual fiesta and Christmas, were looped round the square. Extra lights were hung in the trees and the old stage erected. Trestle tables were put up and some ancient benches were brought out, providing extra seating space.

On the day of the event, we wandered down to the square. It was a beautiful evening, warm and clear. Bats spiralled round the lampposts above the parked cars and the coloured lights glowed brightly against the darkening sky. People filled the square and crowded around the new bar, with its shiny tables and chairs set out for the first time. Adults sipped from plastic glasses of beer, while small children and dogs weaved through the forest of legs.

"I want to stay in the background," I said to Joe. "You know how embarrassing the mayor can be, singling me out."

Joe nodded.

"Let's just stand at the back here and watch," he said. "I'm surprised how many people there are. That stage is beginning to look a bit rickety though."

I followed his gaze and could only agree. The legs supporting the stage were rusty and worn. Not only the stage, but the temporary seating looked antiquated too. Wooden planks had been provided for people to sit on and these were balanced on wobbly-looking trestle supports.

"I can't see Judith and Mother yet," I remarked.

"A drink for you," said a village lady passing with a tray.

We thanked her and accepted the glasses. We didn't sit, but stood under a tree, people-watching, listening to the hum of conversation and looking at the scene.

Our neighbours, Paco and Carmen, sat at one of the round bar tables with their daughter Sofía and her boyfriend, Alejandro Junior. Another couple sat at the same table and an elderly man completed the party.

"Who are those people sitting with Paco and Carmen?" I asked Joe, nodding in the direction of the bar.

"I'm guessing, but I reckon they're Sofía's boyfriend's parents. I can see a family resemblance and I bet the old man is the boyfriend's grandfather."

I agreed with Joe and stared at them all with interest. So this was the millionaire family? They were nicely dressed, as was everyone at the

THE GRAND OPENING

gathering, but they didn't look any different from anyone else. Paco, Alejandro and the old man were deep in conversation, while Alejandro's wife chatted with Carmen. Alejandro Junior and Sofía had eyes only for each other.

The Spanish practice of keeping the same names in the family always confused me, so I mentally called them Alejandro Junior, Alejandro and Alejandro Senior.

The Ufarte family were seated at the next table. Mama Ufarte had her smallest son on her lap and was smiling, trying to stop his chubby little hands reaching for the glasses on the table.

Beside her sat Papa Ufarte, leaning back in his chair, legs stretched long under the table. Grey-haired Granny Ufarte dozed in the next chair, oblivious to her surroundings.

The twins, noisily sucking at the straws stuck in their Coca Cola bottles, shared a chair, their glossy black hair glinting orange from the artificial lights.

Lola Ufarte, dressed in a scanty top that accentuated all her curves, sat still, a little smile playing over her lips. When the crowd parted momentarily, I understood why she was smiling. Under the table, Papa Ufarte's foot caressed hers.

I sighed, but a familiar, nasal voice broke into my thoughts.

"Ah, Beaky and Joe! What do you think of our grand opening?"

With the Andalucian accent that turned a 'V'

into a 'B' and Pancho's way of talking through his hooked nose, I would always be Beaky to him.

"Hello, Pancho," said Joe and shook the mayor's hand. "It's a good turnout, isn't it?"

"The new building looks very nice," I said. I stepped back and stood very close to Joe, having had to escape the mayor's attentions in the past. "I'm very pleased it could finally be finished, I know how Spain is struggling with money at the moment."

"We were lucky," Pancho explained. "We had help from some private sources. If it had not been for benefactors like *el Señor* Alejandro Fernández Rodríguez, I do not believe the building would be open today."

"*El Señor* Alejandro Fernández Rodríguez?"

Pancho turned slightly, throwing his hooked nose into profile. He flapped his hand in the direction of the bar.

"The Rodríguez family is sitting at the table with your neighbours. The old man is very generous. He is nearly eighty years old, but he never forgets he grew up in El Hoyo."

Ah, so I was right. The old man was Alejandro Junior's grandfather, another Alejandro.

"There's Judith and Mother," Joe broke in. "I must go and help them, excuse me."

He strode off, calling and waving to attract their attention, leaving me alone with the mayor. *How could you leave me on my own with Pancho?*

"Beaky," said Pancho in a low voice, his eyes

THE GRAND OPENING

boring into mine. "Beaky, if you ever want a, err ... private chat with me, I have a very nice room in the Town Hall."

I stared back at him, trying not to look as uncomfortable as I felt.

"Thank you," I said grimly, deliberately misunderstanding his words. "Joe and I don't have any problems, but if we do, we'll come and see you."

By now, a group was gathering on the stage and people were drifting over, some sitting on the wobbly benches, others standing in clusters, waiting for the speech to begin.

"I will see you later, Beaky," said Pancho. "Now I must make my speech, but perhaps we can arrange to meet? You could give me some lessons in English, *no*?"

No, I thought, but was saved from answering by a lucky incident. Two dogs hurtled past, followed by Paco's young dog, Yukky, in panting hot pursuit, almost knocking the mayor off his feet. I managed to escape before he could collect himself.

"Has that dreadful old sleaze-bag been bothering you again?" boomed Judith, appearing at my side.

"Judith! Mother! How are you both?" I turned to greet them.

Mother looked amazing as usual. Few people would have guessed she was in her nineties. Needing very little support from Joe and Judith, she stood straight and tall, her white gloves resting lightly on their arms. Today she wore cornflower blue and her clutch bag and court shoes matched perfectly. Tiny blue enamel cornflowers decorated her ears and her silver hair was caught up into a sophisticated chignon.

"Mother, you look wonderful," I said, kissing her papery cheek, sniffing the familiar smell of Chanel No.5.

"Thank you, dear," she smiled.

"Mother, we're going to find you a seat," announced Judith, taking charge. "Let's get you sat down before the wretched speeches start. Goodness knows how long they'll be and I don't want you standing."

We walked to the front as a group, but only just in time. The makeshift benches were already mostly occupied by elderly villagers and finding a place for Mother to sit would be difficult.

"Excuse me," said Judith, addressing a grey-haired gentleman in Spanish. "Is this place free? My mother needs to sit down."

To my surprise, I recognised the elderly man. It was Alejandro Senior, the millionaire benefactor, Alejandro Junior's grandfather. He glanced up, his eyes widening when he saw Mother.

"Of course," he said, standing courteously, allowing Mother to settle herself. He bowed over her hand. "I am Alejandro Fernández Rodríguez and I am enchanted to meet you."

THE GRAND OPENING

"Pleased to meet you," purred Mother and I caught a wicked look in her eye.

"Now, tell me what you've been up to," said Judith, turning back to Joe and me, satisfied that Mother was comfortable.

We chatted until the mayor addressed the crowd, but out of the corner of my eye, I could see Alejandro Senior and Mother. Judging by their body language, I could see they were enjoying each other's company enormously.

All went well with the speeches and Pancho's voice droned on. The adults listened but the kids continued to play and the dogs barked.

"...and without your very good friend and mine," Pancho was saying, "without Alejandro Fernández Rodríguez, our wonderful new community building would not have been possible." The mayor, scanned the crowd for Alejandro. "Alejandro? Where is Alejandro?"

Alejandro Senior had been so captivated by Mother, he hadn't been paying attention. Mother's gloved fingers tapped him lightly on the arm, indicating the stage. Alejandro tore his eyes from her to look at the mayor.

Realising he was being called, he raised an arm and rose to his feet to an explosion of applause from the villagers.

Unfortunately, the sudden noise had an unexpected effect.

TOMATO AND PAPRIKA CHUTNEY

This Andalucian recipe is usually made in the winter months. Using hot smoked paprika and red chilli, this chutney/salsa has plenty of bite and goes very well with cheeses, serrano ham and other cured meats.

Ingredients

- 1kg (2.2lb) fresh ripe tomatoes
- 2 large onions
- 6 garlic cloves
- 1 red chilli pepper
- 250g (9oz) brown sugar
- 1 tsp hot smoked paprika
- 175ml (6 fl oz) red wine vinegar

Method

- Chop the tomatoes, thinly slice the onion and slice the garlic cloves.

- Add all of the ingredients to a deep pan or Spanish "Olla".

- Bring to the boil then turn down the heat and simmer gently for 60 minutes, stirring regularly.

- Turn up the heat and bring to the boil once more until the mixture becomes dark and sticky.

- Pour the mixture into jars and leave to cool before sealing.

- This chutney will keep for up to 8 weeks.

5

MOTHS AND YESO

The spontaneous burst of hand-clapping and cheers as Alejandro Senior rose to his feet set off the village dogs. They began barking excitedly then galloped as a pack into the throng, which parted to let them through.

"*Madre mía!*" shouted Paco and Carmen from somewhere. "Bianca! Yukky! Come here!"

"Copito, Canelo!" shouted the Boys.

"Fifi!" shouted the Ufartes.

But there was no stopping the dogs. None of them ever obeyed any commands anyway, even when not excited. Today, the pack was large, comprising weekenders' dogs, Geronimo's three and some strays who went along for the ride.

"Poor things. Those stray dogs should be caught and cared for," I once said to Geronimo.

"There are too many of them," he said, "but

they are useful. Dogs keep foxes away from our chickens."

The Grand Opening and the possibility of scrounging tit-bits had attracted them all. And for some unknown reason, the applause had sent the pack off in a frenzy.

The panting, baying mob of canines ran alongside the front of the stage, past Joe, Judith and me and almost bowled over the now standing Alejandro Senior. He stumbled backward and sat down heavily on the wobbly bench. The sudden weight proved too much and it tipped over, throwing Mother and Alejandro Senior together in a jumble of arms and legs.

Hands shot forward to help the elderly pair back to their feet.

"*Madre mía!*" everybody said, concerned.

"Mother! Are you all right?" asked Judith.

"I am so sorry," said Alejandro Senior, gripping Mother's arm.

"Please don't worry," said Mother, a little shaken but as serene as ever. "I'm absolutely fine."

As Alejandro Senior brushed himself off, I stole a glance at Mother's face. She was smiling, a naughty gleam in her eye. Our eyes met, her lips twitched and one eyelid dropped in a tiny wink. She'd enjoyed it!

Order was restored and the speeches continued until the building was declared open. We mingled a little and Judith hailed friends and caught up with their news. Food was uncovered and the dogs now snuffled the ground, looking for dropped morsels.

I kept an eye on Alejandro Senior and Mother, but they never stirred from their seat on the bench. They sat close together, deep in conversation, oblivious to the party around them.

We left the festivities earlier than most. In our experience, Spanish parties could continue well into the night.

"I think it went well, don't you?" said Joe.

"Apart from Pancho asking me for private English lessons. How *could* you leave me on my own with him?

"You didn't agree, did you?"

"No, of course not. I hope he forgets all about it."

"Interesting meeting Alejandro Senior, wasn't it?" said Joe, unlocking our front door.

"Yep and if I'm not much mistaken, Mother has got herself a toy boy."

Joe paused. "You're joking, of course..."

"I'm not," I said. And I wasn't.

As I took a last look round the kitchen, I noticed a couple of moths crawling up a cabinet.

Oh no... Let's hope it's just a couple of stray ones, I thought, then yawned and went to bed.

The next morning, I nibbled my toast as Joe tucked into his customary muesli.

"I think they've changed the recipe for this," said Joe, speaking with his mouth full. He took a swig of coffee. "It tastes okay, but it's kind of lumpy."

"We'll try another brand next time," I said, absently staring out of the window at the beautiful day. The blue sky was almost too bright for my eyes. One of our chickens launched into the Egg Song and a cock crowed somewhere in the village. The telephone rang and Joe disappeared before the second ring.

"Vicky?" Dogs barked in the background.

"Morning, Judith."

"Have you got Mother with you? She didn't come home last night. I just took the old gal a cup of tea and her bed hasn't been slept in."

"What? No, she's not with us! What time did you leave the party?"

"Oh, about half past two, I think. Mother said she wasn't ready to go and said she'd get a lift home later."

"Really? Gosh, I hope she's okay..."

"Oh, cancel that, dear! A car's just drawn up outside. Good lord, you should see it! I think it's a Mercedes, a flashy, black one. One of those posh cabriolet jobs. The roof's folded back and yes, Alejandro is driving it. He's getting out now and opening the door for Mother. Must go! Speak to you later." The receiver was hurriedly replaced and the line cut.

"I was right," I said to Joe, chuckling. "Mother has got herself a toy boy."

We chortled over that for a while, until Joe

noticed another couple of those pesky moths crawling along the counter.

The next day, to our horror, there were many more of them in the kitchen. As I began to prepare breakfast, they were crawling up the window, the walls and every work surface.

"Finish making the breakfast," I said. "I'm going to look them up on the Internet. This is getting ridiculous."

I typed 'moths in the kitchen' and literally thousands of references jumped up. I picked one at random. Yes, that photograph was most definitely our moth. I read further.

> *'Food moths, or pantry moths, are generally pale in colour and about 1 centimetre long. At first you may see only one or two individuals, but before long, they will multiply quickly. They can often be found in bags of bird seed or dried goods.'*

Yes, we'd discovered that to our cost. But we'd dealt with that, the chicken grain had been disposed of. I read on.

> *'Food moths lay their eggs, which hatch into larvae and will then continue their life-cycle by weaving cocoons in any crevice they can find before emerging to start the cycle again.'*

Did we have food moths breeding somewhere in our kitchen? It seemed very likely. After all,

MOTHS AND YESO

we'd had a plague of them and a few could easily have sneaked into the house and started breeding. I wondered where they were hatching and read a little more.

> *'You may notice tiny grubs swinging from thin threads from cupboard doors. You may see empty cocoons on the folds of paper bags and the corners of food packets or boxes. It is advisable to check your flour and cereal for clumps. Close examination will show that the clumps seem to be held together with little strands, like spiders' webs...'*

My hand flew to my mouth in horror, just as an anguished howl rent the air. I abandoned the computer and ran to the kitchen, already pretty sure what I might find.

"My muesli! They've been hatching in my muesli!"

"The moths?"

"Yes, of course, the blasted moths!" he shouted, his face a picture of disgust. "I've eaten two-thirds of that packet of muesli! I told you it was lumpy! Look at it, it's crawling with the things!"

I took the cereal bowl over to the light and examined it closely. Yes, there were the sticky clumps I'd just read about. And there were the tiny grubs, wriggling happily amongst the nuts and oats.

All other plans were put aside that day as we

systematically went through the cupboards throwing out all the boxes of cereal, bags of flour and packs of rice. Not until we'd washed down every shelf and vacuumed every crevice were we satisfied.

Touch wood, the pantry moths haven't returned.

※※※

In the heart of summer, any casual visitor might be forgiven for imagining El Hoyo was a ghost town. The searing heat chased everybody inside, or under cover. Dogs were too hot to bark and lolled listlessly in the shade and cats hid in crumbling, disused buildings.

Only when the sun had safely set did people venture outside again. At twilight, they promenaded up the hill. Cats mysteriously reappeared and the dogs barked at the cats. The old folk sat in the square and watched the children play while motorbikes buzzed up and down the streets.

In our street, Papa Ufarte sat on his doorstep, quietly strumming his guitar, head bent low as he watched his fingers move over the strings. Granny Ufarte sat in her armchair in the street, dozing. The Ufarte children ran in and out of the house, squeezing past Papa Ufarte and his guitar.

Gradually the music became louder and more insistent. Maribel, Lola and any visiting friends and relations emerged with chatter and chairs. Sometimes one or two of the guests brought guitars and the sound of flamenco and applause soon filled the street.

The ladies chatted, called to each other and laughed. Inevitably toes and feet tapped, then hands were clapped, all in time to the rhythm. One by one, the ladies rose and so began the ancient Andalucian gypsy dance. With heads held proudly and arms high, they stamped and whirled with defiant, explosive steps. Joe and I often stole up to our roof terrace to admire the scene down below.

All too soon, the sultry summer days began to shorten and it was September. Our boxes from Bahrain finally arrived, although by then, they were almost more well-travelled than we were.

They left Bahrain but first holidayed for a while in neighbouring Doha. Then they returned to Bahrain. After that they spent a few weeks in a warehouse in Germany. From Germany they flew to northern Spain. Foolishly, we believed we'd soon be welcoming them home but, instead, they set off back to Germany.

After a long weekend in Germany, they decided to visit Belgium. Obviously Belgium wasn't to their liking, because, yet again, they returned for another week's holiday in the warehouse in Germany.

Every few days I typed in our tracking number, which by then I knew by heart: 1Z97840-

V6-87906. I learned that our boxes had, at last, returned to Spain, this time Madrid. They obviously enjoyed the city, because they seemed rather reluctant to move from there.

I wrote to the company, asking for news. Back came the reply, in English.

> *'Please don't worry Mrs Twead. The shipment is under my personal control. Now, we are showing the documentation to Customs Authorities. We think they will like your documentation and you will meet your boxes soon.'*

Finally, our boxes made their slow way down to us in the south. To be exact, they were delivered to a friend in the next village, as we didn't trust the parcel company to be able to locate El Hoyo.

It was a bit of an anticlimax when they finally arrived. We had to pay another 20 euros for 'country tax' or something and the boxes themselves were battered and had clearly been broken into.

By now we could hardly remember what we'd packed and when we tore the boxes open, most of the stuff was of very little use. All those long trousers, shirts and ties for Joe, the long skirts and long-sleeved tops for me, when would we ever wear them again? They were essential for our teaching career in the Middle East, but here in Spain? I packed them all up again and instructed

MOTHS AND YESO

Joe to store them in the garage, where they remain, gathering dust.

However, packing the stuff away gave me a good feeling of closure. That chapter in our lives, that year in Bahrain as the Arab revolution raged around us, was over, shelved out of sight but not quite out of mind. It had been a stressful experience, one that cannot easily be forgotten.

※※※

Not so many decades ago, El Hoyo had been a mining village. The main road from below did not exist then and the village could only be approached along ancient and well-trodden paths. In those days all provisions and mail arrived by mule.

As the mine prospered, the village thrived and a better road was laid. Even today, when one drives down the mountain, one still sees the remnants of mule tracks and the buildings where travellers and mules stopped for the night.

Receiving mail had always been rather a problem for us. When we moved in, our front door had no letterbox, so one of the first jobs was to buy a mailbox and fix it on the wall. There wasn't much choice at the hardware shop. We could have a square black one, a square black one, or a square black one. Unsurprisingly, we chose a square black one. It wouldn't be until much later that we realised we were wasting our time.

Fixing anything to any wall of our house was a challenge. Old Spanish houses were constructed with rocks and rubble held together with dry, compacted sand. Joe's drill bit would either sink without trace, or hit a flint and emit sparks without making the slightest impression. Joe did his best, but we invariably ended up with a vast, cavernous hole even if we were just attempting to hang a picture. He therefore had good reason to dread the task of putting up the mailbox.

Valiantly, he drilled into the wall and, as usual, copious amounts of dry grit poured out until the drill bit hit a stone and skittered sideways. The mailbox required four holes, so he had to repeat the operation four times and each hole grew alarmingly in size.

The vibrating drill had brought Paco out of his house. He inspected Joe's handiwork, eyed the mound of grit and rubble on Joe's feet and roared with laughter.

"English! What are you doing?"

"I'm putting up a mailbox. I'm drilling out four screw-holes."

A fist would have fitted comfortably inside each hole.

"You are not doing a good job!" Paco said, when he'd stopped laughing.

"I can't help it if these walls are impossible," said Joe, scratching himself irritably.

"Pah! *Yeso* will fix that."

MOTHS AND YESO

So I was instructed to go and make up some *yeso* to fill the holes.

Yeso. For those who are contemplating a move to Spain and have DIY in mind, be warned. *Yeso* will become very familiar to you, but it's not for the faint-hearted.

I don't believe there is an exact equivalent to *yeso* in the UK and we'd never heard of it before we moved. The Spanish building trade use it for everything: plastering, fixing door or window frames, filling holes, whatever.

Wonderful stuff, *yeso*, but only if you handle it with the utmost care and respect.

But nobody told me that.

ROASTED MUSHROOMS WITH ONIONS AND HERBS

A delicious side dish to chicken or a super tasty *tapas* dish with a chilled glass of dry white wine. About 10 minutes preparation, 30 minutes cooking, and will serve 3 or 4.

Ingredients

- 600g (21oz) mushrooms – any kind you like, mixed or just one kind
- 1 large onion
- 4 cloves garlic
- 1 large sprig rosemary, leaves picked
- Large bunch of oregano, leaves picked
- 2 tablespoons extra virgin olive oil
- Salt and black pepper to season

Method

- Preheat the oven to 200°C/400°F/Gas mark 6.

- Peel the onion and slice thinly, peel the garlic and slice lengthwise.

- Wash the mushrooms and slice thickly.

- Chop the leaves of the rosemary and the oregano.

- Pour the olive oil into a large shallow roasting tin, then add the mushrooms, garlic and onion, mix around in the tin so they are evenly covered with the oil. Sprinkle with the herbs, then season.

- Cook in the oven for 15 minutes then remove and pour away any juices. Put back into the oven and cook for a further 15 minutes.

- Place onto a serving dish, sprinkle with some more chopped oregano and serve.

6

BABYSITTING

I cut open the brown paper sack of *yeso* we had bought and tipped a generous amount of the fine white powder into a metal bucket. Then I added water and mixed enthusiastically with a trowel. It didn't take long for it to attain a smooth consistency, like thick custard. I stirred a few seconds more, ensuring there were no lumps. Satisfied, I lifted the bucket and brought it through the house and presented it to Joe.

"Okay," said Joe, grabbing the trowel, "let's mend these holes."

But the trowel didn't move. It was stuck fast into the *yeso*. Trowel, *yeso* and bucket were one united, solid lump, as hard as rock.

"WHAT THE..."

"It can't have set already!" I said.

But it had.

Paco laughed so hard he had to take his cap off to rub his eyes.

"You English!" he gasped. "You must have used *yeso rapido!* You need the regular *yeso!*"

We didn't know there were two types of *yeso*.

Paco stamped off to get some more *yeso*, while Joe and I struggled to rescue the bucket and trowel from the granite grip of the *yeso*. Paco returned and deftly filled the holes in the wall for us. It soon set and Joe drilled the screw-holes again, then mounted the mailbox on the wall, almost perfectly straight.

"There! That's done," he said, standing back to admire his work. "The postman shouldn't have any trouble with that."

We had to throw the bucket and trowel away and we needn't have bothered with the mailbox at all. There it hung, waiting to be fed with post that never came.

I suppose the fact that our house had three doors, opening onto three different streets didn't help. I imagine any postman would find that confusing. Our house wasn't huge, but decidedly quirky.

"Any post?" I asked hopefully, as Joe unlocked the box daily.

"Nope, just moths," was the usual reply.

Our mail arrived in a variety of ways. Usually, it arrived on the fish van, smelling strongly of sardines and calamari. Sometimes it came on the bread van and smelled much sweeter. At other times the phone rang and Marcia from the village shop informed us that she had letters for us.

"There's a small packet from your daughter in Australia, an electricity bill, a postcard from your English friends, they're on holiday in Lanzarote by the way and a letter from the taxman." Marcia may have been well over 80, but nothing escaped her eagle eye.

We'd discovered that UPS and DHL drivers flatly refused to drive up to El Hoyo and devised all manner of excuses to avoid the twisting, winding road to our village. When the phone rang in the morning, we knew it would be a driver, needing to deliver a parcel.

"*Señora* Twead?"

"Yes, speaking..."

"My van is broken, can you meet me in the next village?"

Or,

"*Señor* Twead?"

"Yes, speaking..."

"I cannot drive to your village. Your village does not show up on my navigation equipment."

Joe and I knew how to answer. We'd done it so many times before.

"You know the Repsol service station at the bottom of the mountain?" we said. "The one near Carrefour? Put it behind the counter there."

"Yes! I know it! I'll leave it there." We heard the relief in the driver's voice.

Sorted. So Joe would climb into the car and

drive down the mountain to collect our waiting parcel from the nice staff at the Repsol garage. Soon they recognised Joe on sight and handed over parcels without a word. We were ever grateful for their enduring patience.

The mailbox was not always empty. Sometimes a lonely slip of paper forlornly awaited retrieval at the bottom.

"That proves the postman does know it's a mailbox," Joe said, waving the slip of paper at me.

"What does it say?" I wanted to know.

Joe read it aloud.

"We tried to deliver your packet, but nobody was in. Please collect it from the post office between the hours of 8.00am and 2.00pm."

We'd been in the house all day and nobody had knocked on any of our doors.

"Oh well," Joe would say, "I'll drive down to the post office tomorrow morning. And I'd better check that nothing's been left at Marcia's or the Repsol garage while I'm there."

It always amazed me that we received any post at all.

☘☘☘

September meant that most villagers returned to their homes in the big town below the mountain and returned to work or school. Apart from at the weekends, El Hoyo was quiet and no children kicked footballs, no motor bikes buzzed and no strains of flamenco echoed in the streets.

During the week in the winter months, the sole inhabitants of El Hoyo were Uncle Felix, Geronimo, Marcia at the shop, the Boys and us. The new bar closed its doors, opening them again only at weekends or for festive occasions.

Our grapes hung in giant, fat bunches, ripening faster than we could eat them. Sylvia taught Snitch and Felicity, her two almost-grown kittens, how to crouch still and silent in the thick thatch of vine-leaves, then pounce on unsuspecting sparrows as they pecked at the plump grapes.

One afternoon that September, there was a polite knock at our door. Joe went to open it. I was in the kitchen and stopped clattering plates to listen.

"*Hola,*" said Joe.

"*Hola,*" came the reply. "How are you and Veeky?"

"Very well," said Joe and I noted a tone of inquiry in his voice.

I recognized the visitor's voice, it was Roberto. But why were the Boys calling on us?

"Veeky said that when we started our salsa classes down the mountain, you and she would be happy to watch Emilia for us."

"Er, she did?"

"Yes, it will not be for long and we'll leave

everything out for you. Emilia is a very good little girl."

Oh dear. I'd quite forgotten to tell Joe about that conversation I'd had with the Boys weeks ago. It had completely slipped my mind.

"So Vicky offered to babysit?" I heard Joe say, too casually.

I hurriedly dried my hands and remembered some vital jobs I needed to do on the roof terrace. I slipped quietly out of the back door. A few minutes slipped past, then...

"Vicky? VICKY! Where are you?"

I sighed and sheepishly came back down the staircase, preparing myself to face the music. Joe was not pleased. I could tell by the way his lips were pressed together and the agitated scratching of his nethers.

"What's all this about? You offered to babysit for the Boys? Is that right?"

"No, I didn't offer... They just kind of assumed it would be okay."

"Well, it isn't okay! Why didn't you just say no?"

"I couldn't. They just kind of sprang it on me. You wouldn't have been able to say no either."

"Humph! Well, their salsa classes start next week. I'm not happy about this."

"Oh, we'll probably enjoy it. Emilia looks like a lovely little thing. We can get into practice in case we have grandchildren one day."

When the day came around, Joe and I rang the

Boys' doorbell. We'd all agreed that it made more sense to watch Emilia at their house. They had all the baby equipment and toys there and our house was not really baby-proof.

"Come in," said Roberto, who had little Emilia balanced on his hip.

We followed him inside and I tried not to stare round the room. It was gorgeous. Everything was either cream or white, including the floors, walls and three-piece suite. A few clever paintings adorned the walls and tasteful ornaments were artfully displayed. The glass dining table and side tables were polished to a dazzle. At the far end was a gleaming kitchen with American-style fridge and stone counters. This was nothing like our cottage.

"Everything is ready for you," said Roberto. "We have shut the dogs in the garden, so they will not bother you. Emilia has had her meal and her bath. You can put her in her highchair and give her this yogurt to finish off, if you like. She is already in her sleep-suit, so you will not need to change her. But we have left spare nappies and things here just in case."

Federico patted a pile of nappies on the sofa and gestured to the changing mat, lotions and talcum powder we might need.

"Do you need reminding how to change a nappy?" asked Roberto.

"Of course not!" said Joe. "We've had children too. It's one of those things you never forget."

BABYSITTING

Little Emilia studied him solemnly with her dark, brown eyes.

"As I say, I do not think it will be necessary to change her. When she's had her yogurt, you can just play with her until we get back."

Federico indicated the big, white box in the corner, brimming over with toys.

"If she gets tired and falls asleep," went on Roberto, "that is okay."

"We'll be fine," I said. "Go and enjoy yourselves."

Now that it was time to go, the pair seemed reluctant to leave. Federico straightened a couple of already straight cushions and Roberto kissed the top of Emilia's head and finally handed her over to me.

"There is a bottle of juice on the side, if you think she is thirsty."

"Don't worry, we'll be fine," I said again.

Reluctantly, the Boys left. Emilia's pudgy hands grabbed the chain round my neck and cooed.

"You are lovely!" I told her.

And she was. Her skin was perfect, soft and clear and her hair was a crown of dark golden curls. She smiled and cooed all the time and smelled delicious. I turned to Joe.

"Do you want to hold her?"

"Okay."

I handed her to Joe and she beamed into his

face. He smiled right back at her and I knew everything was going to be all right.

Unfortunately, it was a Tuesday and my favourite TV program was on. Joe and I had already discussed this and we'd agreed, if he felt comfortable, that I would shoot home and watch my show. It was only on for 45 minutes and I'd be right back. I couldn't watch it on the Boys' TV because it was an English show, not on Spanish channels and our video recorder wasn't working.

Now it was my turn to be reluctant to leave.

"Are you sure you'll be okay?" I said for the third time. "I won't go if you're not one hundred percent sure."

"Go! Enjoy it. We'll be fine, won't we, Emilia?" Emilia smiled back at him. "I'm going to put her in the highchair, give her that yogurt and then we'll play for a while. You'll be back by then."

"Okay, if you're really sure…"

"Go!"

I left them on the sofa, playing 'This Little Piggy went to Market', Emilia's giggles filling the air. There is no language barrier with babies and it didn't matter a bit that she didn't know what a piggy was.

Three quarters of an hour later, I hurried back and tapped lightly on the door.

"Come in quick," said Joe, letting me in. "I've had a couple of little problems."

He was holding Emilia, who beamed at me.

BABYSITTING

"What sort of problems?" I asked, coming in and closing the door behind me.

"Well, I put her in her highchair and tried to give her the yogurt. It was really difficult! She kept grabbing the spoon and the yogurt went everywhere. I forgot how hard it was feeding babies."

"Ah! That's why she's wearing a different sleep-suit? Well, you seem to have managed okay."

"Left a bit of a mess I'm afraid... Yogurt everywhere and this little one could do with another face and hand wash. Couldn't you, Milly-Molly?" He tickled her and she squirmed, chuckling.

"That's okay," I said, "you keep her amused and I'll have a wipe round."

I walked over to the highchair, which was coated liberally with yogurt. Yogurty smears decorated the floor, end table and the white leather couch.

"How did the yogurt get this far?" I asked curiously.

"Well, that was my second little problem. She was covered in yogurt, so I put the changing-mat on the floor and managed to get her sleep-suit off and I thought I'd change her nappy at the same time, but she wouldn't keep still. I'd forgotten how wriggly babies are, it was like a wrestling match and she thought it was hilarious. Anyway, she flips over and zooms off. I'm telling you, she's so fast! She crawls like a demon!"

I was listening as I wiped the surfaces with a damp cloth. "Well, no harm done. You caught her in the end."

"Yes, but it was quite a chase, under the table, behind the couch, behind the chairs. One big game of hide-and-seek. She was laughing and giggling the whole time, she thought it was all a huge joke."

Satisfied that I'd de-yogurted everything and restored the Boys' room to its former pristine glory, I concentrated on Emilia.

Joe sat down on the couch with Emilia on his lap. I plonked myself down beside him and took the baby's fat little hands and sponged them off. Then I wiped her face.

"There we are!" I said. "Good as new."

Emilia beamed at me, but unfortunately that wasn't quite the end of the story.

EGG AND ANCHOVY TOAST TAPAS

A fabulous tasty snack or addition to the *tapas* table.

Ingredients

- French style baguette, cut into rounds and lightly toasted on each side
- 1 jar anchovies
- 3 eggs
- Splash milk
- Salt and pepper
- Olive oil

Method

• Beat the eggs in a pan with a little milk, salt and pepper.

• Cook over a medium heat stirring all the time until the scrambled eggs are cooked.

• Drain the liquid from the jar of anchovies, remove the anchovies and cut into small pieces. Then mix with the scrambled eggs.

• Drizzle a little olive oil over each toasted round of bread, spoon a little of the egg mixture on top.

• Serve with parsley and tomatoes.

7

GOLF

Emilia gurgled and reached for the pink rabbit that Joe was jiggling in front of her. She really was an incredibly happy baby, very easy to amuse. She cooed at the rabbit, grabbed it and sucked at one ear.

"Vicky, can you smell something?" said Joe.

I sniffed the air. "Oh dear, I think I can..."

"Has she filled her nappy?"

I leaned over and sniffed Emilia at close quarters, as one does.

"No, I don't think so. She just smells of talc and baby lotion."

Joe sniffed again. "It's in the room somewhere."

We both looked around at the sparkling clean floor. Nothing. I jumped up and peered under the table and behind the chairs. Nothing.

"I can't see anything," I said, "and I can't smell it over here."

"Now, let's think," said Joe. "Hmm... Now, if you were a really cunning, clever babypoop, where would you hide?"

I went back to the couch and sniffed again. "Oh no, I think it may be..."

"...behind the couch," finished Joe.

He passed Emilia to me, got up and peered round the back of the couch. It was a huge, heavy corner affair of the Chesterfield type. However, there was a gap behind it.

"That's where it must be," said Joe, scratching himself. "She crawled behind there with her nappy off and she took ages to come out."

"I don't fancy trying to move this couch," I said.

Joe scratched himself and thought for a second. "Pass me some tissues, I'm going to crawl behind."

He dropped on all-fours and pushed himself behind the sofa. Emilia and I watched as he forced himself in.

"Yep, I see it." His voice was muffled and I didn't envy him his task. "Got it, I'm coming out."

At that precise moment, a key turned in the lock and the door opened. Emilia squeaked and bounced, arms outstretched toward the Boys.

"We're back," said Roberto, taking Emilia and kissing her curls. "Has she been good? Was everything okay?"

GOLF

"She's been as good as gold," I said, but my eyes were drawn to Joe's rump, which had just appeared like a full moon, reversing its way out from behind the sofa.

Roberto and Federico watched in surprise as Joe shuffled out backwards and got to his feet. I held my breath.

"I found it," said Joe, passing a toy clown to Emilia. "How was the salsa class?"

"Good, thank you," said Roberto and Federico nodded his bald head. "Thank you for looking after Emilia. Same time next week?"

"Of course," said Joe, cheerily. "No problem." He waved to Emilia and hurried to the door, grabbing my arm to steer me out. "Come on, Vicky, we must go."

"Thank you again," said Roberto, as Joe bundled me out of the door.

"Well, that was a quick exit," I said.

Joe was moving so fast I could barely keep up with him.

"Why are you walking all funny?" I panted when we were halfway down the street, Joe still racing ahead. "Joe! For goodness' sake, slow down! And you look all sort of lopsided. Why are you walking like that?"

"Tell you in a minute," he hissed.

As Joe unlocked our door, I fired off the other question that was burning in my head.

"Joe, what did you do with the babypoop?"

"I wrapped it up in the tissues and then I heard the Boys come in."

"You didn't leave the poop there, behind the sofa?"

"No..."

"So where is it now?"

He rolled his eyes and pulled a face. "That's why I'm in such a hurry and why I'm walking funny, I was trying to avoid squashing it. I've got it here. I didn't know what to do with it, so I shoved it in my pocket."

※※※

In El Hoyo, summer extended well into September and October, although daylight hours lessened. The sun was still hot and the skies were usually cloudless. Autumn hadn't arrived in full and there was no need for winter clothes.

The Ufarte twins and their older brothers went back to school and we didn't see so much of them. The whole family spent most of the week in their other house in the city, although Lola often stayed behind in El Hoyo.

We carried on baby-sitting for the Boys until they finished their salsa dancing course. There were no further mishaps, but one conversation made me smile. As we arrived one evening, we heard Federico scolding his little dog.

"You are going outside, Copito. The English are coming to watch Emilia while we are out and I don't want you pooping behind the couch like you always do."

Joe and I stared at each other.

"What? So that was *dog* poop I picked up from behind the sofa?" Joe hissed.

I nodded. "Yep, seems like it."

"I put *dog* poop in my pocket?"

"Probably..."

ⵣⵣⵣ

As the weeks went by, we'd become quite friendly with Sofía's boyfriend's family. Alejandro Senior, the grandfather, was a gentleman, but also a bit of a rascal, as we'd discovered the night of the Grand Opening. As far as we knew, he was still courting Mother and we wondered where that relationship was heading.

Alejandro Senior was always friendly and polite, but there was a shrewdness behind those eyes that Joe and I recognised. We knew he had built his business up from nothing and it was still thriving despite the terrible recession that had hit Spain.

Paco invited us round for a quick beer but as usual the evening had developed into another party. I was in the little kitchen with the women, but we could hear the men in the next room shouting their political views.

Eventually, the topic turned to golf, one of Alejandro Senior's favourite subjects, although it baffled Paco. Alejandro Senior was sprightly for his age and regularly enjoyed a round of golf with his son Alejandro and grandson, Alejandro Junior.

"Come out with us for nine holes," Alejandro Senior said to Joe. "The weather is still good and you will enjoy it! It keeps me young, you know, all that fresh air and exercise."

"I haven't played for years," Joe said, "and I wasn't very good then."

"Nonsense! It does not matter," said Alejandro Senior, clapping him on the shoulder. "It is only a bit of fun amongst ourselves. Do you have any clubs?"

"Well, yes, if I can find them. They've been in the garage for years, I'd have to dig them out and I don't know if they're any good any more."

"Paco, you'll come, won't you?" said Alejandro Senior, swivelling in his chair to face Paco. "Forget about work for once and come and play a round of golf with us."

"Pah!" said Paco, thumping the table with his fist. "Golf? I've no time for golf! It's September and I have grapes to press and wine to make! I've no time for golf!"

"You should try it," said Alejandro. "It is very therapeutic."

Paco shook his head vehemently. "Count me out," he said scornfully. "I've no time to waste on silly games."

"Well, are you going to say yes?" I asked Joe later.

GOLF

"I think so, it might be fun," he answered, a little doubtfully. "That's if my clubs have survived in the garage all this time."

I sensed that he was a little uneasy about the planned outing. It had been a number of years since he last played golf and he probably didn't want to make a fool of himself.

We dug out the golf paraphernalia, cleaned the bag, oiled the wheels of the trolley and packed the pockets with new golf balls.

"Those sticks scrubbed up quite well," I remarked, "considering how long they've been mouldering in the garage."

"Clubs. They're golf clubs."

"Whatever."

A date had been set and I kept catching him in the garden making practice swings, his hands gripping an imaginary golf club, his eyes focused on some distant point on the mountainside.

The day arrived and the sky was uncharacteristically dull, with leaden clouds moving in.

"You'll be fine," I said as Alejandro Senior's flashy Mercedes drew up, all three Alejandros inside. "I think you're wise to take your waterproof jacket though, it looks like it might rain."

Joe stowed his golf stuff in the boot, climbed into the car and they swept away. Waving to him and the three Alejandros, I hoped they'd have a good day. It would do Joe good to get out and do something different.

I enjoyed my day of solitude and used it for writing and pottering in the garden. Time flew past and I heard Joe's key in the front door. He entered looking exhausted.

"How did it go? Did you have a good time?"

"Hang on, let me put this golf stuff away then I'll tell you all about it. I'm putting it all back in the garage, I won't be using it again."

Oh dear. That sounded ominous. I made some coffee and waited for Joe to come back in. He returned, hung his jacket on the back of the chair and plonked himself down.

"Did the weather stay nice for you?" I asked.

"Yes, a few spots of rain at one time, but nothing much."

"What was the course like?"

"Beautiful. I dread to think how many hundreds of gallons of water they use to keep it so green."

Water is a precious commodity in any part of Spain and golf courses are notorious for using copious amounts of it.

"Well, what happened?" I was getting impatient. "Didn't you enjoy it? Why won't you be playing again?"

Joe took a sip of coffee, then began.

"Before we started, Alejandro Senior said they always put ten euros on the game, winner takes all. I was fine with that and handed over my ten euros, even though I knew I'd lose. From the first hole, I could see that all three Alejandros were really good, I reckon they spend more time playing golf than they let on. You should see their equipment. All the latest stuff, really expensive clubs. Anyway, I played superbly, couldn't believe how well I hit that ball, especially with my old clubs. Alejandro Senior claps me on the back and says we should put another ten euros in the pot. Then we go on to the second hole and I'm still playing like a pro." He paused, recalling the wonderful shots he'd played.

"So then what happened?"

"I got a birdie on the second hole, you know."

"Oh, poor thing! Did you hurt it?"

"Don't be obtuse. It means I was one under par."

"Oh." I wasn't even going to ask what that meant. "Then what?"

"They all congratulated me and Alejandro Senior said we should add another ten euros to the pot, just to make things interesting. I didn't really want to, but the other two Alejandros agreed, so I did. And then everything went pear-shaped..."

"How?"

"I couldn't hit a ball straight after those first two holes. I played like an idiot. All the Alejandros said it was just a bit of bad luck, but I knew my first two holes were a fluke and now I was just playing my usual standard."

"Oh dear."

"My golf trolley started squeaking as I pulled it along, then one of the wheels went wonky. And every hole I played was worse than the last one. If there was a bunker, my ball landed in it. I even managed to hit a fence. All three Alejandros stood there watching me make a complete hash of every shot… It was awful."

"Oh dear."

Joe scratched himself and sighed. "The worst hole was the sixth," he recalled, shaking his head. "I managed to hit my ball into the rough and it bounced off a tree. It took a while to find it, wedged under a root on the ground. Impossible to play, so Alejandro said we'd have to apply the penalty rule."

"What's that?"

"He said I'd get a one-stroke penalty, but I could pick up the ball and drop it over my shoulder, then play it from there. So I did that."

"And?"

"Well, that's when a funny thing happened. I dropped the ball and it just vanished. Completely disappeared."

"How could it vanish?"

"I don't know! We all searched for it, but we couldn't find it. Honestly, it was a mystery! The grass wasn't particularly long there and it wasn't on a slope and there weren't any roots or holes. We spent ages looking for that ball, but we never

GOLF

found it. Anyway, it meant I had to use a new ball and lost yet another stroke."

"Oh well..."

"It didn't make much difference, my score was diabolical by then anyway. I won't be playing again. Apart from making a complete idiot of myself, it cost me thirty euros."

"Who won?"

"Alejandro Senior, of course. He pocketed the 90 euros. No wonder he's a millionaire."

"Well, it's a pity you don't want to play again."

"Enough, I don't want to think or talk about golf anymore. What's for dinner?"

Unfortunately, not everybody was willing to drop the subject. Whenever we saw Alejandro Senior, he delighted in talking about that golf day again and describing Joe's unlucky shots in lurid detail. The time Joe's ball hit the fence, the ball that plopped into the ornamental fountain, the ball that flew backwards and the ball dropped over the shoulder, vanishing into thin air.

Strangely, I solved the mystery of the disappearing golf ball. When I was tidying up and hanging Joe's jacket back in the wardrobe, I found something. Nestled in the hood of his waterproof jacket was the golf ball he had dropped over his shoulder. I told Joe, but we didn't share our knowledge with any of the Alejandros. No doubt we wouldn't hear the end of it.

One day, we were invited to see the

Alejandros' grand family home in the village. The invitation came because we had been talking about our chickens and Alejandro (Alejandro Junior's father) mentioned that they kept a lot of animals at their house in El Hoyo. Would we like to see their house and animals?

Of course we would!

ANDALUCIAN BEEF WRAPS

Similar to Mexican fajitas, this simple Andalucian beef wrap dish is ideal for lunch and supper. The beef can be substituted with cold chicken and you can add a variety of other ingredients such as avocado, beetroot, spinach leaves or apple.

Serves 3

Ingredients

- 6 flour tortillas
- Cold cooked beef, cut into thin strips
- 2 small tomatoes
- ½ cucumber
- 1 small tin sweetcorn
- 2 spring onions
- Grated cheese
- Aioli (garlic mayonnaise)

Method

- Chop the tomatoes into small cubes.
- Roughly peel the cucumber and finely dice.
- Clean the spring onions and slice thinly.
- Warm the tortillas according to the packet instructions.
- Place one tortilla onto a plate and add a little bit of spring onion, cucumber, tomato and sweetcorn.
- Then add a few strips of beef, a little grated cheese and top with aioli.
- Roll up the wrap and enjoy!

8

A VILLAGE SECRET

Alejandro Junior and Sofía led the way, arms entwined, heads close to each other. Paco walked with his childhood friend, Alejandro, deep in conversation. Although I was chatting with Carmen and Alejandro's wife, I could hear Joe and Alejandro Senior behind us, Alejandro Senior giving Joe some unwanted tips about the best choice of golf club in wet weather conditions on an uphill slope.

We walked past the village square and eventually came to a halt at the gates and massive walls of their house at the edge of the village. Joe and I had walked past the house many times before and the unseen guard dogs on the other side of the high walls had always barked and snarled a warning. It's not hard to guess the size of a dog from its bark and the dogs behind these walls, we knew, were big. Alejandro's wife caught my apprehensive expression.

"Don't worry, they're tied up during the day when we're here in the village," she said.

Alejandro tapped a code into the alarm system, then used two separate keys to unlock the gates. We all trooped in and I looked around.

The paved yard was big enough to park at least twenty cars. A mountain of firewood was stacked neatly against one of the far walls and, apart from a few large potted plants and a stone-built barbecue, there was little else to catch the eye. A wrought-iron gate, set into the far wall, overlooked what appeared to be tilled land.

Three huge dogs, part grizzly bear, part wolf, were chained to the wall, barking furiously, lips peeled back, straining to reach us. I felt very sorry for them, they probably didn't have much of a life. Being permanently isolated and waiting to shred an intruder, was, I thought, not an ideal existence for a dog.

"Come into the house," said Alejandro's wife. "I will show you around.

I'm not sure what I was expecting, but the house wasn't ostentatious. I reminded myself that although it belonged to millionaires, it was a village retreat, just one house of many.

The kitchen was huge, dominated by a massive fireplace so big that a whole family could warm themselves at once. Now I understood why they needed so much firewood. A vast table stood in the middle of the room, big enough to seat sixteen people, but the room was homely in spite of its size.

As Carmen and Sofía had probably seen the house many times before, they didn't accompany us on the guided tour. Alejandro Senior lit a fat cigar and also stayed behind with them in the kitchen. Paco, Joe and I followed Alejandro Junior, Alejandro and his wife.

"This is our bedroom and another two bedrooms and the bathroom..." said Alejandro's wife.

Joe and I oohed and aahed. The rooms were nice, very Spanish but unremarkable. Each was modestly furnished, the bedrooms with crucifixes on the walls above ornate iron bedsteads, the bathrooms typical of bathrooms anywhere. Alejandro's wife chattered on while her husband waited patiently. Paco looked bored and stole glances up the corridor.

When there were no more wardrobes to show off, Alejandro walked to the end of the corridor and tapped at another alarm box on the wall beside a heavy, locked door. A broad grin decorated Paco's face.

"Now you will see something!" said Paco.

Fascinated but puzzled, Joe and I exchanged glances. Alejandro pushed the door open and stepped inside, beckoning us to follow.

More bedrooms? I wondered. But why should these be locked behind an alarmed door? Alejandro groped for the light switch and an enormous room, the size of a barn, appeared in front of us. It was a bodega. Joe and I gaped at the polished-wood barrels, each neatly labelled stacked up on shelves that rose to the ceiling.

"My father, Alejandro Senior, started this collection," said Alejandro waving his arm to take in the room.

"Wow..." said Joe. Words had failed us both.

Alejandro fussed with some meters fixed to the wall. "Humidity and temperature adjustments," he explained.

In addition to the banks of wine barrels, racks of wine bottles, tilted slightly, lined the walls of the room. By now Paco was laughing at the expression on our faces.

"English! I bet you did not know this was here in the centre of El Hoyo," he roared.

"No," we said, shaking our heads in disbelief.

Paco laughed. "You are honoured! Most of the villagers do not know about this!"

"There are some very valuable wines here," said Alejandro. "Rare labels, some very old wines, some wines that do not exist anywhere else."

"Are they all valuable?" I asked.

"No, sometimes we buy them just because we like them. Sit down, I will show you."

In the centre of the room was a round, wooden table, with stools pushed under it. Paco sat and we followed suit. Alejandro's wife excused herself and retreated to the main part of the house.

"Hmm..." said Alejandro to himself, leaning in to read the labels on the barrels. "This one, I think... You will like this, it is a merry little wine with a hint of cranberry." He turned the tap and ruby wine spurted into the glass held under it. "And maybe this one... Full-bodied, honest and earthy, a robust and courageous wine."

Paco jumped up and took the full glasses from him, plonking them down on the table in front of us. Alejandro was still carefully inspecting each cask.

"Ah yes," he said, "this amusing little wine has a bit of a kick... Oh and this one... Underestimated, rather young, but fragrant with a suggestion of almonds..."

Soon the table-top was covered with an alarming number of filled wine glasses.

"English!" roared Paco. "Try some! Tell Alejandro and his son what you think."

What Joe and I knew about wine could be written on a thumbnail, we either liked a wine or we didn't and that was the extent of our expertise. This was going to be a challenge.

"Er, do we taste it and spit it out?" I asked, looking around for a bucket.

"No, we already know they are good. Taste and enjoy them."

"Pah!" said Paco, thumping the table. "This room holds the best wine collection in Andalucía, apart from the wine I make from my own grapes, of course."

Joe and I exchanged nervous glances and I picked a glass from the dazzling display in front of us. I sipped as Alejandro hovered on one side and his son on the other.

"Take a proper taste!" roared Paco. "You cannot make a decision from a sip the size of a raindrop!"

Obediently, I took a healthy slurp.

"Mmm... Very nice," I said.

"But what about the taste?" Alejandro wanted to know.

"Err..." I sipped again and tried to remember a few things Alejandro had said. "Unpretentious. Maybe a trace of almonds?"

I struck lucky.

"Excellent!" exclaimed our host. "That is precisely what I would have said. Joe, what do you think?"

I passed the glass to Joe and he sampled it as Alejandro's eyes bored into him.

"Oh, I agree with Vicky."

"Good, finish that off and we'll discuss the next." Alejandro was already pushing another glass towards me.

I swigged and racked my writer's brain for some suitable comment to bestow upon this one. "A sunny little wine," I tried. "A fresh, open-air taste."

Alejandro nodded. "Indeed, a very good description," he said.

I passed the glass to Joe, who was gaping at

me. He raised it to his lips.

"Well? Your opinion, Joe?"

"Oh, I agree with Vicky."

Satisfied, Alejandro handed me the next and the next. Each time I had to come up with a new description and as the wine took its inevitable hold, my verdicts became more flowery. It was beyond the limits of my Spanish vocabulary, but Alejandro Junior's English was excellent and he interpreted for his father.

"Ah, a playful wine!" I said. "I sense a hint of irony with just a twist of summer twilight in the mountains."

I was talking complete rubbish, but Alejandro Junior dutifully translated and his father seemed impressed. Alejandro glanced at Joe, eyebrows raised in question.

"Oh, I agree with Vicky," said Joe hurriedly.

"And this one?"

Sip, sip, pause. I was getting into my swing now. "Um, a melodious blend with hidden depths, rather a witty little wine with a riddle in the aftertaste. This wine has a passion and a personality all of its own."

Judging by the narrowing of Joe's eyes, perhaps I was going a bit too far. Alejandro Junior translated.

"Good! Good!" nodded Alejandro. "Joe? I take it you agree with Vicky."

"Oh, definitely," said Joe. "What she said."

At last the glasses were empty and Joe and I

staggered out of Alejandro's bodega. We'd spent half an hour tasting wine and I don't believe Alejandro, Alejandro Junior or Paco had touched a single drop. Back in the kitchen, Alejandro Senior rose to meet us.

"Do you want to see the animals?" he asked.

"Yesh please," we said.

Alejandro Senior led us past the three snarling monsters and through another gate to a field. Vegetables grew in neat rows and a worker was hoeing the soil. I had my camera with me and snapped it all. We skirted the cultivated land, heading for the barn at the end. Tethered to a fence was a young horse, pawing the ground with one front hoof.

"He's not broken in yet," said Alejandro Senior approaching him confidently.

The colt's nostrils flared and his eyes rolled in warning, showing their whites. Alejandro Senior patted his neck and the horse stood still, accepting the attention but not enjoying it, still fearful. I fumbled with the camera, snapping pictures.

Just then, Joe sneezed. The young horse, startled, swung round and aimed a kick at Alejandro Senior. Alejandro Senior skipped back and aimed a kick at the front end of the horse.

Very rarely, one takes a photo that one knows is extraordinary and I knew I had just accomplished that by accident. The old man and the young horse formed a perfect circle, each aiming a kick at the other. The backdrop of rolling mountains, the field and the blue sky, contributed to what I was convinced would be an exceptional photo.

"Wait until you see this photo," I said to Joe. "I think it's a bit special."

I didn't enjoy the animal tour, although I tried hard to hide it. All the animals were provided with food and water but I silently deplored their living conditions. In one shed white rabbits were being reared for the pot. There was a huge white buck in one tiny cage and mothers with their babies in other equally small cages. I don't think eating rabbit meat is wrong, but I do believe that every animal deserves a decent quality of life.

The chicken shed was no better. The hens were housed in small cages and had no opportunity to stretch their wings or scratch the ground. The shed was artificially lit and Alejandro Senior explained that the lights were left on to fool the chickens into thinking it was still daylight so they would lay more eggs.

After seeing terrified quails scattering in the last shed, I was ready to go home. We thanked our hosts and left soon after, heads still befuddled by the wine-tasting session.

"You certainly waxed lyrical in the bodega," Joe said.

"Well, you weren't much help with your 'I agree with Vicky.' Couldn't you come up with anything better?"

"You seemed to be doing fine all by yourself."

Halfway home, I remembered the photo I'd taken. I stopped and scrolled through the day's photos, searching for it. And it was superb, even on the camera's little digital display. I couldn't wait to see it full-size.

"Here, let's have a look," said Joe grabbing the camera. "Where is it?"

"Click the button on the left and scroll through. It's quite near the end."

"I can't see any photos."

"Which button did you press?"

"This one."

I craned forward to see which button he was indicating. It was clearly marked, although the print was tiny. *'Eliminar todas'*.

"You're joking?"

"No, why?"

"You've just deleted all the photos I took today."

"Oh."

I had lost my masterpiece and all the photos stored in the camera. We would have to rely on our wine-blurred memories to recapture that remarkable day.

♀♀♀

One evening in October, much to my surprise, Joe answered the phone when it rang. He didn't call me, so I didn't bother to listen. He came back into the kitchen scratching himself furiously.

"That was Judith. She really should lock those dogs of hers away when she's making a phone call, I could hardly hear a word she said."

"How is she? How's Mother? Is everything okay?"

"Yes, they're all fine. She rang to ask us a favour. She's invited some friends of hers from the UK to come and stay for a weekend. They've booked their flights and now she's discovered that the wife is allergic to pet hair."

"Don't tell me she wants us to take all the dogs and cats!"

"No, but it's nearly as bad..."

"What then?"

"She wants us to put her visitors up here."

"What? Who are these people?"

"They're the vicar and his wife from the village she used to live in."

"You're joking! I hope you made some excuse!"

"I couldn't think quickly enough. I said it would be okay."

"Joe! You didn't!"

"I didn't know what to say!"

"Oh, for goodness' sake!"

Well, it was too late to invent an excuse now. We'd just have to make the best of it. Perhaps I was being uncharitable, but I really wasn't looking forward to having strangers sharing our house, particularly a man of the cloth and his spouse.

WILD MUSHROOMS WITH EGGS

Hi Victoria,

We have had a sudden glut of mushrooms, a mushroom block (what it's grown in) seemed a good idea but little did we realise quite how many mushrooms we would get! This recipe originates from the Basque country. It is a quick and simple dish making a tasty light lunch. We have changed the recipe to suit our taste as originally it was served with a raw egg yolk. We prefer the egg fried or poached.

Jo

Ingredients

Per serving:

- 200g (7½oz) of wild mushrooms (oyster or ceps are best)
- 1 clove of finely chopped garlic
- 2 tbsp good olive oil
- 1 or 2 large eggs
- salt and pepper to taste
- crusty bread to serve

Method

- Clean and trim the mushrooms (do not wash, wipe clean if necessary) and thickly slice if large.
- Heat the oil in a large pan over a high heat. Add the garlic and fry for 1 minute (do not burn).
- Add the mushrooms cut-side down and cook for 1-2 minutes until brown.
- Turn and continue to cook for another 1-2 minutes.
- Season with sea salt and ground black pepper to taste.
- Meanwhile fry or poach the eggs to personal taste.
- Place the eggs on a warmed plate and spoon the mushrooms round the egg.
- Serve with crusty bread and a good local wine.

Kindly donated by reader, Jo Stadelwieser.

9

THE VICAR AND HIS WIFE

As the days went by, I became more and more anxious about the impending visit by the vicar and his wife. I worried about our house. Would our guests be comfortable? Would they remember to duck their heads through some of the smaller doorways? Would they mind the electricity switching off without warning? And would they notice Joe's scratching?

As luck would have it, our guests' visit would coincide with El Hoyo's annual fiesta, which was another source of worry for me. Would they be able to stand the thump of music all night? What about the constant fireworks?

As the village prepared for the fiesta, I prepared the house, cleaning every nook and cranny. Judith had promised to whisk the vicar and his wife away every morning, so they would

THE VICAR AND HIS WIFE

only be with us late evenings and at breakfast time, but I wanted everything in order.

On the Friday, Geronimo fired rockets into the sky at midday, heralding the opening of the fiesta and start of the festivities. As the day wore on, more people descended into the valley. The village was packed with local families and their friends and relations, the cars jamming the narrow streets and parking in every available space.

At around nine in the evening, our guests arrived, shepherded by Judith. She introduced us to the Reverend James Andrew Montgomery and his wife, Mavis. To my relief, I liked the vicar instantly. He had a kindly face with a smile that never seemed to leave his lips. His shock of white hair nearly matched his dog collar and his eyes were good-natured and friendly. I wish I could have said the same for his wife, Mavis.

"We're very pleased to meet you," Joe said, shaking hands and I followed suit.

The vicar's handshake was warm and reassuring, but shaking hands with Mavis was like clutching a bunch of dead twigs.

In contrast with her husband, Mavis was bony and angular with elbows that jutted out sharply and gimlet eyes that stared out from behind a pair of spectacles hanging from a gold chain about her scrawny neck. Her eyebrows were pencilled in and gave her an air of permanent surprise, while her lips were pale and pressed together.

"It's very kind of you to take us in," said the

vicar, smiling. "We're so sorry if we've put you out at all."

"Not at all!" I said, lying through my teeth. "Did you have a good journey?"

"Very smooth and pleasant..." the vicar began, but his wife cut across him.

"The poor vicar found the flight terribly cramped," she said, "and the food was appalling. I had to send it back and ask for something else. My husband wouldn't dream of complaining, of course, but I knew it would upset his sensitive stomach."

"It wasn't *that* bad, Mavis, dear."

Mavis pursed her lips, which was to become a familiar mannerism to us in the next couple of days. Joe said her mouth looked like 'a pussycat's bottom' and he wasn't far wrong. She also had a habit of jerking her head from side to side as though checking to see if somebody was creeping up on her. Her hair had been set into orderly rows of sausage curls, but sprayed so heavily they never moved.

"Well, I'll leave you to it, m'dears!" said Judith. "Toodle-pip and I'll see you in the morning." And with that she was gone.

"Er, what should we call you?" I asked the vicar as Joe portered their cases upstairs.

"Oh, just..." he smiled, but Mavis was already chiming in.

"My husband is accustomed to being

THE VICAR AND HIS WIFE

addressed as 'Reverend'", she said, "but 'Vicar' will do as we're on holiday."

"Okay. Well, let me show you around," I said. "I hope you'll be comfortable here with us."

The vicar chatted amiably as we toured, but Mavis stayed silent, her head flicking from left to right, as though searching for places I'd forgotten to dust.

"Would you like to see outside?" I asked when we were in the kitchen. My hand rested on the handle of the back door, ready to open it. "It's dark, but we have outside lights in the garden. I'll show you the chickens, although they'll be asleep now."

"Oh, I don't think so," said Mavis, pursing her lips. "We wouldn't want the vicar to catch a chill."

"A snack, perhaps?" I asked, as Joe joined us. "Or something to drink?"

"I think the vicar would like a nice warm milk, if you have it," said Mavis. "We'll take it up to bed. Nothing to eat, thank you, the vicar never goes to bed on a full stomach. It's been a very tiring day for my husband and he needs his full nine hours of sleep every night."

Joe had been heading for the drinks cupboard but changed direction and pulled a saucepan from the rack instead.

"I hope you'll sleep okay," I said. "I'm afraid the dancing in the square is going to start soon. I hope it doesn't keep you awake."

"I have terrible trouble sleeping," said Mavis. "I shall take one of my sleeping pills."

"Oh, the noise and music won't worry me," said the vicar and gave me a tiny wink that I couldn't quite interpret.

Our house had a quirky layout. It had a bathroom and cave bedroom downstairs, while upstairs there were another two bedrooms, a bathroom and a little kitchenette. Unless we had visitors, we rarely used the upstairs rooms and could shut the door at the top of the stairs. When the vicar and his wife climbed the stairs to bed, they shut the door behind them and Joe and I looked at each other.

"Well!" I said.

"Isn't that Mavis awful!" groaned Joe. "Thank goodness they've gone to bed. I don't think I could stand being around her for long. Shall we have a drink?"

We hadn't eaten yet, but a drink was very welcome. Joe poured us a couple of glasses and we sank onto the kitchen chairs. Relaxing, we discussed our visitors further.

"He's nice," I said, "but she's..."

"She's dreadful! A dragon! How does he put up with her?"

"Does she ever let him speak?"

"I bet she does the sermons in church!"

We drank and giggled over the She-Vicar for a good half hour until I suddenly heard a familiar noise.

THE VICAR AND HIS WIFE

"Ssssh! That's the door at the top of the stairs opening! They're coming back down!"

We both sat up straight and waited. Quiet, slippered footsteps came down the stairs, through the dining room and into the kitchen. It was the vicar. Resplendent in a dressing-gown with JM embroidered in gold on the breast pocket, he stood there, grinning broadly at us.

"She's asleep," he said. "She won't wake until the morning. Is that offer of a drink still there?"

Of course it was! Joe pulled out a chair and I poured him a stiff brandy.

"Please call me James," he said. "I sometimes forget I have a name, I'm so used to being called 'Reverend' or 'Vicar'. Actually, my middle name is Andrew, but Mavis objected to having JAM embroidered on my towels and dressing-gown pockets."

Within ten minutes, we were the best of friends, laughing, joking and swapping stories. James was hilarious and if his sermons were as good as his stories, I was sure the pews in his church were packed full every Sunday.

"Can we go outside?" he asked. "I'd love to see the garden and your chickens."

It was a wonderful, warm balmy night. We switched on the garden lights and took our drinks with us. James was fascinated by the sleeping chickens, roosting on their outside perch. Each hen sat so close to her sister that they looked like one continuous chicken with seven sets of claws locked onto the roosting rail.

"I never knew chickens snored!" he said.

"Oh, they always do," we assured him.

"Silly birds are still sleeping outside," Joe added. "When winter sets in, they are going to get cold. We'll have to train them to sleep inside somehow."

Even in the middle of October, winter seemed a long way off. The air was heavily scented from our jasmine bush and the sky was black velvet spangled with a million blinking stars. The band in the square began to play and the villagers clapped and cheered. Behind our walls, nobody could see us, but we heard children scamper past up the street, dogs barking, men discussing politics and ladies chattering, all heading for the square. The village was waking up for the fiesta.

One drink followed another until my stomach growled.

"We haven't eaten yet," I said. "We've got a big, hot curry to reheat, would you like some, James?" Joe and I love spicy food.

"Curry? I'd love some!"

"It's hot…"

"Perfect, the hotter and spicier, the better!"

We sat outside until the early hours, eating, drinking and listening to the fiesta. Sylvia and her almost-grown kittens, Felicity and Snitch, appeared from nowhere. When the kittens saw we had nothing to offer them, they chased each other and romped behind the flowerpots.

"This is a marvellous place to live," said James. "I can understand why you're so happy here. I love our village in England, but this lifestyle takes some beating."

"I know," said Joe. "We're very lucky."

"Do you wear your dog collar every day?" I asked curiously.

"Vicky!" Joe said, scolding me. "It's called a clerical collar!"

"That's okay, Joe. I call it a dog collar too. Yes, I tend to wear it every day. Mavis prefers me wearing it and I don't really mind."

When the church bell chimed four times, we knew it was two o'clock. I yawned.

"It's late," I said. "The church clock always repeats itself. I think I'm ready for bed."

"Me too," said Joe.

The Reverend James Andrew Montgomery stood up and stretched.

"Yep, bed for me too," he said. "It's been a wonderful evening, thank you both. I'll see you in the morning and please," he tapped his nose conspiratorially, "not a word to Mavis."

Joe and I watched him depart and lingered in the garden for a few moments more.

"Who would have thought it..." I said.

"I don't think this visit is going to be so bad after all," said Joe.

We cleared the table as the band thumped out

its music. It would carry on for many hours yet and tomorrow night would be an even bigger occasion. The chickens, undisturbed, snored on, although Sick-Note coughed occasionally.

The next morning the vicar and his wife appeared at 8 o'clock, dressed and ready for the day. Mavis's curls were all in place and James looked bright and refreshed.

"Did you sleep well?" I asked.

"Oh yes, thank you," answered Mavis. "I was worried that the fiesta might keep the vicar awake, but he says it didn't bother him at all."

"That's good," I said and caught one of James's tiny winks. This time I understood it.

The chickens were laying well and I'd cooked scrambled eggs for breakfast. Joe poured the tea and I served the toast and eggs.

"That looks delicious," said the vicar. "Thank you!"

"Just a slice of dry toast for me, please," said Mavis primly.

"Salt? Pepper?" I asked James.

"Oh no," Mavis broke in. "The vicar never touches spicy food of any kind. He's a martyr to his delicate stomach."

I managed to keep a straight face and not think of the large plate of curry the vicar had devoured late last night. I would keep his secret. Joe was already lifting the first forkful of scrambled egg to his mouth when Mavis threw both hands up to her face in horror.

THE VICAR AND HIS WIFE

"Wait!" she cried.

Joe froze, eyes bulging, mouth still open, loaded fork hovering.

"The vicar hasn't said Grace yet!" said Mavis in hushed tones, then pressed her thin lips together, closed her eyes and bowed her sausage curls, waiting.

"I'm sure the Good Lord would forgive us if we missed it just once, my dear. We're on holiday after all," said the vicar mildly. When the sausage curls bowed even lower he sighed and mumbled a quick blessing.

Thankfully, Judith arrived soon after and spirited our guests away for the day. But not before I had the chance to say a line I'd always wanted to say...

"More tea, vicar?"

El Hoyo at fiesta time is madness. Marching bands come out of the hills. Processions form. Contests take place and clowns perform. Flamenco dancers writhe and stamp. Fireworks shoot into the sky, day and night. One year, the village square was filled with foam to play in, another year, coloured plastic balls. We loved it all. If we didn't join in, we would stand on our roof terrace looking down at all the activity.

Late that evening, the vicar and his wife returned, having spent a pleasant day with Judith sightseeing. They'd toured Almería and its castle and driven into the mountains to eat in a whitewashed village restaurant.

"Judith had to drop us miles away tonight," complained Mavis. "We couldn't drive into El Hoyo at all because the road is blocked with all the parked cars. I was very worried about the vicar's hip. He's not supposed to exert himself too much."

"I was fine, dear," reproached the vicar. "Good exercise and I enjoyed the walk. There certainly are a lot of people in the village at the moment."

"It's like this every year," I said. "Saturday is the main day of the fiesta. The dancing will go on until four or five in the morning. The band just carries on playing until the last people leave."

"Good heavens!" said Mavis, tossing her perfectly cylindrical iron curls at the thought. "Well, the vicar and I shall be in bed. Could I trouble you for some warm milk to take up with us? I know my husband must be exhausted after our busy day today."

"No trouble at all," I said and heated the milk.

Off they went upstairs, Mavis firmly leading the way. Did I see James give me a tiny wink? I thought so. The door at the top of the stairs closed behind them.

"I'm willing to bet that's not the last we've seen of the Reverend James Andrew Montgomery tonight," said Joe.

I agreed with him.

ROASTED PEACHES

Towards the end of the summer, which is as late as early October for us, peaches are available in huge amounts at really cheap prices so we look for inventive ways to use them.

Ingredients

- 2 large peaches, cut into 4 or 6 thick slices and stone removed
- 2 tbsp honey
- 1 tbsp unsalted butter
- 55g (2oz) caster sugar

Method

- Preheat the oven to 220°C/425°F/Gas 7.

- Heat a nonstick frying pan and then add the butter, sugar and honey. Cook for a few minutes until the sugar has dissolved.

- Add the peach slices to the pan, stir well to coat in the sticky syrup and allow to caramelise for a few minutes.

- If your pan is oven proof, transfer directly to the oven or place the peach slices in a shallow baking tray and cook for 10-15 minutes.

- Remove from the oven, transfer to a serving plate and serve with a scoop of ice cream and a sprinkling of chopped almonds

10

THE FIESTA AND COLD WATER

Just before midnight, the door at the top of the stairs opened again and Joe and I smiled at each other. We heard the now familiar footsteps coming down the stairs.

"It's only me," grinned the Reverend James Andrew Montgomery. "Mavis is out like a light, she took a double dose of sleeping pills. The band is even louder tonight."

Far from complaining, his foot was tapping in time to the beat that permeated even the thick walls of our house. I noticed he was fully dressed this time and the dog collar had gone.

"Shall we take a drink outside?" suggested Joe.

The vicar raised his white eyebrows. "I rather thought we'd go and join the fun in the square," he said. "But yes, I wouldn't mind another glass of that marvellous wine of yours!"

It was another balmy night and we enjoyed a leisurely drink outside in the garden. We told James about the fiesta goings-on that day and he described their sightseeing visit to Almería. He was impressed by the castle. Although some of it is in ruins, there is still much to see. Built high on a hill by the Moors a thousand years ago, the encircling fortifications protected 20,000 people in the town. To this day, gypsies still live in the caves at its foot.

"I didn't know Almería is an Arabic word meaning 'mirror of the sea'," he said.

We didn't know that either.

James drained his glass and set it down.

"Well," he proposed, "shall we wander on down to the square?"

The closer we got to the square, the louder the music became until we could hardly hear each others' words above the pounding beat.

"This certainly beats our village fêtes in the rectory garden!" James shouted into my ear.

The square and its surroundings were a seething mass of people. The new bar was packed, every seat taken. Stalls, manned by dark-skinned Moroccans, sold plastic toys, hot-dogs and firecrackers. Dogs barked soundlessly, unheard above the music. Marcia sat on a straight-backed chair in her shop doorway, her fingers busy with knitting, her eyes playing over the crowds like searchlights. Geronimo sat on the edge of the stage, swinging his legs, his Real Madrid scarf

THE FIESTA AND COLD WATER

draped around his neck. He lifted a bottle of beer to his lips to drink and I saw another two bottles lined up beside him, awaiting his attention.

People were dancing in family knots: mothers, fathers, grandparents and children. I saw Lola and Papa Ufarte dancing with the twins, while Maribel sat on a bench, jiggling a pushchair containing a sleeping toddler. As I watched, the twins tired of dancing and chased away to join a group of children near the stalls.

Paco, Carmen, Alejandro and his wife, Sofía and Alejandro Junior danced nearby. Beside them, Alejandro Senior clasped Mother to him, one arm encircling her waist, the other clasping her hand aloft as he deftly guided her through the other dancers. Paco caught sight of us, waved a greeting and beckoned us over.

"Shall we?" I asked, eyebrows raised in question. I knew James and Joe couldn't hear me. The music was unfamiliar, but the rhythm was mesmeric, making my feet itch to dance.

I didn't expect James to follow, but he did. We joined Paco's family group and jigged and swayed with them, drinking in the Spanish party atmosphere. The heat, the sounds, the smells, the happy faces and the vibration of the music seeped into my bones as it always did. I was loving it and judging by his face, so was the vicar.

One tune melted into the next and I lost all sense of time. We rarely wore wristwatches and it would have been impossible to hear the church clock strike the hour above the music. Joe caught his breath and stopped dancing for a while, but the Reverend James Andrew Montgomery was in his element. He adapted his steps to the changing rhythm, a broad grin stretched across his face as he whirled and tapped. He didn't look like a man who suffered from a painful hip to me.

At around two o'clock, Geronimo jumped off the stage and rummaged beneath it. He backed out with an armful of wicked-looking fireworks, great rockets packed with explosive. I knew what was going to happen next and it wasn't my favourite aspect of Spanish life.

"Watch!" I shouted to James, pointing to Geronimo.

He swung round and I saw his eyes widen. The band finished their number, paused, then backed away from Geronimo who had joined them on the stage. Now everybody watched as Geronimo held a firework aloft, pointing it at the sky. He set light to the touch-paper then allowed the firework to burst from his grasp and shoot into the air.

"Good grief! That's so dangerous!" said James. "What about Health and Safety?"

"This is Spain, James."

One by one, Geronimo let the fireworks off and they arced into the night sky, exploding with a bang that shook the village. The villagers clapped and cheered every time until the last rocket had been set free. Then the band struck up again and the dancing continued with even more gusto.

Some time later, I was still on the dance floor. Occasionally I took a rest and so did Joe, but there was no stopping the Reverend James Andrew Montgomery. He gyrated, bounced and bobbed, only his white hair giving any clue to his age. Perhaps he could trace some Spanish ancestry back somewhere, because that night his feet were made for dancing. Paco kindly brought us some drinks, which we accepted gratefully, then carried on dancing.

I don't know what time it was when it happened. Without warning, the village was thrown into total blackness. Every streetlight and coloured bulb fizzled out and the music ground to a halt as the electricity died. For five minutes, the villagers laughed and called, their voices floating through the darkness. Some lit cigarette lighters and held them high, the light casting strange shadows on their faces. Joe grabbed my arm and we stood still, waiting for the power to be restored. This was a common occurrence, particularly at fiesta time.

Just as suddenly, the lights came back on. As I blinked, adjusting to the sudden brightness, a couple standing quite close to me jumped apart guiltily. The crowd cheered and applauded the return of the electricity, but not everybody was in high spirits. As the music struck up and the cheering crowd settled down, a single voice cut through.

It was Maribel. Like me, she had seen her husband and her sister Lola in that close embrace. Like me, she had seen the pair spring apart guiltily. Now she stood, one hand with the knuckles turning white as she clutched the handle of the push chair, her other hand jabbing in fury, her mouth a slash of accusation.

I don't know what she shrieked at the pair, I didn't understand the words, but it made the hair rise on the back of my neck. This was a woman in shock, a woman who had just witnessed her own worst nightmare, a woman wronged, outraged. The people standing close by, me included, shrank into themselves and turned away. It was too painful to watch. As his wife screamed and stamped in fury, Papa Ufarte had the grace to look ashamed. Lola just lifted her chin in defiance.

I caught Carmen's eye. She raised her brows and twitched her shoulders in an almost imperceptible shrug, an 'I told you so' signal that I understood perfectly.

For me, the evening was spoiled and I wanted to go home. I didn't feel like dancing any more although the crowd around us was already swinging in time to the music, swallowing up the harrowing scene. Joe was ready to leave too, but the Reverend James Andrew Montgomery was not. He hadn't seen the distressing drama unfold and his toes were still a-tapping.

THE FIESTA AND COLD WATER

"Don't worry, I can find my own way back," he shouted over the music as Joe handed him a spare key. "I'll see you in the morning!"

When we left him, Sofía and Alejandro Junior were teaching him some flamenco steps and he barely waved goodbye.

Joe and I didn't say much on the short walk home, both deep in thought. We did smile, however, when we saw Little Paco sitting on a doorstep in the shadows with his arm around a pretty young girl. Little Paco was growing up.

There wasn't much of the night left and we slept soundly through the little that remained. Next morning, when James and Mavis came down for breakfast, nobody would have guessed that the vicar had danced the night away.

"Did you sleep well?" asked Joe innocently.

"Like a log!" returned James, beaming.

"Well, I'm surprised," said Mavis. "I was worried that the stroll around the castle yesterday would have aggravated your hip problem. One shouldn't overdo it at our age, you know."

Nobody said a word.

Judith came to collect our visitors and we said our final goodbyes. I wasn't sorry to bid Mavis or her prim pussycat-bottom mouth or her rows of iron sausage curls farewell, but evenings would be quieter without the Reverend James Andrew Montgomery.

It was Sunday and the fiesta finished with another flurry of fireworks in the early evening.

Village doors were locked and all the cars drove away up the mountain and out of the valley. Joe and I were saddened to see that Maribel Ufarte had also quit the village, taking her children and the unborn baby away, but leaving her husband and Lola together in their house.

※※※

In El Hoyo, months often slipped quietly by without a fuss, but that October was not one of them. The fiesta and the visit by the vicar and his wife were closely followed by another: the Gin Twins' visit.

Of course they were as badly behaved as ever and I dread to think how many bottles of gin they consumed between them. But we had a blast. We went exploring villages, got lost numerous times, lazed by a friend's pool, played Rude Scrabble (rules supplied upon application) and ate and drank far too much. My face ached from laughing. After a week of riotous living we bade them farewell until the next year.

The following October event wasn't so amusing. Workmen appeared in the village and began digging holes randomly. Before we had a chance to find out what was happening, our water supply was switched off. It stayed shut off for two entire days, reappearing without warning. First a rusty trickle dripped from our taps, then a more enthusiastic jet of clear water appeared.

THE FIESTA AND COLD WATER

We assumed that maintenance on the village water supply was complete, but we were mistaken. For nearly a week, the water was randomly shut off and then resumed without warning.

One time, Joe was taking a shower, happily singing away. I could hear him as I typed at my computer.

> "It's been a hard day's night,
> And I've been working like a do-o-g,
> It's been a hard day's night,
> I should be sleeping like a... (pause)

VICKY! There's no blasted water! Those idiots have turned it off again!"

"Oh dear."

"VICKY? Where are you? I need to get this soap and shampoo off!"

"Okay, I'm coming..."

We always kept a few bottles of water in case of emergencies. And I had no choice, did I? I *had* to grab our bottled water from the fridge and throw it over his head and body to rinse the soap and shampoo.

Yes, it was icy cold.

Yes, he did bellow profanities.

Yes, it did make him shudder and dance.

And yes, I *did* enjoy doing it...

Unfortunately, Joe wasn't the only one to suffer a cold shower that autumn.

Nowadays, most chickens are bred to lay eggs happily whether there is a cockerel present to fertilise them or not. The hen lays her daily egg then abandons it, no thought of incubation or childcare troubling her thoughts. However, just occasionally, something goes awry.

One day, Three decided she didn't want to be parted from her egg. Instead of jumping down and carrying on with her normal daily pursuits of eating, preening and dustbathing, she chose to sit on her egg and stare into space.

Instead of roosting with her sisters, Three stayed with her egg all night. The next day and the next, she laid more eggs and still she stayed sitting on the nest. Three had definitely 'gone broody' and we had no idea how to deal with her.

Of course the eggs would never hatch, however long she sat on them. We tried removing the eggs, even though she pecked at our hands as we stole them from beneath her. It made no difference, she just sat on the empty nest, staring straight ahead.

Every now and then she left the nest, jumped down and produced an enormous, smelly poop. She snatched a beakful of food, took a few sips of water, then hurried back to her nest. According to the Internet, this is all normal behaviour for a broody hen.

Poor Three began to look a little ragged. She must have been hungry and uncomfortable, but

THE FIESTA AND COLD WATER

still she remained immobile on that nest. We were at a complete loss how to help her.

"Pah!" said Paco, slamming his fist onto our kitchen table, "I will show you what I do with such a hen!"

"You won't hurt her?"

"No, of course not! Now, watch me."

Paco filled a bucket with cold water and carried it to the coop. We watched, round-eyed. He grabbed poor Three and carried her, flapping and protesting, to the bucket of water.

"Oh no!" I gasped as he held her upside down and dunked her, headfirst, into the cold water.

"*Uno, dos, tres,*" counted Paco, then set a soaking wet and shocked Three on the ground. "Now she will forget all about the eggs."

The chicken shook her feathers in a blur and water droplets flew off. She stood still for a moment, having a deep think, clearly disoriented. Then she realised she was ravenously hungry and pecked enthusiastically at the grain. After a good drink of water, she settled down to preen her feathers and take a dustbath.

All thoughts of egg incubation and starting a family were forgotten.

🐔🐔🐔

That November, strong winds ripped through the valley, snatching the last crisp leaves from our grapevine. Over-ripened grapes still hung from the vine's branches, attracting wasps and fruit flies. Frequently the grapes dropped with a splat on the patio below, leaving black sticky stains. Now that the leaves were stripped away, we could see the grapes and cut them down. It took several hours, an unpleasant job, dodging wasps and smearing ourselves with decomposing fruit that already smelled alcoholic.

Chickens eat everything, it doesn't matter how unpleasant it may seem to us. I've seen a video of a chicken catching and swallowing an entire live mouse. They'll eat dead or live cockroaches, potato peelings and their own eggshells, which are supposed to be good for them.

So when we threw the rotting grapes into the coop, the chickens dived on them. Perhaps it was my imagination, but I'm sure the fermenting grapes caused the girls to stagger to bed that night.

By November, the wind had lost its hair-dryer warmth and had a chilling edge to it. The sun was still warm but nights were long and cold. We stockpiled our logs and lit the wood-burner a little earlier each day.

But now Christmas approached and as with every year, Carmen and Paco came round bearing gifts of home-grown tomatoes, a bottle of red wine and a poinsettia. The tomatoes were useful for homemade tomato soup and the wine was most welcome too. However, as always, the poinsettia filled me with dread.

THE FIESTA AND COLD WATER

When I was a child, I thought a poinsettia was a breed of dog, but now I know it's a magnificent red and green plant. Every poinsettia I've ever owned begins to die as soon as I accept it. This one was no different and I could hear the leaves dropping off as I typed.

But that Christmas I was given another gift. The most unexpected, welcome Christmas present I could ever wish for. A gift that would probably change our lives for ever.

FRISCO OMELETTE

All these ingredients are grown in abundance in Spain and this is a great recipe for camping trips.

Ingredients

- 2 fresh eggs
- Chopped onion
- Chopped green olives
- Chopped black olives
- Chopped mushrooms
- Season to taste: salt, garlic, paprika, etc.

Method

- Put all the ingredients into a small jar and shake vigorously.
- Fry in small pan, turning when ready.
- For the sweet version, add chopped apple in the jar.

You can make these omelettes at home and also on a small portable stove on the road.

Kindly donated by Rocky Frisco, Tulsa, Oklahoma.

11
NEWS

"Mum?"

"Karly, what a nice surprise! Are you okay? Is Cam okay? What time is it in Australia?"

"Um, ten o'clock at night."

"Oh. Early morning here."

"Mum..."

"Yes? Karly, what's the matter?"

Hushed voice, full of wonder. "Mum... Mum, I'm *pregnant*, we're going to have a baby!"

"What? That's FANTASTIC news!" I dance around the room, squealing. "Joe! JOE! Karly and Cam are going to have a baby! Karly's pregnant! They're going to have a *baby!*" Then, more soberly, "Karly, are you sure?"

"Yep! I did the home test and it came up positive. We kept staring at it and didn't believe it so I did another test and it still came up positive. So then I made Cam do a test."

"You made Cam pee on the little stick?"

"Yes, just to make sure it looked different. And it did."

"Wow! That's just the *best* news ever!"

"I know…"

"Gosh! I'm going to be granny…"

"I know…"

"So, when is it due?"

"I'm not sure, August I think. It's about the size of a poppyseed at the moment."

"Oh my! I can't believe you're going to have a baby!"

"I know! Neither can we! I wish you didn't live so far away."

"Don't worry. I'm definitely coming over. Even if we can't both come, I'll be there."

"Are you sure? It's such a long flight and so expensive."

"I'm sure." Wild horses wouldn't stop me.

"When I've had my doctor's appointment and had my first scan we'll have a better idea of dates."

"Okay, I'll wait to hear from you, then I'm booking that flight to Australia."

12

DEATHS

'At five weeks, your baby is the size of an apple seed. It is starting to form tiny organs...'

In January, while we were warm and snug inside at night, our chickens still insisted on sleeping outside in the elements. Creatures of habit, they ignored the cosy perch inside their coop, and insisted on flying up to the exposed outside perch. Whatever the weather, neither harsh winds nor freezing rain would induce them to sleep on their rail under shelter.

"Daft birds," said Joe one morning as the chickens flapped down from their perch, soaking wet and shivering after a stormy night. "How can they be so stupid? Our last batch of chickens always slept inside under cover, why won't these?"

DEATHS

We tried to break the silly habit. We spoke to them severely, explaining it was for their own good and that they'd catch pneumonia if they stayed outside. Poor Sick-Note's cough grew worse and we were convinced the cold nights outside were the cause.

One night we watched a documentary on TV about brains. It seems a chicken's brain is about the size of a wine-gum so perhaps our expectations were too high. It was very likely our hens were incapable of reasoning that roosting under shelter was a much better idea. Through the window, I watched the clouds thickening as night fell. The temperature was already down to freezing; it would probably snow.

"Let's manually put them on the inside perch for a few nights," I suggested. "Perhaps they'll get the idea then."

That night, as it began to grow dark, we caught them one by one and put them on the perch. There they sat, locked on, until we turned our backs to catch the next one. Then down they jumped, ran outside and up to their accustomed outside perch.

"This is getting ridiculous," said Joe, lifting Venus down for the third time and carrying her protesting inside. "We need to wait until it's dark."

Chickens can't see in the dark at all, so it was a good plan. When night fell, Joe's routine was to 'put the girls to bed'. He plucked each girl from the perch and took her inside. Seven times a night he repeated this action until every chicken was safe and sound inside. Our thinking was that the girls would wake up in the morning, realise that they'd had a pleasant night and choose to sleep inside in future.

Not so. Our chickens weren't the brightest bulbs on the Christmas tree. For weeks Joe continued the nightly ritual. He trudged down to the bottom of the garden, lifted each chicken off the perch and put her inside. But they never learnt.

"That's it!" said Joe one day, toolbox in hand. "I'm going to remove the outside perch, then they'll *have* to use the inside one."

I heard the sounds of drills and hammers and demolition work coming from the chicken coop. Joe came back in, pleased with his work.

"I've removed the perch completely," he announced. "I think we've finally solved the problem."

That night we waited until the garden was in darkness, then visited the chicken coop. Were our girls sleeping inside, snug and warm?

They were not.

The inside perch was empty, but outside, huddled on the ground in an untidy heap of feathers under the place where the perch used to be, were the chickens. Exasperated, we took them inside the henhouse and placed them on the perch.

DEATHS

Sleeping outside proved to be too much for Sick-Note. Sadly she died that week and we buried her on waste ground near the cemetery. The evening ritual of putting the girls to bed continued all winter, ferrying the chickens inside.

But, months later, when the weather had turned warmer and the ferrying wasn't really necessary, our girls surprised us one night.

"Well, cut off my legs and call me Shorty!" said Joe. "You won't believe where the girls are perched now!"

With no warning, the girls decided that their indoor quarters were preferable after all and we never had to move them again.

𐀀𐀀𐀀

When I finish reading a good book, I always experience a sense of loss. It's exactly the same when I'm writing. When the final chapter is completed, I'm left with a void, a gap that needs filling. That's how I felt when *'Ole!'* was finished that winter, but I felt reluctant to start the next book. I had all my notes, photos and material poised for *Camel*, but I just didn't want to start it. I think that year in Bahrain shocked us more than we realised and I wasn't ready to relive it all.

So, at the beginning of 2012, I was looking for any excuse not to write, but I needed a project. And it appeared, as if by magic and it had been buried in our house all the time.

In 1993 my parents both died within three months of each other. Neither of them talked much about their childhoods or family, but I knew that my father was the youngest of several siblings and that my mother was an only child estranged from her mother.

What I *didn't* know was that my father's eldest brother had been an adventurer and explorer and was proclaimed by the newspapers of the 1930s as 'the World's most travelled motorist'. (My mother hid a huge, much darker, more shocking secret too, but I wouldn't uncover that for another twelve months.)

I'm ashamed to confess that we still had boxes stored from our move to Spain in 2004. They remained unpacked and unexplored until the day I decided I really should sort through them and throw away useless stuff. The first box I tackled was filled with odds and ends that had belonged to my parents. Some china ashtrays, a few pictures, kitchenware and odds and ends. But at the very bottom was a bound manuscript, brown with age.

I read the old-fashioned copperplate writing on the cover. *'Horizon Fever' by Archibald Edmund Filby.* I guessed this was the work of my uncle Archie, who had died long before I was born. I opened the manuscript and found newspaper cuttings pasted in. Dated 1938, the headlines shouted, *A Marvellous Motor Trip!* and *London to*

Cape Town and Back. It seemed that my uncle had been quite a celebrity in his day.

I read reports of his broadcasts and saw grainy photos of a small, bespectacled man smoking a pipe, dressed in a suit and sitting on the running board of an ancient car.

I turned the flimsy, typewritten pages. I had stumbled upon Archie's memoir, written 80 years ago. Here were his own words describing his 37,000 mile journey from London to the bottom of Africa and back again in a series of dilapidated motor cars, including a Model T Ford. It was the project I had been searching for and, as if by magic, it emerged genie-like from the bottom of a box.

"Look what I found," I said excitedly to Joe. "This has been buried here all this time!"

Together we pored over it and were mesmerised by Archie's tales of his journey through Africa. How things had changed since he bashed out these words on a typewriter! He wrote about big game hunting, the natives, swimming in the Nile with crocodiles, mining for gold and crossing the Sahara. For a while, one of his companions was a monkey, another a stray dog, until it was killed and dragged up a tree by a leopard.

Joe and I looked at one another. This was it. We had our next project.

"I'll transcribe it all," said Joe. "It's not going

to be easy with all those crossed-out words and the 'e' not working on Archie's typewriter."

I emailed my brother in the UK, who told me that he had scrapbooks belonging to Uncle Archie with photos he'd taken on that African trip. He scanned them and sent them over.

Gradually, we pieced the jigsaw together. It seemed that Uncle Archie intended to have *Horizon Fever* published, because an address label of a publishing company in London, now defunct, was still pasted on the back cover. Archie died of malaria at the age of 43, less than three years after he had written the book, so we were pleased that we could put the book together ourselves and finally share Archie's stories with the world. His exploits were fascinating, but it was even more interesting getting to know this uncle I had never met through his own words.

As Joe worked away on *Horizon Fever*, I reluctantly began *Camel*. However, soon the words began to flow and I was happy in my own little writing world again.

※※※

Some mornings, ice skinned the puddles and the mountains were dusted with icing-sugar snow. As the sun rose higher in the sky, the snow melted away, except on distant high peaks where it clung on with grim determination.

Joe and I kept the wood-burner stoked and

DEATHS

abandoned the hob, preferring to cook on the wood-burner instead. We were warm and the chickens didn't seem to mind the low temperatures outside. With fluffed-up feathers, they appeared twice the size that they were in the hot summer months.

All the village cats now had thick winter coats. Gravy never reappeared, but we saw a great deal of her sister, Sylvia and Sylvia's two kittens, Snitch and Felicity. We didn't feed them regularly, but sometimes left scraps outside.

Then the time arrived when we heard caterwauling coming from the garden, even with our doors tightly shut. The cycle of nature had swept round once again. Every village tomcat had crowded into our garden and was sidling up to Sylvia, following her every move.

Sylvia appeared indifferent, even annoyed by their presence. She growled at them in warning, but it was an elaborate act. If she felt they weren't paying her enough attention, she'd drop the 'playing hard to get' pretence to roll on her back, tail sweeping the ground, paws waving in the air. If that didn't entice them, she'd slink up and turn her hindquarters to them, coyly watching the reaction over her shoulder as she offered herself wantonly. But she held all the cards. She permitted a tomcat to mount her only when *she* was ready and not a moment before.

Snitch and Felicity watched their mother with huge eyes from under the shelter of our garden table. They needn't have been nervous; the tomcats were far too preoccupied to be bothered with the youngsters.

That year, the biggest, most powerful, well-endowed tom in the village was a jet-black cat Joe insisted on calling Black Balls, for obvious reasons. I hurriedly shortened the name to Blackie. We guessed that many of the village kittens born that spring would be black and as the weeks rolled by, Sylvia's waistline expanded and we knew she was pregnant again. We would have to wait a few months to see if Blackie was the father.

February is probably Spain's wettest month, as well as the coldest. El Hoyo is snuggled at the bottom of a valley and grey clouds often hid the mountains surrounding us, making us feel as though we were in an isolated world, smothered under a silver blanket.

However, even in deepest winter, the valley never looked lifeless. The wild fig and almond trees lost their leaves, but the orange and olive trees retained theirs. Not to be outdone, the almond trees burst forth, their waxy, pinky-white blossom like edible decorations crafted from sugar. But the orange trees dashed off with the prize, now hung with bright fruit that weighed down the branches and begged to be picked. As distant snow-covered peaks jabbed at the sky, it seemed strange that oranges could ripen and be picked in midwinter.

DEATHS

Outside our kitchen door, our grapevine was a tangle of dead-looking branches over our heads. For the first time, neither Uncle Felix nor Paco arrived to prune it for us, so I decided to take matters into my own hands.

"How hard can it be to prune a grapevine?" I asked Joe.

Joe looked at me blankly and shrugged.

"You just chop it, I guess."

I shouldn't have asked him. Had I wanted to know something about the molecular structure of hydrogen sulphide or (heaven forbid) something about the Fourier analysis of waves, he might have helped. If I'd asked him to list all the American Civil War battles and their commanders, or the dates of every significant writer from Samuel Pepys onwards, he might have been useful.

But gardening is not one of Joe's strengths. Joe calls every flower, regardless of size or colour, a pansy.

Having been away for a year, the shrubs had become rather unruly and I'd asked him to help me in the garden. We had a beautiful jasmine and a plumbago that grew together, intertwined. The blue plumbago flowers lasted for months and when the snowy jasmine flowers peeped through, it was my favourite part of the garden.

"Could you just tidy it up a tiny bit?" I asked him, handing him the secateurs. "Just neaten it up, nothing more."

Then I turned my back to get on with other jobs.

Big mistake.

"I've finished," he called some time later and I came to view his labours.

Joe stood there, beaming, obviously well pleased with his efforts, the garden shears hanging loosely from one hand. Piles of green foliage, blue and white blossoms and branches were piled on the ground, already wilting. The plumbago had been reduced to a foot-high stump and the jasmine was nearly as bad. I stared with horror.

"It would have taken too long with the secateurs," he said, "so I used the big shears."

I couldn't speak. To be honest, I felt quite tearful.

The plumbago, unsurprisingly, gave up and died. The jasmine eventually recovered and took over the space. I loved the blossoms and the fragrance of the jasmine, especially during summer evenings, but I sorely missed the cheerful splash of blue that the plumbago had provided.

Yes, the grapevine needed pruning, but this was not a job Joe could be trusted with.

"If Uncle Felix and Paco don't turn up by the end of the month," I announced, "I'm going to have a go at doing it myself."

BROAD BEANS WITH HAM
HABAS CON JAMÓN

Serves four people as a *tapa* or you could serve it as a dish in its own right.

Ingredients

- 250g (9oz) shelled broad beans
- 3 tbsp good quality olive oil
- 1 onion finely chopped
- 1 or 2 slices of medium thickness serrano ham, chopped
- Chopped fresh parsley to taste
- Salt and pepper to season
- Crusty bread to serve

Method

- Bring a pan of salted water to the boil.
- Add the beans and return to the boil, continue to boil for 4 minutes.
- Drain and place beans in cold water to prevent further cooking.
- Unless the beans are very young, peel off the outer skins. Meanwhile heat the oil in a large pan over a medium heat.
- Add the onion and fry for 4-5 minutes until cooked but not brown.
- Add the beans and stir in the parsley and ham. Check taste before seasoning, as the ham is salty.
- Transfer to a warmed serving bowl and drizzle with olive oil.
- Serve with crusty bread and a good local wine.

Kindly donated by reader, Jo Stadelweiser.

13

PRUNING

'Your baby is now the size of a raspberry. Those little arms and legs are wriggling around like crazy...'

By the middle of March, Paco and Uncle Felix still hadn't appeared to prune our grapevine. I spent a lot of time under its twisted, naked branches, gazing up, considering how best to tackle the job.

I turned to the Internet for assistance.

'Prune the 12 renewal buds so that there is always one more bud growing from the tip. Allow the renewal buds to extend and grow one bud length. The fruit develops on the new growth that springs from the renewal bud. Keep it short during the dormant season and the plant under control.'

I've always liked gardening, but this was a little baffling. Twelve renewal buds? I stared up at the vine and did a little counting. This wasn't going to be quite as simple as I'd thought.

"I've sharpened the clippers," said Joe. "Are you sure you don't want me to help?"

"Quite sure, thanks," I said, recalling the ugly slaughter of the plumbago. No, I was not going to allow the same thing to happen to our beloved grapevine.

I took a deep breath, trying to remember the rules I'd just read about new growth and old growth, renewal buds and fruiting spurs. Then I positioned the cutters and snipped. The first branch tumbled to the ground.

An hour later, my feet were surrounded by fallen branches. I had a stiff neck from looking up, sore eyes from squinting against the bright sky and blisters on my hands from the clippers. I was exhausted, but satisfied that I'd done a fairly good job. In fact, I was feeling rather pleased with myself.

Vine branches and twigs make perfect kindling, so Joe and I chopped them into short lengths and stored them away to dry, ready for next winter.

A week or so later, we heard the clattering of hooves up our street and voices. Then a fist pounded on our door.

"English! English!"

PRUNING

"Hello Paco," said Joe, opening the door to admit our neighbour and Uncle Felix.

As always, Paco burst in and his presence dominated the room, in sharp contrast to Uncle Felix who shrank a little every year. Uncle Felix's flat cap was pulled down over his eyes and he shuffled behind Paco, his fourscore years evident. Uncle Felix's mule tried to follow her master inside, but she'd been tethered to the window bars so only succeeded in pushing her head into our living room.

Uncle Felix's mule was showing her age, too. I put out my hand to pat her and noticed white hairs growing amongst the grey. She ignored my gesture of friendship, but I wasn't affronted. Uncle Felix's mule had eyes only for her master, whom she adored.

The entire village chuckled every time the mule managed to escape, which was often, and watched her trot the streets in search of Uncle Felix. She usually found him in the square and her trot would quicken, her ears stood tall and, with a little whinny of delight, she clopped over to nuzzle the old man.

"Uncle Felix and I have come to prune your vine," bellowed Paco, waving his industrial branch-cutters.

The mule took a last look round the room, rattled her ears and withdrew to munch on the plants in my window-box.

"The vine?" I echoed weakly.

"This year Uncle Felix and I have come much later than usual because the winter has been quite dry. It would be a mistake to do it earlier. Today is the perfect day to prune your vine."

I stared at him in dismay, aware that I'd committed a massive crime and I was about to be discovered.

"Er, Vicky has..." Joe began.

But Paco wasn't listening and was already pushing past us to the kitchen and out of the back door. Joe and I exchanged worried glances and followed reluctantly.

"¡Madre mía!" roared Paco. "What has happened here?"

Uncle Felix sank down onto the bench in shock. He removed his flat cap and rubbed his head, his faded old eyes sweeping the already-pruned branches above.

"What has happened here? This is a massacre! This grapevine has been butchered!" bellowed Paco. "Who is responsible for this abomination?"

Just for a brief second I considered blaming aliens, or burglars that had broken in and savaged our vine.

"Er, it was me..." I stammered. "I pruned the vine..."

"¡Madre mía!" shouted Paco. "Did you hear that, Felix? Veeky pruned the vine!"

Uncle Felix rolled his eyes and shook his head sadly for a full thirty seconds.

PRUNING

"Joe, what in God's name were you thinking, allowing her to touch the vine?"

"Well, I..."

"What do women know about the art of pruning a grapevine? Why did you not stop her? You should have done it yourself, or waited for me and Uncle Felix."

"I tried to stop her," said my traitorous partner in life, thoroughly enjoying himself. "But you know what's she like. I told her she was doing it all wrong."

I gaped at him.

"Look at this! Can you believe she cut this branch here?" said Paco, smacking the offending branch with the flat of his hand. "And this one? ¡Madre mía!"

"I know," said Joe, swinging round to look at me severely. "I remember telling her not to cut that one."

I stared at him, mouth open.

"It is a disaster," pronounced Paco. Then he sighed deeply. "We will do our best to put it right, but if this vine produces decent grapes this summer, then my name is Julio Iglesias."

I'd heard enough. I slunk back into the kitchen, head hanging, eyes downcast. I boiled the kettle and set out the brandy, resisting the urge to take a large swig straight from the bottle. My actions were punctuated by *snip-snips* from outside. I peeped out of the window and saw Uncle Felix directing operations from his seat, waving his arm and pointing up at branches that required further attention. Joe stood aside, an insufferably smug expression on his face. I gritted my teeth and rummaged in the freezer for a bag of mackerel that had been lurking right at the back for several months. I caught sight of Joe's slippers by the door and viciously kicked them behind the kitchen bin.

By the time the job was finished, Paco was in a good mood again.

"I'm sorry I pruned the vine," I said as the men trooped back into the kitchen. I didn't look at Joe.

"Never mind," said Paco, sitting down heavily at our kitchen table. He reached over and slopped a generous glug of brandy into his glass of coffee. "But next year, wait for me and Felix, or let Joe do it."

I nodded meekly.

The grapevine sorted, conversation began to flow at the same speed as the brandy disappeared. Although Uncle Felix was frail and hunched, he hadn't lost the ability to drink brandy. His ancient, crooked fingers curled around his glass and rarely released their hold.

"Uncle Felix is 84 years old now, you know," said Paco.

Uncle Felix beamed proudly.

"Or are you 85, Felix?"

Uncle Felix thought hard, then shook his head. He was never a man of many words. Being a shepherd, he'd never learnt to read or write and I doubted if anybody knew his real age, including himself.

"Never had a day's illness, have you, Felix?"

Felix shook his head proudly and I knew what was coming next.

"Never seen a dentist, have you, Felix?"

The old man beamed, exposing pink gums. I waited for the next comment and mouthed the words silently. I wasn't disappointed.

"And he has never been with a woman!" Paco's fist slammed down on the table in triumph.

Uncle Felix shook his head again, still grinning from ear to gnarled ear as though he had achieved something extraordinary.

"Tell the English about your new TV," commanded Paco. Uncle Felix just beamed, so Paco took over. "He has a brand-new widescreen plasma TV!" roared Paco. "The whole family clubbed together and bought it for him."

"In his cottage?" I asked.

"Yes!"

I blinked at the thought. I hadn't been inside Uncle Felix's cottage, but Joe had. It was very primitive, with thick, crumbling walls and a corrugated asbestos roof. It consisted of just two rooms with earth floors flattened by age. Uncle Felix lived, cooked and slept in one room, while his mule and two chickens occupied the other. I tried to imagine a wide-screen TV in that cottage and failed.

"He loves that matchmaking show on the TV in the afternoons. Never misses it. You know the one where couples come together? You love that show, don't you, Felix?"

I thought I knew the one he meant, a little like a Spanish *Blind Date* for the elderly.

Uncle Felix grinned and released his glass long enough to tap his two forefingers together, side by side, signifying a couple getting together.

So Uncle Felix's decrepit exterior hid a romantic and sentimental heart? Who'd have thought it? If only he had met a lonely shepherdess in the mountains in his younger days...

The conversation switched to Mother and Alejandro Senior whose torrid affair was the talk of the village.

"Good luck to them," said Joe. "I hope I'm that lively when I get to their age."

If I let you reach that age, I thought.

"Has anyone seen Maribel Ufarte and the children?" I asked.

"Bad business, bad business," growled Paco. "Juan Ufarte made a big mistake there. Lola will be off soon, you mark my words, chasing some other man. Then Juan will have nobody. A bad business."

The conversation turned to other village matters, like the new bar and the council's decision to cut down on the number of dumpsters in the village to save money.

PRUNING

"I was talking to the mayor only last week," said Paco. "He said the council has to save as much money as possible. The coffers are empty. Oh and Veeky, he mentioned you."

"He did?"

"Yes, he said you promised to give him private English lessons."

I stared at Paco, horrified. I thought that had all been forgotten.

"The mayor is thinking that he should speak good English and maybe attract more English people to the village. English people have lots of money."

We'd come across this misconception many times before. Spanish people always thought the British were a hugely rich nation. We tried to explain that although salaries were higher in Britain, so was the cost of everything, including property, food, transport, utilities and taxes. In fact, we knew very few people in Britain who owned two houses, whereas in Spain it is common for families to have a house or apartment in the city and a house in the countryside.

We went on to discuss Spain's floundering economy and the latest Spanish football triumphs. Eventually, Paco and Uncle Felix stood up to leave and we walked them to the front door. The mule gave a little snicker of delight when she saw her beloved master.

Paco leaned in to Joe and delivered his parting

shot. He lowered his voice but I still heard the words clearly.

"Listen, Joe, never, *never* let a woman loose on grapevines. That is a man's job."

"Well, that was a nice visit, wasn't it?" said Joe brightly, closing the front door and following me back into the kitchen. "Always good to hear the village gossip."

I said nothing, still seething.

"Have you seen my slippers? I'm sure I left them here by the door."

"Did you?"

"Yes, how strange... Never mind, perhaps I put them somewhere else. What are we having for dinner tonight?"

"I've defrosted some mackerel."

"Mackerel? I hate mackerel!"

"Yes. I know."

※※※

The Almería area has often been described as the vegetable basket of Europe. Ugly plastic greenhouses stretch for acres in some areas, the perfect growing environment for tomatoes, peppers and aubergines, all year round. They are a terrible eyesore, ruining glorious views, but they are a necessary evil. Spain was in the grip of a financial crisis and unemployment was rocketing, so this greenhouse industry was now more important than ever.

PRUNING

Almería is also a big supplier of citrus fruit. Joe and I never wearied of driving alongside the orange and lemon orchards. In the depth of the Spanish winter, the trees hung with luscious fruit.

Thanks to the generosity of the Spanish, we were never short of oranges. If we ever stopped our car near an orchard, a farmer would beckon us and fill our arms with oranges.

And although our garden may have been too small to grow orange trees, we didn't even need to leave home in order to be supplied with oranges.

MACKEREL PATÉ

The preparation time for this paté is just 10 minutes, but the mackerel will require 20 minutes in the oven.

Ingredients

- 2 whole mackerel, baked
- 150g (5oz) cream cheese
- 2 garlic cloves, minced
- ½ tsp lemon juice
- 6 basil leaves, chopped
- Salt to taste

Method

- Clean, then bake the mackerel in tinfoil in a preheated oven at 180°C/350°F/Gas Mark 4, for 20 minutes.
- Cool and flake the mackerel into a *cazuela* or mixing bowl.
- Add the rest of the ingredients and mix well (can also be put through a food processor).
- Serve with crackers or fresh crusty bread.

14

ORANGES AND THE LAW

'Your baby is now the size of a prune. Bones and cartilage are forming and fingernails and hair are starting to appear.'

At the bottom of our mountain was a roundabout, one of many. We were accustomed to seeing an elderly farmer sitting on an upturned crate beside his ancient car at the side of the road.

In winter, although the Spanish sun is always warm, the air can be cold and the wind often has a biting edge. The old man wore woollen gloves and a scarf, his shoulders hunched in a heavy coat. Under his flat cap, he watched the traffic pass, waiting for people like us who couldn't resist his wares.

I turned to Joe. "Stop the car," I said. "I want to buy some oranges."

ORANGES AND THE LAW

He rolled his eyes, but applied the brakes. I knew what he was thinking. We had more than enough oranges given to us by villagers in the bowl at home. But I also knew he agreed with me. Spain was going through tough times and most people were struggling financially. We could easily afford 5 euros for a bag of oranges.

The crates stood in a row on the verge, tilted slightly, so that passing motorists could see the gorgeous display. A few had rolled into the road and been crushed by tyres.

"Very fresh," the old man assured me and I knew he was telling the truth. The glossy, green leaves still attached to some of the golden fruit hadn't even begun to wilt.

I held the carrier bag open and the old man poured an entire crate in, muttering with annoyance as some big oranges threatened to escape. I paid him and carried the bag back to the car. It was so heavy that it cut into my fingers.

When we arrived home, we found a bulging bag had been left on our doorstep. Oranges and lemons. Some kind villager had left them for us, as they often did. I sighed and took them through to the kitchen. It had been been a long day and a gin and tonic with a few fresh lemon slices wouldn't go amiss. Joe put the car away, but didn't come back empty-handed.

"Somebody left these for us," he said. "They were hanging on the garage door handle."

"What are they?"

Silly question.

I became very inventive with oranges. We ate them all through the day and a jug of freshly squeezed orange juice was a permanent fixture in our fridge. I made chicken à l'orange, orange curd, orange sponge cake, orange upside-down pudding and orange mousse with caramelised oranges (thank you, Hugh Fearnley-Whittingstall).

It's a pity the body is unable to store vitamin C because I'm sure Joe and I had enough in our systems to last until we were at least 300 years old. We never caught colds and perhaps we could thank the oranges for that.

Of course all those oranges generated yards and yards of peel. It occurred to me to do a spot of research to find out whether orange peel can be recycled in any way.

Oh yes, apparently there are many colourful uses for discarded orange peel.

1) Orange peel firelighters

I was keen to try this one as we always needed firelighters to start the stove in winter. I followed the instructions by placing our peel on a tray in the sun to dry. A couple of days later, I went to see how my firelighters were coming along. They were swarming with ants, so many that the peel appeared black, not orange and organised lines of ants were marching in from all directions. Failure. I threw the peel, ants and all, into the bin.

2) *Orange peel cleaning product*

This one looked easy. All you had to do was place the peel in a jar, cover with vinegar, screw the lid on tight and wait two weeks. After a fortnight, I needed to strain the vinegar, throw the peel away and my cleaning product was ready to use.

All went according to plan, although the liquid smelled more of vinegar than oranges. Unperturbed, I set to work. I dampened a cloth with the mixture and began wiping the furniture. It worked beautifully. I looked at my cloth with satisfaction. It was now grey with the dirt that my new cleaning product had lifted. I scrubbed some more. It was then that I realised I was not only removing dirt, but also the varnish. The remainder of my homemade orange peel cleaning product was poured down the sink.

3) *Orange peel rose table centre-piece*

Oh, please! Life was too short to start sculpting orange peel into little roses. Joe would never have noticed anyway as he'd be far more interested in what was on his plate.

4) Orange peel insect repellent

Hmmm... That could prove useful. *"If you mix orange peel and water, then spray the solution outside your home, you will prevent ants from coming in,"* began the article. Rubbish! I'd already seen my orange peel firelighters swarming with ants. I believed the orange water would *attract* ants, not chase them away. I certainly wasn't going to waste my time with that one.

5) Orange peel bird feeder

With three or more hungry cats in the garden? Probably not a good idea.

6) Scary teeth

"Why not fashion yourself some orange peel Halloween teeth?" asked another article.
"Because it's March," I grumbled.

7) Adorable orange peel boats

Are you kidding?
No. Enough.
So I carried on throwing away all our orange peel, satisfied that at least I'd tried.

ORANGES AND THE LAW

I'm not good at breaking the law; it makes me nervous and twitchy. I don't believe I ever did before we moved to Spain, but circumstances changed.

The problem was our car. It was brand new the year we came and although we used it for carrying heavy stuff and firewood up the mountain, it still ran beautifully and the mileage was ridiculously low. It was a four-wheel drive, a Suzuki and we loved folding back the soft roof in the summer as the sun beat down, allowing the wind to blow through our hair. (Well, mine, anyway, as Joe was rather lacking in that department.)

The jeep was a right-hand drive and had British number plates and we knew we should get Spanish registration for it. We tried. We hired a lady to do the paperwork. She hired an official to check over the car and make notes about its specifications. Back came the report. Our car didn't exist. It could not be found on any of the Spanish files.

"Never mind," said the lady, tapping her clipboard with a polished fingernail. "We can find a way round that. It'll cost a bit more, of course."

Of course.

Several months down the line, we had imported new headlights from Japan at huge expense, removed the tow bar and paid to have all sorts of other modifications made.

All cars must be put through the ITV

(*Inspecciòn Tècnica de Vehiculos*) and we were confident that our car would pass with flying colours, considering all the modifications that we'd made. In the UK, the MOT, or Ministry of Transport test, is carried out at appointed garages. In Spain, the procedure is different. There are designated ITV stations dotted all over the country. We made an appointment and drove there.

In Britain, you just leave your car and pick it up later, but in Spain you actually stay in the car as the mechanics swarm all over it like insects over a carcass. They crawled underneath, spun the wheels and fired instructions at us to switch things on and off. At the end, we were informed that the car had failed because of a headlight technicality.

"Do you realise we've thrown a couple of thousand euros at this car and it still isn't right?" said Joe. "I think we should just sell it and buy an ordinary Spanish car instead. Otherwise we'll have to go through all this paperwork again and I bet it won't ever pass, whatever the garage does."

"But who is going to buy a right-hand drive Brit-registered car, without an ITV certificate?"

We both loved that car. It was reliable, functional, lovely to drive and easy to park in our garage. Neither of us wanted to get rid of it. The weeks slid by and we continued to use it, illegally. I was a nervous wreck every time we went out, jumping at the sight of police cars, convinced we would be pulled over, questioned and fined.

It's rare to see any police presence on our mountain roads so when Joe drove to the seed merchant to buy more grain for the chickens, he wasn't expecting any problems. It was a lovely sunny day and the roads were empty.

When he approached a service station on the outskirts of a neighbouring village, he decided he should fill up with petrol. Checking behind him in the mirror, he turned left and swung onto the forecourt without bothering to indicate as there was no other traffic on the road.

Unfortunately, he hadn't looked carefully enough. He'd failed to notice the police motorbike tailing him. Worse still, Joe's left turn and lack of signal had forced the policeman to brake violently.

On the garage forecourt, Joe switched off the engine and waited, head drooping, for the inevitable. The policeman drew up alongside, killed his engine and angrily pulled off his crash helmet. Joe looked at him sheepishly.

"Dangerous driving," announced the policeman. "You failed to signal when you turned off. You have broken the law and you could have caused an accident. I need to see your ID, proof of insurance and the car's paperwork."

Glumly, Joe produced his passport, which was all he had with him. The policeman glanced at it, then patted the pockets of his own leather jacket and checked his panniers for something.

"You need to produce the rest of your paperwork within one week," said the policeman, scribbling Joe's name and registration number on the back of a cigarette packet. Obviously his official notebook had gone missing, or perhaps he was off duty. "Take them to the police station, or you will be fined."

Tucking the cigarette pack back into his pocket, he replaced his helmet, turned the ignition key and roared off up the empty road.

"We've got a week," said Joe gloomily when he came home and told me all about it. "A week to pass the ITV or get a new car."

"There's no way we can get an ITV, so I guess we'll have to buy a new car, even though we don't want one."

"And what do we do with the old car?"

"I don't know. Just park it in the village somewhere for now. Ask Paco what people do with old cars. Perhaps there's a car scrap place we don't know about."

It was a depressing thought to abandon our perfectly good car to rust amongst crashed and broken vehicles in a scrap yard.

The following day we started looking in earnest for a replacement vehicle. In the city, we parked at the first car showroom and started browsing the vehicles on display on the forecourt. We were so engrossed we didn't notice when a

ORANGES AND THE LAW

tall, skinny man with fair curly hair strode up to us.

"Joe! Vicky! How are you?"

"Kurt! Good to see you!"

Kurt was the German estate agent who had found our house in El Hoyo for us, nearly ten years ago.

We exchanged chitchat. Kurt and his Spanish lawyer wife now had two children. Selling houses was no longer a profitable career, but Kurt had fingers in numerous pies. He was active in local politics and also had an interest in the restaurant in the next village. We told him about our year in Bahrain and life in general.

"Are you looking for a car to buy?" asked Kurt.

"We are," said Joe, "although we don't really want to part with our old car. Are you looking for a car, too?"

"Ja, I promised my vife I vould look for a fun vehicle ve can use to pull our little boat to the beach in the summer. A small RV vould be good, perhaps."

Joe and I stared at him.

"Like that one?" Joe asked, pointing to where our vehicle was parked.

"Ja, exactly like that one."

To cut a long story short, Kurt loved our car. The fact that it didn't have an ITV certificate didn't bother him at all as he was a man of many contacts. He didn't mind that it was a right-hand drive, either. We shook hands on the spot and Kurt was pleased with his purchase, although being German, he wasn't one to rave. He had secured a bargain for 1,000 euros and we had sold a car we thought was un-sellable. He found us another car in another garage, a rather boring Volkswagen Polo, but it suited our needs.

The next day, we sealed the deal and drove our new car home. Kurt, delighted with his acquisition, drove away in our jeep with a tiny smile on his face. I was sorry to see it go.

"What luck!" said Joe for the millionth time.

Now we needed to take all our paperwork to the police station in the next town, a job neither of us fancied.

Finding the police station was the first hurdle. We asked at the supermarket and were directed to a shabby-looking building down a side street. It was all locked up so Joe knocked politely on the door.

ORANGES AND CINNAMON

A different take on oranges, good enough to serve as a dessert with a dollop of ice cream.

Ingredients

- 6 sweet juicy oranges
- 100g (3.5oz) sugar
- Ground cinnamon

Method

- Peel the oranges and slice crosswise.
- Place in a large dish, sprinkle with the sugar and dust with cinnamon.
- Chill in the fridge for 30 minutes.
- Serve sprinkled with a little more cinnamon.

15

OWLS AND KITTENS

Your baby is now the size of an onion and can yawn, hiccup, roll, twist, kick, punch, suck and swallow.'

"Knock again," I said. "Perhaps they didn't hear you."

We could hear voices and laughter through the door. Joe knocked again, a little harder and the door swung open.

"Good morning, we've brought all our car's paperwork as requested," said Joe.

The policeman looked blank. I could see past him into the police station where his colleagues were playing cards, seated round a table.

"Anyone know anything about an elderly English couple bringing in their vehicle's paperwork?" the policeman called over his shoulder.

"No," chorused the uniformed card players from within.

"But we were asked…" began Joe, but was halted in mid-sentence as the policeman waved us away and firmly shut the door.

We stared at the closed door and then each other.

"Well!" said Joe.

"I guess that's that, then?" I asked.

"If they don't want to check it, that's fine by me," said Joe.

We turned away and walked back to the car. I didn't like the new car much, but at least we were no longer breaking the law.

We spoke to Kurt a couple of days later. I asked him if his wife liked our old car and approved of the purchase. Kurt was not known for his sense of humour, but allowed a little smile to cross his face.

"*Ja*, I told my vife, look at this picture of a car. Do you like it? Then I showed my vife the photo on my phone. My vife said she liked it very much, then she looked at the photo again, very exactly. 'Isn't that our garage?' she asked. 'I can see our boat there and the toys of the children.' I said, '*Ja*, I haf bought this car as a surprise. Come to the garage and meet our new car.'" Kurt's face split into an uncharacteristic grin.

"Oh, I'm pleased it's gone to a good home," I smiled.

"*Ja*, my vife likes it very much and the children, they like it very much. And ve all laugh very much at the little prank I made."

☥☥☥

Joe and I, as well as the villagers, accepted that Maribel Ufarte had left with the children. Although Lola and Papa Ufarte were now a couple, I don't think anybody believed theirs would be a lasting relationship. Sometimes we heard raised voices through the walls and the sparkle seemed to have left Papa Ufarte's eyes. He still sat on the doorstep strumming his guitar, but the exuberant flamenco music was gone, replaced by long, sad, haunting melodies.

Then, one day, we saw Papa Ufarte leaving. His car was parked outside their house and he was loading it with clothes, shoes and personal paraphernalia. When I saw him carry out both his guitars and stow them in the back, I knew he wasn't planning to come back anytime soon.

"I don't know where he's gone," said Carmen when we discussed it over a glass of coffee and *churros*. "Maribel told me she wouldn't have him back."

"Perhaps he's found a place of his own in the city," I said. "Or perhaps he's moved back in with his parents?"

"*Claro*, very possible," Carmen replied. "A great pity. But you mark my words, that girl, Lola, won't stay single for long."

Lola left the village soon after and the house was closed up, as empty of life as it had been when we first moved into El Hoyo so many years before.

Spring brings many wonderful things, but perhaps one of our favourites was the scops owl. We'd only seen one once as it sat on a wall at the roadside in broad daylight. Scops owls are tiny and if it hadn't swivelled its head as we drove by, we probably wouldn't have noticed it.

We stopped the car and Joe and I stared at the beautiful little bird. Not to be outdone, it stared back at us. In fact we all stared at each other for a full minute before it launched, sweeping away into the valley on silent wings.

Although it's rare to *see* one, hearing scops owls is a nightly occurrence. Usually there would be just one trying to attract a mate, but some nights two or three of them would compete.

Scops owls don't say "Twit-Twoo" like owls are supposed to. Scops owls are perfectly happy with just a "Pooo" every twenty seconds or so, repeated over and over again. So the conversation went rather like this:

Scops Owl #1, "Pooo."

Scops Owl #2, "Pooo."
Scops Owl #3, "Pooo."

Our valley resembles a Roman amphitheatre. Even the smallest sound travels and can be heard by all, particularly at night. The bark of a fox or the grunt of a deer sounds as though the animals are mere yards away when they are probably on the other side of the valley.

Joe and I loved to stand on our roof terrace at dusk, listening to the owls trying to out-pooo each other.

Joe is not a good mimic. Whenever he tries to copy a foreign accent it comes out sounding Pakistani. However, he is very good at imitating these owls and his 'pooo' is almost perfect. Three scops owls in the valley was an opportunity too good to miss.

"Pooo," said Owl #1, from somewhere high in the valley.

"Pooo," agreed Owl #2, his voice echoing from our far right.

"Pooo," added Owl #3, somewhere to the south of us.

"Pooo," said Joe, beside me.

Utter silence.

What? An interloper! A gatecrasher competing for the attentions of a lady owl? Oh, horror!

We giggled as we imagined all three owls' expressions as they swivelled their heads, trying to work out where this uninvited upstart newcomer might be perched. I imagined them ruffling their feathers in annoyance, their yellow eyes piercing the gloom in an effort to see this cheeky infiltrator.

Having got over the shock, the owls pulled themselves together and resumed their hooting. But so did Joe. Now we had a quartet, all in perfect time. Occasionally a fox would bark, but the four performers refused to be distracted. The three owls took turns to hoot, leaving time for Joe to chime in at the end of the sequence.

"Pooo," said Owl #1.

"Pooo," said Owl #2.

"Pooo," said Owl #3.

"Pooo," said Joe.

I left them to it. I had supper to prepare and I could rely on Joe to carry on with the good work.

Half an hour later, I called a reluctant Joe inside.

"Two of them gave up," said Joe, triumph in his voice. "It was just me and the southerly owl left."

"Eat your supper," I said, "before a lady owl comes knocking on our door looking for you."

Of course spring meant that new litters of kittens were being born all over the village. Tiny mews could be heard from ruined cottages and nooks and crannies. As the bolder ones emerged, it was obvious that Black Balls had been busy. Where many of the previous generation of kittens had exhibited Siamese traits, the vast majority of this year's kittens were coal black.

We suspected that Sylvia had a litter stashed away somewhere, but we didn't know where. So it was with some surprise that we saw her daughter, Felicity, who was barely a kitten herself, carrying a kitten into our garden. She climbed down the trunk of our vine and dropped the kitten on the ground, staring at us with huge green eyes.

"Joe! Felicity has brought a kitten into the garden! She must have stolen it!"

"Perhaps she's taken one of Sylvia's?"

"What shall we do?"

The little black kitten, eyes still closed, squirmed and mewed.

"Well, we can't interfere. We'll just have to wait and see what happens. Perhaps Sylvia will hear it and come and collect it."

I watched Felicity all that day through the kitchen window. First she stashed the kitten behind a pile of flowerpots, then she sprang up the vine again and vanished.

"Joe! She's abandoned Sylvia's kitten and gone up the vine!"

"Leave it, let's see what happens next."

Felicity reappeared at the top of the vine. The vine leaves were young, not fully grown yet and we could easily see what she was carrying. Another kitten.

"Oh no, she's bringing another one!"

Felicity climbed down and deposited the second kitten behind the flowerpots with the first. Now both kittens were howling.

"Look who's coming," said Joe, pointing up the garden.

Sylvia was walking towards the house. Surely she must pass the kittens' hiding place? She would most certainly hear her babies yelling.

"Good, she'll rescue them now," I said, hugely relieved.

Sylvia did hear the kittens. Unhurriedly, she walked over to the flowerpots, had a look and a sniff, then turned her back on them. Joe and I stared at each other. The truth dawned on us at the same time.

"Those kittens aren't Sylvia's, they're Felicity's!"

"I didn't think she was old enough!"

"Well, she obviously is!"

During that day, Felicity tended to her two offspring, only leaving them briefly to gobble the scraps we left out.

"Looks like we have more cats in the garden," said Joe, "and what if Sylvia brings hers, too? We can't look after all those cats."

"I agree. We can't have them multiplying in the garden. But what do we do?"

It was a problem we had faced many times.

We'd taken in the Siamese family a couple of years before and had been lucky enough to find homes for them in Germany. However, we were fully aware that finding homes for Spanish feral cats was next to impossible. The Spanish don't like cats much and even their pet cats are rarely neutered. Thus the feral population continues to expand and multiply.

In this case, the problem was taken out of our hands. Felicity changed her mind about her babies' nursery and carried the kittens away during the night. She didn't take them far. She decided that the cavity behind the air-conditioning unit on the Ufartes' roof would make a suitable home. As the evenings stretched longer, Joe and I could sit in the garden at dusk and watch the two kittens grow and chase each other around the Ufartes' chimney, silhouetted against the orange sky.

As spring swung towards summer, countless shades of green smothered the mountainsides, interspersed with dabs of multicoloured wildflowers. The village kittens grew larger and bolder and began to show themselves. Flushed out by the fish van's hoot, they scampered after their mothers to crowd around the van in the square, hopeful that a fishtail or a scrap might be flung their way.

Uncle Felix tethered his mule in a different place every day and she feasted on lush new

OWLS AND KITTENS

growth. Sometimes I caught sight of Uncle Felix's tiny frail figure early in the morning, leading her to pastures new. He'd stay with her awhile, watching her crop and giving her an occasional pat. Then he'd make his slow descent back down the mountain.

Visitors began to arrive. The crafty cuckoo's call echoed around the valley. The swallows and house martins returned and refurbished their nests under the eaves of the cottages.

Joe and I also welcomed our own visitors, a stream of family and friends escaping from the UK's dismal weather, eager to bask in the Andalucian sunshine.

Since returning from our year away in Bahrain, we'd managed to do a fair amount of decorating. We'd repainted most of the interior and outside, using gallons of white paint. I wanted everything looking nice before the next batch of visitors arrived.

Joe strained his back, so much of the decorating rested on my shoulders. He also managed to scrape his knees when kneeling on the roof, bruise his thumb by trapping it under a plank of wood and gash his finger changing a light bulb.

Yes, everything looked wonderful, ready for the summer, except for the chicken house. The chicken house was badly in need of sprucing up and we still had an unopened tub of paint. Joe pulled the lid off and we stared at the paint in dismay.

"That doesn't look right," I said. "It looks pink!"

"Just needs a stir," Joe said and tapped the lid closed.

JUDITH'S EASY LEMON CURD

Ingredients

- 700g (25oz) caster sugar (Judith says she uses ordinary granulated sugar and it seems fine and nobody has complained!)
- 1 block butter - 225g (8ozs)
- Finely grated rind and juice of 6 large lemons
- 8 large eggs

Method

- Put sugar, butter, grated lemon rind and lemon juice in a heatproof basin.

- Place the basin over a saucepan half full of simmering water, making sure the bottom of the basin does not touch the water.

- Over low heat, stir the mixture until the sugar has dissolved and butter melted. (Judith says, "I now find a very short period of time in the microwave to melt the butter helps!!")

- Add lightly beaten eggs and stir until mixture is thick enough to coat the back of a wooden spoon.

- Pour into prepared jars and keep in the fridge once the lemon curd is cold.

Recipe kindly donated by reader, Judith Benson. (A different Judith to our friend in the next village.)

16

A SANDWICH

'Your baby is now the size of a small pineapple and all five senses are in working order.'

Buying paint in Spain is not difficult as there is very little demand for any colour except white. Having an old, traditional house, we were very happy to follow our neighbours' example and paint everything white. It always looked fresh and there were never any colour-matching issues.

When we removed the lid of the last 5-gallon tub of paint, Joe grabbed a stick and started stirring. Much to our surprise, it still looked pink.

"Perhaps it's just separated," Joe said, stirring even more energetically.

"It's most definitely pink," I said glumly.

And the more he stirred, the pinker it became.

"Well, I've had enough," grumbled Joe. "I'm

not going down the mountain to buy more paint. The chickens will just have to put up with a pink house."

I opened my mouth to argue but something unexpected stopped me in my tracks. A small tractor was passing our house, heading for the farmland above. That wasn't unusual. These reliable little work-horses were a familiar sound as they chugged up the steep hill past our back gate, pulling trailers carrying farming paraphernalia and produce.

But the next event was unusual.

CRASH!

Startled, our chickens shrilled their alarm call while Joe and I froze, listening. After the initial crash we heard a series of loud thuds, then rolling sounds, followed by the tractor braking, then a torrent of Spanish curses. After a brief pause, the tractor continued on its way with the farmer's curses fading as he turned the corner at the top of the road. Joe and I opened our back gate to look outside.

It was a scene of carnage. Red juice splatted the street and shattered watermelons lay strewn around, all jagged edges and pink glistening flesh. The tailgate of the farmer's trailer must have dropped and his load of watermelons had escaped, bouncing and rolling down the mountain road.

Joe and I gaped at the mess, then silently collected all the undamaged watermelons, rolling them into a pile for the farmer to collect when he returned. As for the huge shards of damaged watermelons, we knew who would appreciate them.

As we daubed pink paint on their house, our chickens feasted on watermelon.

Our first visitor, my niece Becky, arrived. She offered to help paint the chicken house, which was very kind of her. Except there was a problem. Becky was absolutely terrified of the chickens.

"They won't hurt you," I said, "they're really gentle."

Becky was brave, but the painting session was a noisy one. Every time a chicken got too close, she'd shriek and make a dash for the gate.

Nevertheless, the chicken house was eventually painted. Surprisingly, the finished job looked rather good, if a little, um … pink. Some of the chickens had pink streaks where they'd rubbed against the wet paint, but they soon wore off.

We learnt a lesson from the experience. When buying paint, always check, then double-check that the label says *blanco*, not *arcilla*. *Arcilla* actually means 'clay' but, I promise you, it's pink.

Very pink.

※※※

Before visitors arrived, they often asked if they could bring anything for us from England, items that we couldn't purchase in Spain. We usually asked the Gin Twins to bring bayonet-type light bulbs as the Spanish screw-in type didn't fit our English light fittings. We asked niece Becky to bring Italian seasoning as we missed our spaghetti bolognese.

"Do you have any requests?" I asked Joe as our latest batch of visitors were preparing to fly out.

"Yes! I've been craving bacon. Can you ask them to bring a few packs?"

Delicious serrano ham and all kinds of wonderful pork products are easy to buy in Spain, but good old English sausages and bacon are impossible to find.

Of course, during our year's stay in Muslim Bahrain, pork hadn't been on sale at all. I estimated we hadn't tasted bacon for at least 10 years. I hadn't missed it at all, but it seemed that Joe had suddenly developed a hankering for it.

"I can't stop thinking about bacon," Joe said with a dreamy look in his eye. "I'm fantasising about it. I can almost smell it."

"No worries, I'll ask them to bring some."

Our visitors arrived and so did three packs of bacon. Joe thanked our friends but as soon as they'd left the room, he started complaining.

"Only three? They brought only three packs? Don't they realise I've been suffering terrible bacon withdrawal symptoms?"

A SANDWICH

"Don't be so ungrateful. It was kind of them to bring any at all."

"Well, don't plan any bacon-based meals while they're here. I want to save this little lot until after they've gone. I'm hiding this."

True to his word, he tucked them away at the back of the fridge behind the sauces and ketchups that were seldom moved.

We enjoyed our friends' stay but as we took them back to the airport, I felt Joe's impatience.

"What's the matter with you?" I asked as we drove home. "Why are you driving so fast?"

"No reason."

"Yes, there is. Something's on your mind, that's for sure."

"I don't know what you mean." Joe drummed his fingers on the steering-wheel, feigning nonchalance.

"Come on, what's on your mind?"

"Well, if you must know, I'm planning a sandwich."

"You're what? You're planning a ... *sandwich?*"

"Yep, we're going to stop at the supermarket and I'm going to buy some fresh bread, lettuce and tomatoes. I've been dreaming about this. I'm going to make the best bacon, lettuce and tomato sandwich in the world."

Back in our kitchen, Joe unpacked his purchases and laid them out. Then he reached for a pack of bacon, running his fingers over the smooth, cold plastic before snipping it open with scissors.

"Now, don't interfere, I'm making this myself. I've been rehearsing it in my mind for days. You don't want one, do you?"

"No, thanks, I'll just make myself a coffee."

Joe lit the hob and heated a little oil in the frying pan. He peeled several slices of bacon out of the pack and laid them lovingly into the hot oil where they sizzled. Humming to himself, he poked them gently with a spatula, moving them around a little.

"I'd forgotten how good bacon smells when it's cooking," I said.

"Don't think you're getting any of this, you're too late. I offered and you said no. This is all for me."

"Don't worry, I don't want any of your wretched bacon."

Joe was in a world of his own as he carried on with his preparations. He pulled off a few choice leaves from the iceberg lettuce and sliced a tomato with surgeon-like precision. Then he cut the freshly baked bread, still warm from the bakery.

The scene was set. The BLT was almost ready.

"Stop staring at me, you're putting me off."

"Sorry, I can't help it," I said, shaking my head. "I've never seen you so engrossed in making a sandwich."

Joe spooned and spread mayonnaise on the bread and laid out the bright tomato slices evenly,

A SANDWICH

topping them with the crispy lettuce. Then, with a flourish, he placed the bacon slices on top, finishing off with another slice of bread. I had to admit it, it did look good.

He stood back and stared at the sandwich waiting on the plate.

"What a sandwich," he whispered. "Not so much a sandwich as a work of art."

"Well, go on then, eat it!"

"Not yet, I need to take a photo of it first."

Having snapped it from all angles, he went to put the camera away.

"Don't you dare touch it while I'm gone."

"Huh! I value my life too much."

When he returned, he stared at the sandwich again.

"Are you going to eat it now?" I asked.

"Yes, but there's no rush. This sandwich was made with love. It's probably the best sandwich in the world. You can't rush these things."

"Oh, for goodness' sake, just eat it!"

But he couldn't. He'd invested too much into that sandwich. It was just too beautiful to eat.

Having circled it a few times, he finally picked up the plate.

"This sandwich deserves to be savoured. I want to be alone when I eat it."

I rolled my eyes, exasperated. "Oh, for goodness' sake! Do whatever you want. I'm going to get some writing done."

I left the room to allow him to continue his

love affair with the sandwich in peace. An hour or so later, I went back into the kitchen.

"How was the sandwich?" I asked, but the kitchen was empty. There was no sign of Joe or the sandwich.

I went out into the garden. Joe was nowhere to be seen. I went up the outside staircase and found him on the roof terrace, fast asleep on the sunlounger, the empty plate still in his hands.

"Joe?"

He woke up with a start and sat upright.

"How was the sandwich?"

He looked at me, then stared at the empty plate.

"I never ate it!"

"What do you mean?" I asked, puzzled.

"I just sat down and stared at it. I was imagining biting into it and deciding which end to start. I wanted to savour every second. I guess I must have fallen asleep."

"So where is it?"

We both looked down at the floor. There was the sandwich. Well, most of it. The once glorious sandwich had fallen apart and the tomato slices had tumbled out and were already covered in ants. The creamy mayonnaise had disappeared, melted into the bread. The lettuce was limp and wilted from lying in the sun.

And where was the bacon?

Gone.

A SANDWICH

"Cats," I said, picking up the mess and putting it back on the plate.

"Blasted cats!" said Joe furiously. "I can't believe it! The cats sneaked up and stole my bacon while I was asleep!"

"If you had just eaten the stupid sandwich instead of worshipping it, this wouldn't have happened."

"I can't believe I never even tasted it!"

I made Joe (and myself) another BLT. Joe maintained it wasn't anywhere near as beautiful as the first one, but this time he didn't hesitate before eating it. We both agreed it was delicious.

※※※

The phone rang very early one morning. I immediately knew who it was. My daughter had told me that she had a hospital visit scheduled. They were hoping to discover the gender of the baby.

"Mum, it's me!"

"Hi, Karly, good to hear you. Did you find out?"

"Yep! It's a little girl! We are going to have a daughter!"

"Oh my! I'm going to have a granddaughter! Does that mean you're going to stop calling her Wolfgang or Grug now?"

How did the poor little unborn mite get saddled with those names?

"Yep, we've got to start looking at names properly. The hospital says everything is going according to plan and the baby is the right size and everything."

"Oh good, that's great news. And your due date is still early August?"

"Yes. Cam's parents are going to fly down from Sydney and stay a while when the baby is born."

"Okay and I'll book my flight. I think you'll have lots of help in those first couple of weeks and Cam will have time off work to be with you. I'll come over in the first week of September. Can't wait!"

"I can't wait either! I can't wait for this baby to be born and I can't wait to see you!"

"Time will fly, you'll see."

※※※

By the end of June, the sun was often unbearably hot and the villagers were arriving for their summer break. Children played in the streets, mopeds and scooters buzzed and the evening promenade up the mountain road resumed. Only the Ufartes' house remained quiet and empty. Then, in midsummer, we heard activity again and wondered who was living there now.

"I hope Maribel has come back," I said. "It would be nice to see the kids again."

But it wasn't Maribel, or her husband, Papa

A SANDWICH

Ufarte. Lola had returned and to nobody's surprise, she wasn't alone.

Lola's new companion had long, unkempt hair and a furtive way of looking at one. His jeans were torn and dirty and he made no attempt to talk to us or any of the villagers. I didn't much like the look of him and it seemed other people shared my view.

"You mark my words," said Carmen, "that new man of Lola Ufarte's is not to be trusted."

"Do you know anything about him?" I asked.

"No, and that is what worries me. In a village like this, we all know about each other."

We didn't see much of either Lola or her new man. They kept to themselves and rarely emerged from the house except to drive noisily away in a rusty old van with a dangling exhaust pipe that nearly scraped the ground.

And all the time, on the other side of the world, my granddaughter was growing.

CLASSIC BLT TOASTED SANDWICH

The BLT never fails to make Joe's mouth water. Try it with one slice of toast spread with yellow mustard. Makes 4 sandwiches.

Ingredients

- About 12 bacon slices
- 8 slices white bread
- 8 leaves iceberg lettuce, fresh and full
- 8 slices of ripened tomatoes
- 8 tablespoons mayonnaise

Method

- Cook bacon until crispy, then drain on paper towels.
- Toast the 8 slices of bread.
- Spread 1 tablespoon mayo on each slice of toasted bread. (More or less, to taste)
- Add 1 slice of lettuce to 4 pieces of mayo-spread toast.
- Add 2 slices of tomato on top of lettuce.
- Arrange 3 slices of bacon evenly on top of tomato. Break bacon slices in half to fit, if needed.
- Add 1 slice of lettuce on top of bacon.
- Put the remaining 4 pieces of mayo-spread toast on top to finish the sandwiches.

17

BIRTHDAYS

'Your baby is now the size of a coconut and is getting closer and closer to being able to breathe on her own. Her skin is getting smooth and soft and her gums are rigid. Her liver and kidneys are in working order.'

My daughter, Karly, was speaking to me on the phone from Melbourne.

"We've done some *great* eBay shopping for Grug and bought a second-hand cot, pram and chest of drawers-changing-table thingy and nappy bag. Cam has sanded down and repainted all the furniture and it looks *amazing*. We've saved an absolute *fortune*," my daughter told me on the phone.

"Oh, well done! Any more thoughts about her name?"

BIRTHDAYS

"We're thinking of calling her Bunny after the Duracell advert where the bunny never stops moving. It's okay, I'm joking. We keep changing our minds but we have a shortlist of about six now."

"You'll know which name is right for her when she arrives," I said. "At least you can stop calling her Wolfgang or Grug."

"That's true. What's the weather like in Spain now? It's cold here in Melbourne."

"Hot! We try to go to the beach at least once a week and the doors and windows stay open permanently."

"Well, by the time Wolfgang arrives and you come over, spring should be well on the way here."

It always surprised me how very hot the Spanish sun was. I couldn't touch the handrail of the outside staircase without scalding myself and the chickens stayed in the shade until evening. They looked their very worst in midsummer as they lost feathers and developed bald patches as they moulted.

"They look like roadkill," Joe observed more than once.

"Poor things!"

"They look about ready for the pot," said Joe.

"Sssh! They'll hear you."

We had never eaten our own chickens but we delighted in eating their eggs. No matter how hot the summer became, they always presented us with eggs, which I thought was very generous of them, considering the heat. I'm sure I wouldn't have bothered. The eggs were always rich with gloriously orange yolks. That is until one particular day.

It was a Sunday and I was boiling eggs for breakfast. I hummed to myself as I cut the buttered toast into soldiers and popped the eggs into the eggcups.

"Lovely!" said Joe as he sliced the top off his egg, but his expression soon changed.

"What's the matter?" I asked.

"This egg. It's got no yolk!"

"Don't be ridiculous," I said, "all eggs have yolks."

"Well, I assure you, this one hasn't."

He was right, of course. His egg had no yolk. It was the first of many and, believe me, a breakfast egg with no yolk is no joke.

I looked it up on the Internet and apparently it can happen sometimes. It occurs when something or other inside the hen becomes detached and is most commonly found with elderly chickens. We guessed Regalo was the culprit as she was the most advanced in years, but we never found out for sure.

Naturally, my Facebook friends were full of suggestions. "Make meringues, or an egg white omelette," they said.

But there was something very unappetising about those yolkless eggs and I couldn't bring

BIRTHDAYS

myself to use them. We learned to recognise which were yolkless because the shell was slightly rough and contoured. Whenever Joe or I came across them, we'd set them aside and put them in a carrier bag to dispose of later.

By July, I was getting really excited. In just a few short weeks our granddaughter would be born and I would be jetting across the world to meet her. Joe and I had discussed it at length and reluctantly decided I should go alone. I was desperate to be there to meet and help with the new baby, but we had commitments in Spain, animals to care for and flights to Australia are hugely expensive. Joe would have to be patient.

As our granddaughter prepared to make her entrance into the world, Joe was approaching his own birthday.

When one reaches our age, birthdays cease to be magical and are more of an unwelcome reminder that the years are ticking by. There was no way that Joe could have had a better birthday than the one he had in 2010. That year his birthday coincided with the final of the World Cup, which Spain won. An unforgettable day for the Spanish and for us.

"What do you want to do for your birthday this year?" I asked him.

"Nothing really, it's just another day. Unless you want to ply me with drinks and entertain me with the Dance of the Seven Veils. That would be good, I'd like that."

"Not a chance."

"Well, let's just have a day at the beach and then go for a nice meal afterwards."

"You don't want to do anything different?"

"Nope. No surprises please, I don't want any fuss."

We always go to the same part of the beach and hire sunbeds and a parasol for the day. The sunbeds have thick, comfortable mattresses and the parasols are big Balinese type ones thatched with straw or something similar. What could be better than lying stretched out on a comfy sunbed with a good book in your hand, listening to the waves lap and dozing occasionally?

The Spanish are very sensible about exposure to the sun. They flock to the beach in the morning, but at around one o'clock, when the sun is at its highest, they shake out their towels, pack up and leave. The beach almost empties, until five o'clock when they all return after a siesta.

Very few tourists or expats used the part of the beach that we favoured. At one o'clock the mass exodus began and we soon had the beach to ourselves. Well, almost all to ourselves because we shared it with a couple of ladies a short distance away. A glance told me that they were foreigners like ourselves, perhaps English or German.

I dozed off and awoke to see the pair coming back up the beach after a swim in the sea. Sadly, I noticed that one of the ladies was badly deformed with large misshapen lumps all over her torso hidden by her blue swimming costume. *That's odd, I thought. Poor thing, I'm surprised I didn't notice it before.* I turned away and read my book again.

Some time later I was too hot to read any more.

"Fancy a swim?" I asked Joe, but he was fast asleep.

I walked down to the water's edge just as the two ladies were also returning for another dip. To my astonishment, both ladies looked totally normal and there was no sign of the ugly lumps I'd noticed earlier. As they approached, I heard that they were English.

Once in the water, we struck up a conversation. The ladies were on holiday, staying at a friend's apartment and were full of praise for the area. The sea was gentle that day and very clear. As we chatted, the lady in the blue costume suddenly dipped below the water. The other lady explained.

"Don't mind my friend Lizzie," she said. "She loves Spain so much that whenever she sees a bit of rubbish in the sea, she picks it up."

"I just feel I want to give something back, you know, help keep it all clean," said Lizzie, bobbing up.

She held aloft an old plastic bottle and a dented can. Tucking the offending items into her swimsuit, she sank below again to retrieve more passing trash.

"Ah, that explains the lumps in your swimsuit," I said, when she resurfaced. I was full of admiration. "What a great idea! If everybody did that every time they went for a swim, the seas would be so much cleaner!"

I resolved to copy her example and started right away. Unfortunately, it wasn't difficult to find rubbish and my own swimsuit was soon equally stuffed.

"Where are you going? And what on earth have you got in your swimsuit?" asked Joe as I sauntered past him, my swimsuit bulging more than usual and my hands full of more plastic bits and pieces.

I explained, waving the rubbish at him.

"I'm just off to the bin to dump this lot."

"Do you want any help getting it all out of your swimsuit?" he asked hopefully.

"Thank you, no. I can manage."

After a very relaxing day on the beach, we enjoyed a good meal at our favourite restaurant and Joe indulged himself by ordering a steak.

At that time of year the days are long and it was still light as we drove home up the mountain. The lush green of spring had long gone, burnt brown by the relentless sun. As the sun dipped, the shadows deepened and stretched, making rocks and caves look even more mysterious than usual. I reminded myself that although we had driven that road countless times, it never looked the same twice.

BIRTHDAYS

"I've had a lovely birthday," Joe said. "I've really enjoyed it."

"And it's about to get even better!"

"Is it? Why?" Joe stole a suspicious glance at me, before concentrating again on the winding road ahead.

"Wait and see. When we get to the next bend in the road, the one nearly at the top of the mountain, I want you to stop the car."

"Do you want to look at the view?"

"Yes, but something else as well. A surprise."

"You know I don't like surprises."

"You'll enjoy this one."

There was a handy lay-by at the side of the road with enough room to park the car and enjoy the magnificent view. The sky was streaked orange and peach. In front stretched the Mediterranean sea, blue and dotted with tiny boats. Below us the cliff dropped, great rocky crags jutting out at crazy angles and burnt orange by the evening light.

"So why have we stopped? What's the surprise?"

I opened the back of the car and carefully lifted out a heavy carrier bag. By now Joe's curiosity had been aroused.

"What are you doing?" he asked. "What's in the bag?"

"Get out of the car and I'll show you."

He got out and I opened the bag to reveal the contents.

"Eggs," I said. "All those horrible yolkless eggs. Let's throw them at the rocks below."

I believe there is a secret vandal in all of us. Is there anybody who wouldn't enjoy throwing eggs at rocks? Joe and I stood on the edge of the drop and looked down. A large rock far below jutted out perfectly and we chose that for our target. One by one we threw the eggs, watching them explode as they hit the rock. Very satisfying.

Swimming, sunbathing, a nice meal and finally hurling eggs over a cliff and watching them smash on the rocks beneath. Joe agreed it was the perfect birthday.

※※※

With Joe's birthday over, another birthday was absorbing all my thoughts. A brand new little person in Australia was about to make her long-awaited entrance into the world.

As the due date arrived, Karly had a few problems. She'd developed gestational diabetes, which needed to be monitored, although that didn't bother her as much as restless legs, which drove her crazy.

"If I don't go into labour this weekend by myself, I'll be taken in on Monday to be induced," she told me. "So it looks as though you're going to be a grandmother by Monday at the latest! Cam's parents are flying down from Sydney on Monday so that's good timing. And Nana and Pa (great grandparents) will be here on Tuesday. She'll have quite a reception committee."

We all know that things never go to plan when babies are involved. The weekend passed uneventfully and mother- and father-to-be set off for the hospital.

"Goodbye, house," said Karly. "When I come back I'll be a mother! Goodbye street, goodbye car, goodbye..."

Cam just rolled his eyes.

In spite of being induced, the baby wasn't ready to appear. Nothing happened.

"Not to worry," said the cheery nurse, "come back tomorrow. Things will be moving by then."

On Tuesday, they returned. After a full day waiting, still nothing was happening.

"Well, you might as well go home tonight," said the cheery nurse. "Baby isn't ready yet. Come back tomorrow."

On Wednesday, they went to the park and played in the children's playground. Not even the slide or the roundabout started things moving. The nursery was ready. The crib was ready. The pram was ready. All the little clothes were ready. Karly and Cam were more than ready. But the star of the show wasn't ready.

STEAK WITH PAPRIKA AND HERBS

This steak is a real treat and the herb and paprika coating gives an amazing flavour that complements the steak beautifully. Serves two, and ready in under twenty minutes.

Ingredients

- 2 lean fillet, sirloin, rib-eye or rump steaks about 2 ½ - 3cm thick
- 5-6 sprigs thyme, leaves picked
- 2-3 sprigs rosemary, leaves picked
- 1tbsp fresh basil leaves
- 1tbsp fresh parsley
- 1tsp smoked paprika
- Salt and freshly milled black pepper

Method

- Preheat the grill to Medium.
- Finely chop all the herbs.
- Place the herbs and paprika on a plate and mix well.
- Season the steaks with salt and pepper and then coat with the herb and paprika mix on both sides.
- Cook under the grill according to your preference:

  Rare – 2½ minutes each side

  Medium – 4 minutes each side

  Well Done – 6 minutes each side.

- Serve with a simple salad or chunky chips.

18
LETTERS

The rest of that day dragged by. Joe and I went to bed. The next morning, the 8th August, 2012, the telephone rang.

"Karly? Is that you?" My hand shook as I held the receiver.

A tired little voice filled with awe answered quietly, almost whispering.

"She's here. And she's perfect."

I shrieked and danced around the kitchen.

"Have you and Cam decided on a name yet?"

"Yes. Indy Grace."

"Oh, that's lovely! The name Indy wasn't even on your shortlist, was it?"

"No, but it just seems to fit her perfectly."

Thanks to the wonders of technology, we saw little Indy Grace immediately. The baby was less than an hour old but the good news and photos of

LETTERS

her flashed around the world before mother and baby were even out of the delivery room. My Facebook page was red-hot with congratulations from every continent. I was so happy, I could have burst.

How was I going to be able to wait another four weeks before flying to Australia and meeting Indy? That first day, I couldn't settle to anything and my heart ached to see her.

And so I did the only thing I could think of doing. I wrote a letter to my granddaughter.

Hello Indy Grace,

We haven't met yet, but I'm your grandmother. Welcome to the world, little one. The world is a big place and you and your Mum and Dad live in Australia, on the other side of the world. We live in Spain, but that isn't going to stop us coming to see you as often as we can.

We've been waiting for you to arrive for so long! Yesterday, your Mum went into hospital so that they could hurry you along. But you weren't ready. So your Mum went on a children's slide and a space-hopper thingy and tried all sorts of things to encourage you to come out. But you still weren't ready. Your name, Indy, suits you already.

But now you're here and of course you are the most gorgeous, intelligent, perfect baby ever born - 6 pounds, 12 oz of beautiful baby.

You couldn't have been born to a better Mum and

Dad, or in a nicer place. Your life is going to be filled with love and laughter.

And you are lucky! When you were in your Mummy's tummy, your Daddy called you Wolfgang, then Grug, then Gruglington. Thank goodness they finally settled on Indy.

The world you were born into is a wonderful place and I hope it stays that way for you. I've seen so many changes and technological marvels in my life and I can only guess at the advances you'll see. Perhaps you'll have a holiday home on Mars, or a robot to do all your housework? Perhaps you'll live until you're 150? Who knows!

Have you any idea of how many people wish you well? Not just me and Grumps. Not just family, but hundreds (yes, hundreds!) of lovely people have posted on Facebook, Twitter and have emailed me, all congratulating you on your arrival. (You'll learn about Facebook and stuff later – there's plenty of time for that!)

You'll love Grumps, by the way. He grumbles and scratches himself quite a lot, but he's a big softie. You'll be able to twist him round your tiny finger.

So, little one, you're here at last. In one month, I'll be holding you and I can't wait!

Until then, I shall blow you kisses from Spain. When they arrive, they'll turn into little fairies that flutter around your cradle, watching over you.

Be well, little Indy and I'll see you soon.

Your loving grandmother, xxxx

LETTERS

Time crept at snail's pace. I didn't want to wish the summer away but my heart was in Australia. Life in the village was never fast but now each day stretched more than the last.

Days were long and hot and evenings were quieter than before. No longer was the night air punctuated by the Ufartes' flamboyant flamenco music and dancing in the street. The house next door was occupied but we rarely glimpsed Lola and her new partner and we never chatted with them.

There was something different about Lola's manner, which puzzled me. She had always been loud, super-confident, almost arrogant. Her dress-sense had been designed to catch the eye and the sway of her hips was deliberate.

But the Lola who lived next door now had changed dramatically. Gone were the bangles and strappy sandals. Gone were the skimpy, revealing clothes, replaced by creased shirts and dirty jeans. No longer did she toss her hair in defiance. Instead of holding her head high, she stared at the ground when we approached.

"Have you noticed a change in Lola Ufarte?" I asked Joe.

"No, why?"

"Oh, you never notice anything. Remember, she always used to wear really short skirts and jangly bangles?"

"Yes, I suppose she did."

"Don't you think she's much quieter, almost subdued?"

"Perhaps she's sorry for breaking up that family."

Maybe Joe was right, but when I saw her with lank hair and a slouch in her step, I felt there was more to it.

Whatever the change, Lola and her partner didn't seem short of friends. A steady trickle of people, all strangers to us, arrived in the village at all hours of the day and knocked on their door. Sometimes they stayed for just ten minutes, at other times all day. Sometimes they knocked on our door by mistake, often very late at night and we'd have to redirect them.

༅༅༅

The village was at its fullest, apart from fiesta time, as the villagers escaped from the heat of the cities and reoccupied their cooler cottages in the mountains. Paco and Carmen's house was always filled with friends, relations and barking dogs. Glorious cooking smells wafted down the street and the buzz of conversation could be heard through our walls.

However, there was one house that remained empty. On the other side of the valley, almost hidden by Spanish oaks, was a house owned by Brits. They rarely used it and most of the time the house stood locked and unused. During the summer, some of the youths from the village used the garden to hang out, away from the watchful eyes of their parents. They did no harm, just sitting around the empty pool.

In the last week of August, Geronimo passed our house and stopped to bang on our door.

"Hello, Geronimo," said Joe. "How's things?"

"Bad," said Geronimo, shaking his head.

Joe wasn't concerned. This was Geronimo's stock reply.

"What's the problem?" asked Joe.

"Somebody tried to break into the English house," said Geronimo. "I was walking past it this morning and I saw broken glass. I thought you would want to know."

"Do you think it was the village kids?"

"No," said Geronimo, vehemently shaking his head and causing his long hair to fly. "The kids here wouldn't do that."

And with that, he turned on his heel and walked away up the street, thus passing the responsibility on to us.

"Well, I suppose we'd better go over there and take a look for ourselves," I said.

We walked up the little track that approached the house. Wild fig trees were laden with summer fruit. Summer-baked acorns crunched under our heels as we walked round the property.

The attempted break-in was obvious. The thieves had tried to dig out the burglar-bars but failed, apart from one corner of the living room bars, which they'd managed to pry loose. The sliding shutters beyond had been forced open and the window-glass shattered. Glass and bits of rubble littered the ground. Despite the damage, we doubted if anyone had succeeded in getting in because the resulting gap was so small. Only a monkey or a contortionist could have gained entry.

"Can you see in?" I asked Joe.

"Not a chance. It's pitch dark in there and the gap's so small. I don't believe they managed to get in."

I'd brought my camera and had an idea.

"What about if I take some photos? We can't see in but the flash will go off. The photo should show if anything's been taken."

I carefully stretched my arms through the broken window and snapped a few photos, pointing the camera this way and that, relying on the flash to capture any evidence.

We scrolled through the pictures with interest. All looked fine to us. I could see an end table and a sideboard and everything looked tidy and undisturbed.

"I'm sure they didn't manage to get in," I said.

We'd met the English owners of the house and I had their email address. I emailed them the bad news.

LETTERS

Hi,
I hope you and the family are all well.
Sorry to be the bearer of bad news, but one of the villagers alerted us to the fact that somebody has tried to break into your house. They've tried to get in through your front door, but didn't succeed. They have also bent the window bars and broken the pull-down shutter and smashed the glass of the living-room window.
The gap is very small between the bent bars and the wall (see pic below) so I don't think anybody managed to actually get in, though they've left a bit of a mess with the broken glass. I stuck my camera in and took some photos. I think you'll agree that everything looks okay. (see pic below) (The photos I sent can be viewed in free Photo Book 4)

Back came the reply.

Hi Vicky,
They DID get in! There was a flat-screen TV on that low table and a computer on the sideboard. Could you please report it to the police? And find some workmen to fix everything?

"Oh no," Joe grumbled, giving his nethers a mighty scratch. "That's all we need. How are we going to find workmen in August? The whole of Spain closes down in August."

"Well, we'll have to report it to the police and

take it from there, I suppose. I'll transfer the photos onto the iPad so we've got something to show them."

So Joe and I drove down the mountain and went to the *Guardia Civil* offices in the city, armed with the photos.

They examined the pictures and consulted each other.

"Are you the owner of the house?" asked an officer.

"No, it belongs to an English family. It's a holiday house."

"Do you have their details?"

"Yes," I said, passing them the paper I'd brought with the owners' names, address, telephone number and email address.

"I'm afraid we can't do anything without a fax number," they said. "We need to fax the documents to the owner."

"But we have the email address."

"No," they insisted, "we must have a fax number."

"A fax number? Who has a fax machine nowadays?" said Joe as we drove home after our failed journey. "Why couldn't they just scan and email the documents?"

I emailed the owners and wasn't surprised when they admitted to not owning a fax machine, but they rushed out and bought a 'splitter' or something.

Meanwhile, I contacted Julio, our builder, who

spoke very good English. He kindly came to look at the job although he was supposed to be on holiday, as it was August. However, he couldn't do anything, as it was August. And no glazier was open, as it was August.

I returned to the *Guardia Civil* offices and was dealt with by a different set of officers. I explained the whole thing again and triumphantly produced the owners' fax number.

"Fax number?" they said. "We don't need that."

"But your colleagues said you needed a fax number!"

"We can make some investigations, but I doubt if we will ever find out who did this crime. If you would like us to start investigations, you must leave your passport with us."

"*My* passport?"

"Yes, your passport."

"But I need my passport! I can give you other identification."

"No, we can't do anything without your passport."

It was at that point that I gave up. I was due to fly to Australia in a few days and I was NOT willing to surrender my passport.

We passed Julio's telephone number and email address to the home owners, and, as far as I know, when September arrived, Julio returned and fixed everything. I imagine the *Guardia Civil* did nothing but I may be doing them an injustice.

Suddenly, I was packing my suitcase with warmer clothes and little gifts for Indy.

"Are you sure you are going to be okay?" I asked Joe yet again.

"Of course I will. Stop worrying. I'm perfectly capable of looking after myself. Just go and enjoy yourself. I'll email you every day."

Departure day arrived and I packed my precious computer and last minute stuff. I wasn't looking forward to the 24-hour journey across the planet, but it was going to be worth it.

FIG JAM

Just four ingredients in this delicious jam and one of them is water! (Recipe kindly donated by reader, Judith Benson.)

Ingredients

- 1 kilo (2.2lb) figs
- 1 kilo (2.2lb) sugar
- 125ml (4½fl oz) water
- 45 ml (1½fl oz) lemon juice

Method

- Clean and cut the figs up quite small or chuck in a food processor.
- Dissolve the sugar in the water.
- Add the juice of the lemon and boil for 10 mins.
- Add the figs and cook for about an hour.
- When set, transfer to jam jars.

19

BEARS, SPIDERS AND PENGUINS

I love Australia. I love the vivid light, the vast open spaces, the crazy plants and animals. I love the informality of the Australians, the way they dress in shorts and go shopping barefoot. I love their openness and friendliness.

And now I had another reason to love Australia: my daughter was there, married to a lovely Aussie man and they had a baby.

The plane touched down in Melbourne very early in the morning. As I made my way outside to look for my daughter and son-in-law, I shivered. They say Melbourne can experience four seasons in one day and that early September day was definitely winter, especially after the sunshine of Spain.

Then, all thoughts of climate vanished as I saw them. A flurry of hugs and kisses, all of us talking at once and the first sight of my granddaughter. Four weeks old, oblivious, rosy with sleep, warm and smelling faintly of milk and baby powder. Had my own children ever been so small? Of course they had, but how quickly we forget.

The timing was perfect. Cam had finished his paternity leave and was going back to work. I felt I could be useful helping with Indy and giving her mother a break to catch up on some sleep or have her hair done. Indy was a good baby and Karly was a natural, relaxed mum. Each day melted into the next, filled with laughter, nappies and mountains of washing.

Looking after a newborn meant we didn't go on many outings, but Australia still provided plenty of wildlife to entertain me. The garden was home to a pair of possums who peered at me from the fence as I hung tiny baby items on the washing line. I pushed raw carrots into the fence to lure them so that I could watch them feed.

"Watch out for drop bears," Karly warned. "Don't walk under the trees."

"Drop bears? What are drop bears?"

I knew all about koalas but hadn't heard of drop bears. I'm a huge fan of David Attenborough and nature documentaries and I know quite a lot about bears. I know about polar bears, black bears, grizzlies, sloth bears, sun bears, giant pandas and even spectacled bears. But I'd never heard of a drop bear.

"They're very dangerous, look out. They're

related to koalas but they're carnivorous. They sit in the trees looking down, waiting to drop on prey passing underneath."

"You're joking!"

"No, honestly! I never knew about them before I moved to Oz, either."

I was dubious. I knew my daughter too well. She and Cam had warned me about Cam's parents' two fierce dogs. They said they were a matching pair of Mexican fighting dogs and that I should be extremely wary of them. The Mexican fighting dogs turned out to be a couple of very timid elderly Chihuahuas.

"You have to be really careful when you walk in woods round here because of the drop bears," Karly repeated, "but you can take precautions."

"Like what?"

"Well, apparently, if you carry a handkerchief soaked in your own pee, that puts them off."

I stared at her.

"Or if you smear Vegemite on your neck," she added.

We were both laughing now.

"And if you hold a fork behind your ear, that's good. Drop bears really don't like that. And if you talk with an Australian accent, you're safer than if you talk with a Pommie accent. Stop laughing! I was told all that stuff when I moved over here and I believed it!"

"Honestly? You believed it?"

"Yes!"

"Well, I don't!"

Later, still chuckling, I looked up 'drop bears' on Wikipedia:

> *A dropbear or drop bear is a fictitious Australian marsupial. Drop bears are commonly said to be unusually large, vicious, carnivorous marsupials related to koalas (although the koala is not a bear) that inhabit treetops and attack their prey by dropping onto their heads from above. They are an example of local lore intended to frighten and confuse outsiders and amuse locals, similar to the jackalope, hoop snake, wild haggis or snipe hunt.*

༓༓༓

Unfortunately, the creatures of Australia don't necessarily stay outdoors. One evening, little Indy decided to become Monster Baby instead of being her usual Angel Baby. Cam was already asleep as he had to be up for work early next morning. Karly and I took it in turns to wheel the pram up and down the living room and finally Indy settled and went off to sleep. Very carefully, Karly picked her up and took her upstairs to her cot.

The next thing I heard was a stage whisper from the top of the stairs.

"Mum! I can't come down!"

"Why ever not?"

"Look!"

I looked at the wall where she was pointing,

halfway up the stairs. There, stock still, sat a huge black spider.

Australia is well known for its variety of scary spiders, from the massive huntsman to the vicious red-back. There are mouse spiders, funnel webs, trapdoor and wolf spiders. Most of them deliver a nasty, painful bite that can make one very ill and treatment should be sought immediately. I didn't know what variety this enormous spider on our wall was, but Karly did.

"It's a white-tail!" Karly hissed. "If it bites you, it's really painful and it'll make you sick and swell up. And if you are allergic to it, you get a reaction like gangrene and it eats your flesh away."

I stared with horror at her and then at the spider high on the wall.

"You're not joking, are you?" I asked hopefully. "Like the drop bear?"

"No! I'm serious! What if it gets into Indy's room?"

I'm a real coward when it comes to spiders. I respect them and am fascinated by their skills and ingenuity, but they still terrify me. Even English and Spanish spiders that are relatively small and harmless, fill me with terror. It's an unreasonable fear which, unfortunately, Karly and my son, Shealan, inherited from me.

I recalled Joe's spider bite. It was swollen and itchy, but a walk in the park compared with a bite from one of these Aussie beasts. The knowledge that I'm allergic to bee and wasp stings and react badly even to humble mosquito bites, didn't fill me with any more confidence.

"What do we do?"

We stared at each other, white-faced and shuddering.

"I can't get close enough to kill it."

"Neither can I."

The spider appeared to be listening and twitched.

"What if it starts running? What if it hides and we can't find it?"

"Okay," I said sounding much braver than I felt. "I'm going to get the Dyson. I'll vacuum it up. Keep watching it in case it moves."

At the top of the stairs, Karly gripped the banisters, eyes locked on the spider on the wall.

I pulled the Dyson out of the cupboard, giving myself a severe talking to as I did so.

Come on, pull yourself together. It's just a spider. You can do this.

I attached the nozzle and pulled out the extension tube as far as it could possibly reach.

"Mum! Quick, it's moving!"

I refused to look. A stationary spider is frightening enough, but a scuttling one is much worse.

I pulled out the cable and plugged it into the wall. The cleaner hummed into life.

Hurry up! You can do this! Just suck it up!

The spider was still again and I swear it was staring at me.

What if it jumps at me?

For a full thirty seconds I stood there, poised, extension tube in hand, unable to do the deed.

Do it!

So, I did. I inched forward and stretched up until the nozzle was beside the spider. It began to scuttle away sideways but the vacuum was too strong. The spider clung to the wall for a second then shot up the tube with a soft thud.

I dropped the tube with a clatter and left the machine running, just to make sure. I didn't want to risk the spider climbing back down the tube and out. I should have felt proud of myself, but I didn't because I hate killing anything. That poor spider didn't know he had entered forbidden territory.

Luckily, neither Indy nor Cam woke up and the crisis was averted. However, for the remainder of my stay, I couldn't help checking out the walls and dark corners for any more lurking arachnids.

Our days were kept busy with baby care, but there was still time for other stuff. Cam and Karly took me to the local park at dusk to watch the possums. Well-accustomed to humans, these possums were tame enough to accept pieces of carrot from one's hand. Wherever you looked, possums ran up and down the trees and allowed themselves to be photographed from just feet away.

As I crouched down to snap a mother sitting on the grass with a baby peeping from her pouch,

BEARS, SPIDERS AND PENGUINS

I didn't see another possum approach, probably hoping I had something edible in my hand. Just as I took the photo, he popped up in front of me, providing me with the most audacious photobomb I have ever seen.

(For those like me who have never heard that word before, 'photobomb' means to spoil a photograph by unexpectedly appearing in the camera's field of view just as the picture is taken.) This cheeky possum did it perfectly, very close up and the resulting photo had us laughing hysterically. (Page 13 of Photo Book 4)

Another evening, we went to the St Kilda area of Melbourne in search of fairy penguins.

These are the smallest penguins in the world, the adult being just 30 cm (12 inches) tall. There is a colony of fairy penguins that nests in the rocks at the end of a long walkway and every evening they return from the sea. Crowds gather nightly to watch the spectacle and there are volunteers who are happy to tell you fairy penguin facts. Flash photography is absolutely forbidden as these penguins have no eyelids and the bright flash can cause epileptic fits.

We parked the car and pushed the pram along the beach just as the sun was dipping into the ocean. We joined the waiting throng, all scanning the sea for a sign of the returning colony. There was an air of anticipation and excitement. They'd arrive soon, we were told and clamber onto the rocks of the breakwater below us.

Twenty minutes later, the sun had all but disappeared leaving just a light patch on the distant horizon. As yet, there was no sign of the fairy penguins.

Unfortunately, six-week-old babies don't give a fig for fairy penguins. Indy stirred, grunted, woke up and yelled, demanding to be fed. No amount of jiggling the pram would pacify her, she was hungry and determined to tell all the waiting penguin watchers about it. Reluctantly, we turned away and hurried back down the walkway.

We never saw the fairy penguin colony swim home or clamber up the rocks, although I did catch a glimpse of one or two hiding amongst the boulders. It was unlikely I'd ever get the chance again because Cam and Karly were planning to leave Melbourne and move back to Sydney in a few months. Their property in Sydney was currently being rented out.

One day, Karly and I discussed the move.

"We can't wait to get back to Sydney and live in our own house again," she said. "And it'll be nice to have Cam's parents nearby. Cam's really looking forward to working for the Sydney company again too and we're hoping the hours won't be so long so he can spend more time with Indy."

"Will you move back into your own house or rent another?"

I knew that their house was lovely and in a

fashionable part of Sydney, but I also knew it wasn't a house designed for a growing family.

"No, we're going to tidy it up and then sell it. It's a beautiful house but it's more for young professionals. It's not really a family house. We're going to need a proper garden and we'd like to live closer to Cam's parents."

It's astonishing how fast a baby grows. I was there when Indy started to focus properly, eyes following her mother and father as they moved around the room. I was there to see her first smile.

But, all too soon, my weeks in Australia drew to a close and I had to leave the little family. Bittersweet, as I missed Joe and our home in Spain, but I didn't want to miss any of Indy's growing up either.

Then I was kissing them all goodbye and boarding the plane back to Spain, wondering what had been going on in the village while I'd been away.

ROASTED TOMATO SOUP WITH PAPRIKA

This soup will certainly warm you up through the generous use of hot smoked paprika, black pepper and plenty of garlic!

Preparation: 15 minutes

Cooking: 1 hour

Serves 6 – 8

Ingredients

- 1 small white onion, diced
- 6 garlic cloves, crushed
- 6 beef tomatoes, roasted
- 2 large red bell peppers, roasted
- 1 tsp hot smoked paprika
- 1 pint chicken stock
- Salt & cracked black pepper to season

Method:

- Roast the beef tomatoes, onion and red peppers until soft and the skins blackened.

- Remove from the grill/oven and wrap in newspaper for 30 minutes – this makes removing the skins easier.

- Heat a drizzle of olive oil in a terracotta casserole or pan and gently fry the garlic.

- Add the tomatoes, onion, peppers and smoked paprika. Mix together and cook for 15 minutes over a low heat.

- Add chicken stock, season with salt and pepper, then gradually bring to the boil before turning down immediately and leaving to simmer for 20 – 25 minutes.

- Strain the soup for a smooth consistency, but for the Andalucian version use a hand blender to puree any larger pieces of tomato and pepper while still keeping the consistency rustic and chunky.

- Serve with fresh crusty bread and decorate with a swirl of cream.

20

SENIOR MOMENTS

"So you had a good time and Indy's gorgeous."

"Of course she is, she's absolutely scrummy and she's such a good baby."

I paused for breath. I think I'd been talking nonstop since I arrived back in Spain. I described how we coaxed smiles out of Indy, what Melbourne was like, what the Australian weather was like, the animals I saw and all sorts of other unimportant stuff. We'd tried chatting on Facebook, but the difference in time always made it difficult. We'd agreed it would be easier to catch up with everything when I returned.

"I'm glad it all went well and it's good to have you back," Joe said.

"Karly and Cam are coming over to the UK and Spain next summer, isn't that fantastic news?

They want to show Indy off to all the British friends and relations."

"That is really good to hear! It's such a long trip to and from Australia, watching Indy growing up from afar is going to be difficult," said Joe.

He didn't need to tell me that. There was already a dark struggle going on inside me. I felt ripped in half. Half of me wanted to stay in my beloved Spain, while the other half of me yearned to pack up everything and move to Australia.

But it wasn't as easy as that. At our age, to move to Australia would mean applying for a horrendously expensive visa. We would need to pay approximately 50,000AUD (£28,000 or $47,000) *each* to be allowed to stay in Australia permanently. I couldn't see how that could ever be possible.

"Anyway, what's been happening in the village while I've been away?" I asked, shaking off my thoughts. "Any gossip?"

"Well, the chickens are fine, laying eggs when they feel like it. Sylvia, Felicity and Snitch are in the garden most of the time. Lola Ufarte and her partner are still next door. I think they are doing some house renovations because they keep drilling into their walls."

"And Paco and Carmen?"

"Yes, they've been up every weekend as usual. It's been grape-pressing time of course. Paco was telling me he no longer does it up in his *cortijo*. He's joined forces with Alejandro Senior and they've built a huge barn down in the valley. He took me to see it and it's got a huge mechanised wine press and modern galvanised barrels storing all the wine. It's all very industrial. There's also a fireplace, a massive one, a kitchen area and a huge table in the centre."

"Paco couldn't afford a place like that!"

"No, but Alejandro Senior can."

"Have you seen Judith and Mother at all?"

"No, but that reminds me. I saw Pancho the mayor last week and he said he'd be in touch about those English lessons you promised him."

"Oh no! What did you say?"

"Don't worry, I told him you were away in Australia."

"Whew!"

It didn't take long to settle back into village life. It was autumn and the leaves of the Spanish oak began to crisp and turn rust-brown as the days grew shorter. And soon it was fiesta time again. It seemed like only yesterday when the Reverend James Andrew Montgomery and his awful wife, Mavis, had been our guests.

The arrival of the villagers, with their friends and relatives, marked the beginning of the weekend's festivities. Over the weekend, the procession carrying the village saint passed our front door as usual. Paco was invariably one of the bearers, but I didn't see him. In fact I hadn't seen him at all for the whole weekend. Neither had I seen Carmen or Little Paco. (Not so 'little' now, Little Paco was seventeen and taller than both his parents.) Instead of Bianca and Yukky barking and shouts and laughter coming from next door, the house was silent and the front door was locked. It was most unusual.

We had seen Judith keeping an eye on Mother, who was dancing in the square with Alejandro Senior. Marcia sat on a kitchen chair in her shop doorway, knitting something shapeless, hairpins slipping from her hair. Uncle Felix appeared and sat on the bench next to the shop entrance. I hadn't seen any of the Ufartes but then I didn't expect to.

On the Sunday night Geronimo let off a final explosion of fireworks and, following the usual mass exodus, the village fell silent once more. It wasn't until a fortnight later that we discovered why Paco and his family hadn't appeared at the village fiesta and it wasn't a happy story.

We'd been making curry and discovered that we'd forgotten to buy sultanas, an ingredient we loved to include. It wasn't disastrous, just irritating. The nearest shops were at the bottom of the mountain, quite a long drive and just not worth the effort for sultanas.

But then we realised we had no plastic bin bags for the rubbish bin. To cap it all, the fire alarm started beeping intermittently, informing us that the battery needed replacing.

"I might just as well go down the mountain

and get some sultanas, a battery and some bin bags," Joe said, grabbing the car keys. "Being a Friday I bet the supermarket will be packed. I'll probably be a couple of hours."

He returned with a glum face, scratching himself irritably.

"What's the matter? I asked, as he dumped the shopping on the table. "Problems at the shop?"

"No, worse. Much worse. I was reversing the car into our garage and I was so busy making sure I had enough space on my side, I didn't check the other. I scraped the car and ripped the wing mirror off."

"Oh."

I was sympathetic because I knew the garage doorway was extremely narrow, but I was also annoyed because he never bothered to fold the mirrors in. It wasn't the first time he damaged them while reversing into the garage, although this time it sounded more serious.

"But that's not all. While I was trying to fix the wing mirror I put the keys down on the bonnet of the car. I couldn't do anything about the mirror so I left it, picked up the shopping and closed the garage door. Just as I snapped the padlock together, I realised I'd made a big, big mistake."

"What?"

"I'd locked the keys in the garage."

"Oh no! Haven't we got a spare key for that padlock?"

"I hope so."

We searched high and low for a duplicate key. We looked in all the obvious places like the key rack and then the not-so-obvious places like the kitchen junk drawer where miscellaneous objects go to die. I looked in old handbags, coat pockets and in the tool shed. No key.

"We'll have to use bolt cutters to cut through the padlock," I said. "Where are the bolt cutters?"

"In the garage."

"Oh."

"And we can't go and buy some more bolt cutters because we can't get to the car."

So we did what we always do in times of crisis. We went next door to ask for Paco's help.

Yukky greeted us as usual with much frantic tail-wagging, pushing his wet nose into our hands. Carmen was there too. She kissed us, but seemed quieter than usual.

"No problem!" said Paco, when we had explained our difficulties. "I have bolt cutters."

It was then that I noticed Bianca lying on a blanket in the corner, her sad eyes watching us. Was that a huge bandage wrapped around her?

"What's happened to Bianca?" I asked.

Paco shook his head.

"A terrible accident," said Carmen, leaning down to fondle Bianca's soft ears. "Our eldest son, Diego, was visiting us at our house in the city. When he left, he reversed his car out and he didn't see Bianca. He felt a bump and heard her cry."

"He had driven over Bianca!" shouted Paco,

smacking his own forehead with the palm of his hand.

"We thought she was dead," said Carmen, shaking her head. "We took her to the vet and he cut off her front leg."

We stared at poor Bianca in horror. I knelt down and stroked her head. I remembered Little Paco's tenth birthday and his disappointment at not getting a puppy of his own. I remembered Paco and Carmen scolding him, saying that there was absolutely *no* chance and that they didn't need another dog. And I remembered the following weekend when Little Paco, with adoration in his eyes, showed us the tiny puppy cupped in his hands. Bianca had thrived and was loved by all.

"Oh, poor Bianca!"

"Pah!" said Paco. "I said we should tell the vet to put her to sleep. Whoever heard of a dog with three legs?"

"Do not listen to him," said Carmen. "He is as upset as the rest of the family. It was Paco who decided we should not go to the fiesta this year. He said she needed peace and quiet to recover. It is the first El Hoyo fiesta we have missed in our lives."

"Come," said Paco, already halfway out of the door. "We will get the bolt cutters and break into your garage."

Paco's bolt cutters sliced through the garage padlock as if it were made of butter, making us wonder why we bothered to padlock it at all. Joe retrieved the keys and stopped scratching himself. We finished cooking the curry and we enjoyed it that night.

"Most expensive curry we've ever had," said Joe with his mouth full, "if you add the cost of a new wing mirror. But this is delicious!"

Bianca made a full recovery and learned how to limp, then walk, then sprint, on three legs. Always a happy dog, she was as cheerful as ever and was soon racing up and down the streets with the other village dogs. It was hard to believe she had only three legs.

Joe's lapse of memory resulting in the keys being locked in the garage was not unusual. To be fair, my own short-term memory seemed not as sharp as it used to be either. But I think Joe's lapses were worse.

Even before we moved to El Hoyo in 2004, Joe had been forgetful. I remember how, one day, we searched high and low for his mobile phone, which he couldn't remember having mislaid. We finally resorted to dialing its number and listening for the ring tone.

"I think I can hear it," I said. "It's very faint but I think it's in the bedroom."

We found the phone in the top drawer of the chest, nestled amongst Joe's socks. We never worked out why it should be there, particularly as Joe almost never wore socks.

On another occasion, we were shopping at the

mall in the city. We parked the car and left it, then spent between two and three hours shopping. Eventually we returned, laden with bags and our shopping trolleys. It was, by now, siesta time and the car park was almost empty, apart from our car.

As we approached our car I thought it strange that I could hear an engine running, with no cars parked nearby. Of course, it was our car. Joe had left the engine switched on for the whole of the time we had been shopping. We were lucky the car wasn't stolen.

On another occasion, he returned from a shopping trip and couldn't find his credit card. He felt in his pockets. Nothing.

"Look in the carrier bags," I suggested.

We searched in the empty carrier bags. Nothing.

"Perhaps you left it in the car?"

Joe went back to the garage and checked the car. Nothing.

"Could you have left it in Carrefour?"

"Well, I suppose it's possible…"

Phone calls to Carrefour confirmed that no credit card had been handed in.

"I'm sorry," said the helpful assistant. "Are you sure you haven't lost a green draught excluder, shaped like a python? Somebody handed in one of those…"

Another blank. I knew Joe had also stopped at the service station. Perhaps it was there?

"Perhaps you left it at the petrol station?" I suggested.

Joe scratched himself irritably. "I don't think so, I paid with cash. I suppose I'd better drive down the mountain and see. If they haven't got it, we'd better get on the phone and cancel it."

21

ZOMBIES AND A FARM

Joe had hurried away to drive back down the mountain, leaving me to think about the problem.

I was nervous by now. Had the credit card been stolen? If so, how would I report it stolen if I didn't have the telephone number on the back of the card?

I'd recently discovered a handy app for iPads. It allowed me to store all my valuable PINs, passwords and documents in a single secure location. Furthermore, I could login and access them from any computer, tablet or smartphone.

Before going to Australia I laboriously saved all our valuable items onto the app. These included our *escritura* (house deeds), photos and the original manuscripts for my books. If the credit card wasn't at the petrol station, I could easily retrieve all the details from the app, then call the bank to have the card cancelled. At least, that was the plan.

Joe returned from the petrol station looking worried. "I didn't leave it there," he said.

"Never mind," I said smugly. "I've got all the details on the iPad. I'll phone right now and report it lost."

But I couldn't find the iPad. I'd used it last but couldn't remember where I had left it.

We searched high and low. No iPad. I'd destroyed our credit card statements so we couldn't refer to those. To make matters worse, the Internet connection was playing up.

"Put the kettle on," said Joe. "I'll feed the chickens and then we'll work out what to do over a cup of coffee."

Two minutes later, he burst into the kitchen.

"I've found the credit card!" he said, waving it triumphantly. "It must have fallen out of my pocket in the chicken coop."

I stared at him blankly.

"When I gave the girls that lettuce," he explained, "when I came back from shopping."

"Ah! Well, that's good! And guess what, I've found the iPad."

It was Joe's turn to look blank.

"Where was it?"

"In the fridge."

"The fridge? How on earth did it get into the fridge?"

I still have no idea.

Every year, October was marked by three events. First came the village fiesta, then the Gin Twins' annual visit, followed by Halloween.

Unfortunately the Gin Twins were never able to be in Spain for the fiesta. As teachers they could only come during the school half-term holiday, which never coincided with the fiesta. However, that year, their visit coincided with Halloween.

And they were ready for it. They unpacked their suitcases to reveal a mountain of Halloween accessories and decorations.

There were streamers with little phantoms dangling from them. Banners proclaiming 'Happy Halloween'. Bags of sweets. Terrifying 'scream' masks for us to wear. Juliet had even brought a pumpkin costume.

On the night of Halloween, Juliet and Sue cooked the evening meal. We were testing some of the recipes that Nadia Sawalha had kindly allowed me to use for my then forth-coming book, *Two Old Fools on a Camel*. But before we sat down to eat, we decorated the front of the house. Up went the banners, streamers, phantoms and skeletons.

"I'm assuming the village kids celebrate Halloween?" asked Sue, pinning up a final skeleton.

"Oh yes, they'll be around, trick or treating."

We stood back and admired our handiwork.

ZOMBIES AND A FARM

The decorations looked good and we were prepared. The sweets were in a bowl by the front door, ready for the first batch of kids. The scream masks lay waiting for us, ready to give the kids a fright. Juliet was already wearing her pumpkin outfit.

The meal was a huge success and we ate far too much. All the time we were listening out for excited children's voices and anticipating a banging on our door. We heard nothing.

"I'm so full," Joe groaned, leaning back in his chair.

"Where are those kids?" asked the pumpkin, sucking up her gin and tonic through a straw decorated with a plastic skull.

"I can't stay up," said Joe, "I need to go to bed."

The Gin Twins and I stayed round the table, chatting. Sue was now a grandmother too, which made me feel very old as I'd taught her son, another Joe. Still no children knocked on our door.

At midnight, the Gin Twins surrendered.

"I'm sorry," said Sue, "I don't think the kids will come now and I need my bed."

"I can't stay awake either," yawned the pumpkin. "I'm going up, too."

I cleared the table and stacked the dishwasher. Then I answered a few emails, by which time it was past 1am. I got myself ready for bed, locked the kitchen door and went round switching off lights.

I was just thinking whether I should blow out the candles on the front doorstep and windowsill when it started. Children's feet raced down the street and I could hear excited voices. Young fists hammered on our door.

"*Truco o trato,*" they yelled. "*¡Truco o trato!*"

Tightening my dressing-gown belt, I grabbed the mask and pulled it on, then seized the huge bowl of wrapped sweets.

"*¡Truco o trato! ¡Truco o trato!*" chanted the impatient voices through the door.

I opened the front door to a crowd of eagerly waiting ghosts, pirates and zombies. Little hands snatched at the candies and within seconds my bowl was empty. I didn't even have time to emit the ghostly howl I'd been practising before the last of the little monsters had galloped away up the street.

I sighed, blew out all the candles and put the empty bowl away. As I retired to bed I reminded myself that 1:30am might be a ridiculously late hour for English kids, but it was quite normal for the Spanish.

"What happened to all those sweets?" Juliet asked the next morning. "Don't tell me Joe ate them?"

"The kids eventually came," I said. "You all missed it."

ZOMBIES AND A FARM

This was the Gin Twins' tenth visit to El Hoyo and it occurred to me that they had never been to Fort Bravo, the permanent Wild West movie set near Tabernas. So that year I decided to leave Joe behind and take them myself. We'd have a girly day out.

When Joe drives, the journey takes about 40 minutes. I wasn't yet used to driving our new car and my navigational skills were sadly lacking. I managed to get us thoroughly lost and, although we finally did arrive, it was not before we first saw a great deal of rural Spain.

Fort Bravo is on the edge of Europe's only desert. Its similarities with the deserts in the American West made it ideal for filming spaghetti westerns like *The Good, the Bad and the Ugly* and *A Fistful of Dollars*. More recently, a *Dr Who* episode was filmed there.

Filming was taking place that day, which was always entertaining to watch. We bought two beers and a coffee from the wench in the saloon, then settled ourselves on a step to watch a shot involving a minister throwing a villain out of the chapel.

All the staff at Fort Bravo dress in costume, so we weren't surprised when a cowboy cantered up to us. We smiled sweetly and Juliet held up her camera to take a photo of him on his horse.

But the cowboy wasn't amused. He reined in his horse sharply and stared down at the three of us sitting on the step with our drinks.

"What do you think you are doing in the middle of the shot!" he shouted theatrically, in a French accent.

Red-faced, we sprang up and removed ourselves, hiding behind the tavern to finish our drinks and giggle at our own stupidity. It didn't spoil our day though. We still had a ride in the mule-cart, explored the whole town, watched the Wild West show and took photos of ourselves with the resident cowboys. Then we drove home, by the direct route this time, drank more gin and eventually toppled into bed.

※※※

If you're ever in the area, do visit Fort Bravo. It's a great day out and some of the resident cowboys are very pleasing to the eye. Oh and look out for a new movie, the French version of *Billy the Kid*. In particular, watch for the scene where a villain is being ejected from the chapel by the minister. Look past the chapel and the reverend. You may see the Gin Twins and me sitting on the steps of the saloon, drinks in hand.

※※※

Close on the heels of Halloween comes All Soul's Day, quite an important day in the Spanish calendar. Every year, a steady stream of villagers visits the cemetery and lays flowers on the graves of departed loved ones.

I'd been told that it was customary in some villages to have family picnics, setting an extra place for the deceased.

By now the nights were colder. The Log Man had made his annual visit and our wood shed was satisfyingly full. We lit the wood stove every evening and abandoned the gas hob in favour of cooking on the wood stove.

Although the days were often warm and pleasant, November did bring occasional storms to Andalucía. The gales blasted through the valley, rattling doors and window shutters. The wind howled down the chimney, blowing smoke into the kitchen whenever we opened the wood-burner's door to toss in another log.

It was on a night such as this that something extraordinary was revealed. Something that cleared up several mysteries but astonished us.

Joe had already retired for the night but I was still up, doing some final editing to *Camel* before dispatching it to my editor and proofreader. The doors and shutters clattered as the wind whipped around the house. I heard a distant banging but thought nothing of it, imagining a loose door or window, somewhere in the village, being thrashed by the wind. The banging continued for a while then abruptly stopped. I forgot about it and went to bed.

The next day dawned, calm and sunny. Midmorning, somebody knocked on our door. Joe opened it and was surprised to see Lola Ufarte on the doorstep, accompanied by her partner.

"Did you hear banging last night?" Lola asked without so much as a greeting.

Joe raised his eyebrows.

"No, I didn't. It was a wild night last night, very windy. Vicky, did you hear any banging last night?" he called. "Lola and her friend are asking."

I left the computer and joined the group at the front door.

"Yes, I did hear distant banging last night. I thought maybe it was a door caught in the wind. Why? What's happened?"

"Come and see," said Lola, turning on her heel and marching down the street.

Joe and I glanced at each other, then followed the retreating couple.

"Look!" cried Lola dramatically, throwing her arm out to indicate their front door. She tossed her lank hair over her shoulder, watching our reaction.

Joe and I stared at the door, or what was left of it. It had been hacked to pieces.

"Oh my …" I whispered, covering my mouth with my hand. "Who could have done that?"

Lola kicked some pieces of the ruined door aside. Her partner shuffled his feet and stared at the ground.

ZOMBIES AND A FARM

"Did they steal much?" asked Joe. "Have you called the Guardia?"

"Oh, the robbers knew exactly what they were after," Lola replied bitterly, ignoring his last question. "Wait. We will show you."

Her partner spat on the ground and stood aside, letting us pass.

I knew the Ufarte cottage well from when Joe and I used to babysit the Ufarte kids. The front door opened into the main room, which was both kitchen and living room. Granny Ufarte used to sit by the fire, the kids sprawled on the sofa or played on the floor and their mother, Maribel, would be cooking at the kitchen end, overlooking it all.

Now the house bore no resemblance to the domestic setup I remembered. The kitchen table, the counters and every available surface were covered in sheets of newspaper. Maribel's row of saucepans and stacked *cazuelas* was gone, replaced by shelves covered in newspaper. There were newspaper-covered shelves taking up every available metre of wall space. I gaped and my look of complete bafflement was mirrored by Joe. All those shelves explained the constant drilling we'd heard, but what were they for?

The Ufarte house used to smell of baking and coffee, but the overpowering smell that hit me today was *very* different. I knew that smell, but couldn't quite place it.

Then I remembered the 'tomato' plants that I'd

innocently raised for Mother a few years ago. They hadn't been tomato plants at all and they stank just like this house did.

"Here, they missed this piece," said Lola, holding up a green sprig from a shelf. "We grow the marijuana plants in the bedrooms and this is where we dry them out. The robbers knew exactly what they wanted."

Joe and I were speechless. We were living next door to a cannabis farm? Here, in El Hoyo? That explained the stream of strangers constantly knocking on their door. That explained Lola's furtive demeanour. And that explained why the couple were in no rush to call the police to report the crime.

Later, we chatted with Paco.

"You did not know?" asked Paco. "Pah, everybody in the village knew what they were doing!"

"We had no idea."

"Every room in that house was full of plants, you could smell them as you passed the house."

"We didn't notice anything. It's illegal, isn't it?"

"Oh yes. You are not permitted to grow more than a few plants for your own use."

"But all the villagers knew about it? Nobody reported it to the Guardia?"

"We talked about it amongst ourselves. But what happens in the village, stays in the village.

ZOMBIES AND A FARM

We protect each other. We never tell outsiders village business."

Lola and her partner replaced the old wooden front door with a modern, white PVC security door. The trickle of unsavoury looking strangers stopped, so we assumed the marijuana farm had closed for business.

🌴🌴🌴

December saw the launch of my third book, and I felt we could relax.

"I think we've had quite enough excitement for one year," I said to Joe. "I'm looking forward to a nice quiet December."

A vain wish because, as the year drew to a close, a gigantic family secret was about to explode into the open and send me reeling.

GOAT'S CHEESE ON TOAST

Not really a recipe - more of a delicious hot snack idea.

Ingredients

- 1 French baguette
- 300g goat's cheese, grated
- 1 tsp sweet smoked paprika
- Parsley

Method

- Slice the baguette diagonally into 12 slices.
- Toast one side of the bread under a grill.
- Remove from the grill and top the untoasted side with the grated goat's cheese.
- Sprinkle lightly with paprika and place back under the grill until the cheese begins to brown.
- Garnish with parsley and serve immediately.

22

ALICE

I should explain. Both my parents died long ago, in 1993, within three months of each other, but I didn't know very much about either of their backgrounds. They never discussed them with us children, but I knew my father was English and the youngest of several children. Finding his eldest brother's memoir, *Horizon Fever*, was a revelation, as I had no idea we had a famous explorer in the family.

I knew even less about my mother's side of the family. I was aware that she was an only child and was estranged from her mother, my grandmother. I never knew the cause of the rift, but on the rare occasions that she mentioned our grandmother, it was accompanied by a snort of contempt. Consequently, we never met our grandmother and I was told that my grandfather had died long before I was born.

My mother was Austrian but she had lived in England so long that her accent was barely perceptible. I was rather proud of being half-Austrian, picturing Austria to be a land of snow-capped mountains and edelweiss and imagining my ancestors yodelling to their goats on the mountain slopes.

The revelations all began with a letter the day before Christmas Eve. Joe had already checked our mailbox for last minute Christmas cards but, as usual, it remained empty. Then somebody knocked on our door. It was an unusual knock, not the customary rap of knuckles or fist, but I recognised it immediately.

"That'll be Marcia," I said. "She can't manage the steps to the front door any more, she's knocking with her walking stick."

I opened the door and was proved right.

"I have a letter from England for you," said Marcia, leaning on her stick.

She pushed away a strand of silver hair from her forehead and a hairpin tumbled to the ground narrowly missing her black cat, which wound itself around her ankles.

"Thank you, Marcia," I said. "But you didn't need to bring it to us. We'd have collected it from you after Christmas."

"It looks important," she said, turning the

envelope over to peer at the back before handing it over to Joe. "It has official stamps all over it."

"Well, thank you," he said. "And *feliz navidad* to you and your family."

Marcia shuffled off up the street, the black cat scampering ahead. Joe looked at the brown envelope in his hand.

"Who is it addressed to?" I asked.

"You. And it has 'Salvation Army' stamped all over it."

"How very odd," I said, taking it from him and tearing it open.

I unfolded one of the sheets of paper inside and started reading aloud.

"*The Salvation Army Family Tracing Centre*
Dear Ms Twead,
You may know about The Salvation Army's service which seeks to locate family members with whom contact has been lost for some reason."

I stopped.

"I haven't lost contact with any family members! I've absolutely no idea what this is all about!"

"Read on," said Joe.

"*We give below details regarding one of our current enquiries and we are writing to you in the hope that you may be the person we are trying to contact. If you believe the information may refer to you, we would be grateful to have your reaction to this enquiry and to know whether you would wish to be put in touch with the enquirer.*"

I looked up.

"Who? Who is trying to trace me?"

"Read on," said Joe.

"*Should you not wish to have contact at this time, please let us know, so that we need not trouble you again.*"

I searched the bottom of the letter. And there it was. Alice Frank Stock.

"Alice? Alice? I don't know of any Alice." I shook my head, confused and dug in the envelope again. "Wait, there's another letter and this is from Alice herself."

"Well, read it out then."

"*Dear Victoria,*

I am calling you Victoria rather than Mrs Twead because we are related. Your mother was my cousin because your grandmother, Anna, was my aunt. The main purpose of this letter is to talk to you about your grandmother Anna. I don't think you ever met her because your mother, for all sorts of reasons, was on very cool terms with her own mother.

I could tell you lots about your grandmother but as I am 94 and almost blind, I would prefer to do this by telephone.

I would be very happy indeed to be in touch with you, or at least make your telephonic acquaintance. Do let me hear from you soon.

Affectionately,
Alice"

ALICE

"Well!"

"Did she give you a number? Are you going to phone her?"

"Of course I will!"

It took a while for me to gather my thoughts before dialling the number. Why had I never heard of this cousin before? Why did my mother fall out with her mother?

I tried to picture Alice. Born in 1918, I imagined her to be very frail. I rang the number at the bottom of the letter and the phone was picked up in Bristol, England, almost immediately.

"Hello? This is Alice."

This was not the quavering voice of a fragile old lady. This was a strong, warm voice, lightly accented.

I introduced myself and the next three quarters of an hour flew past, packed with surprises.

"Your mother was born in Vienna," Alice began. "We were cousins and used to see quite a bit of each other. We even went skiing together when we were children. I still have a photo of your mother and me on skis, I will send it to you. Our family was very rich, you know, because we had land and the textile factories in Czechoslovakia that your great-grandfather had set up. Your grandmother, Anna, fell in love with a dashing Austrian officer, but that didn't go well."

"Why not?"

"Well, he was very handsome, likeable and full

of life. They had a big, flamboyant wedding, but over the years she became impatient with him. He left the army to help run the family textile factories, but he had no head for business. He was spending all Anna's money socialising and having a good time."

"So what happened?"

"Well, I think they both had affairs after your mother was born. Your mother adored her father and when Anna left your grandfather, your mother never forgave her. She was young, of course, but she couldn't accept that her father had gone and she blamed Anna. Did your mother never talk of Anna?"

"Only very rarely. She made it very clear that she no longer spoke to her mother."

"Well, that is a great pity, because Anna was a delightful person, very funny, a good writer and very resourceful. She died in Belfast, you know."

"What happened after Anna and my grandfather split up?"

"Well, when Hitler began his war against the Jews everything changed. I managed to escape to Paris. Anna had the choice of an Austrian or a Czech passport for herself and your mother. Luckily she chose the Czech one. It saved her and your mother's lives."

"Just a second… Are you saying that my mother and all her family were *Jewish*?"

"But of course! We are all Jewish. Didn't you know?"

"No!"

Alice chuckled. "Well, your mother kept that little secret very close to her chest! What religion were you brought up in?"

"We were Church of England. I was baptised and later confirmed. My brother and I were both married in churches. I taught in a Catholic school for years."

"Good heavens! Our family name was Goldschmidt, you know."

I was astounded. This was news to me and I knew for a fact that neither my brother nor sister had any idea of our Jewish heritage.

"So what happened next?"

"Hitler invaded Czechoslovakia and, of course, all the Jews had to flee. Your mother was nineteen and she chose to live in England with relatives who had already settled there."

"And Anna?"

"She went to Ireland. Mother and daughter never saw each other again. Your mother always blamed Anna for the marriage split and losing her father."

"And my grandfather? What happened to him?"

There was a small silence.

"I'm afraid your grandfather died in one of Hitler's concentration camps."

It was almost too much to take in. I discovered that my hand was gripping the telephone receiver so tightly that my knuckles had turned white.

"You didn't know?" asked Alice gently.

"Nothing. I didn't know any of this."

"Anna was a clever lady. If she hadn't chosen the Czech passports for herself and her daughter, they would also have died in the concentration camps."

And I wouldn't exist, I couldn't help thinking. *Neither would my brother and sister. Or my kids. Or Indy.*

"What a terrible waste of life," I said. "Thank goodness they managed to get out in time."

The horror of the holocaust had suddenly become so much more real with the knowledge that my own grandfather had perished in one of Hitler's despicable concentration camps and that my mother, grandmother and Alice had narrowly missed the same fate.

"And what happened to the textile factories? And the land?"

"Oh, Hitler took all those," said Alice. "The family lost everything. Anna came to Ireland with nothing and had to start from scratch."

"What did she do?"

Alice chuckled. "As I told you before, she was a very resourceful lady, very clever. She was good with her hands. She made belts and Tyrolean toys that were so beautiful that Liberty's, in London, placed orders for them. She loved animals and she always had dogs. She discovered she could write and began to write articles for the *Dublin Times*

ALICE

and the *Belfast Telegraph*, even the *Manchester Guardian*. Then she began to write books."

"I write books!" I exclaimed excitedly.

"Do you?" asked Alice and I could hear the smile in her voice. "Ah, then you must have inherited that from her."

"What books did she write?"

"She wrote books about keeping dogs. West Highlands were her favourite. She began to breed dogs for a living. I have the books still, I will send them to you."

"That would be wonderful!"

"Anna's house in Ireland was bombed by the Germans and she boarded with Professor Estyn Evans. They remained friends for the rest of her life. By the time Anna died, she had made many good friends. Professor Estyn Evans wrote a beautiful obituary for her, which was published in the *Irish Times*. I think I am right in saying that the *Belfast Telegraph* wouldn't publish it because she was Jewish, in spite of the fact that she had contributed articles about the war and dogs and other things for years."

"When did she die?" I asked.

"I believe it was the early 1970s."

That would make sense. I vaguely remembered my mother opening a letter and telling my father the news.

"Humph, that's no loss," she had said as she tossed the letter aside.

"Was my mother told that her mother was dying?"

"Oh yes, your mother was notified. It was terribly sad," Alice said and I heard her sigh. "Although Anna had many friends, she longed for a reconciliation with her only daughter, your mother. As Anna lay dying in the hospital, she never tore her eyes away from the ward door. When the nurses asked her what she was doing, she told them that she was waiting for the door to open. She knew her daughter had been told she was dying and she was sure she would come to see her for the last time and make peace. Of course your mother never came, but Anna never stopped hoping and died with her eyes fixed on that door."

After that phone call I sat still for a long time trying to absorb all the information I had gleaned. Those terrible events so long ago that I only knew about from history, were now part of my own history. My emotions bubbled over and it was a long time before I was ready to relate it all to Joe.

A couple of days later, I chatted with my sister on the phone. She was as shocked as I was and had by now also spoken with Alice. We compared notes and memories.

"Jewish!" said Caroline. "I suppose that explains why we never had any relatives in

ALICE

Austria and why those we knew about seemed to be scattered all over the world."

"You'd never guess Alice's age from her voice, would you? I think she's amazing!" I said.

"No, she's as sharp as somebody a quarter of her age. She speaks three languages fluently, as did our grandmother, Anna. Did you know Alice worked for years in the OECD in Paris?"

"Yes, I looked that up on the Internet. Apparently OECD stands for the Organisation for Economic Cooperation and Development and it was set up to stimulate progress and trade after the War, whatever that means."

"Whatever, Alice is certainly no frail little old lady mouldering away in a nursing home," said Caroline. "I can't wait to meet her in person."

Over the weeks and months that followed, I had many more conversations with Alice and she often had another nugget of family history to relate, something she had just recalled.

Coincidentally, 'ancestors' was a subject that was also beginning to occupy the minds of the villagers. In fact, it became a hot topic, one that was set to divide families and cause major problems in the months to come.

23

THE CEMETERY

Our house stood just a pebble's throw from the village cemetery and funeral processions would pass our front door.

The first time this happened, many years ago, I was on my own in the living room. At the time, we had one small, quite high, window overlooking the street, too high for people to look inside. I looked up when I heard the tramp of many feet approaching. To my astonishment, a coffin sailed past the window. Being high, the window didn't reveal the bearers, which resulted in the unnerving sight.

I'd always loved El Hoyo's cemetery. It was far more intimate than any cemetery I've seen in England. Surrounded by white walls, the graves were neat and well maintained. An ancient yew tree, a favourite place for nesting birds, cast its

THE CEMETERY

shadow over the sleeping inhabitants. Apart from the graves, rows of niches were set into the walls. Each niche had a shiny brass plaque and was often accompanied by a portrait photograph of the departed.

From our vantage point on the roof terrace, we could look down on the cemetery. One beautiful January day, Joe and I climbed the stairs to enjoy the view. The sky stretched blue and clear and the almond trees had already burst into flower, their pinky white blossom fresh against the mountain backdrop.

"There's a lot of activity around the cemetery today," remarked Joe, turning his head to speak to me.

But I had gone. I had ducked down and was crouching by his feet.

"Vicky, what on earth are you doing down there?" he asked, astonished.

"I'm hiding!"

"Hiding from who? It's only Pancho the mayor showing some men around."

"I know," I hissed. "I don't want him to see me. He might remember those English lessons he keeps banging on about."

But the mayor and men were engrossed in whatever they were doing, so I bobbed up again to watch.

"They've got clipboards," I said. "and they are measuring things."

We watched as the mayor, deep in discussion,

led the men outside the cemetery where they made notes and took more measurements along the wall.

There was quite a large patch of waste ground beside the cemetery and it seemed to both Joe and me that the party was discussing extending the cemetery. We'd both noticed that it had become very crowded and had wondered where the next newly deceased deceased villager would be laid to rest.

The mayor finished his discussion and shook hands with the men. They departed in one direction while he headed towards our house. My heart sank.

"If he knocks on our door, I'm not in," I instructed Joe.

Sure enough, Pancho did knock on our door.

"Don't you dare let him in," I ordered Joe through gritted teeth.

"I have to, it might be important."

"Then don't tell him I'm here!" I hissed, as Joe headed for the door and I darted into the kitchen.

"*Buenas tardes*, Pancho," said Joe, opening the door. "How are you?"

"Ah, Joe, I am very well. I was just at the cemetery and I thought I would call to arrange those English lessons your wife promised me. Is Beaky in?"

Hidden behind the kitchen door, I made a face and rolled my eyes. I waited for Joe's reply, not really trusting him to keep my presence secret.

THE CEMETERY

"Oh, I'm sorry, Vicky isn't here," answered Joe as I exhaled with relief. Then, neatly changing the subject, "Yes, we … I mean I … saw you were there. Are you thinking of enlarging the cemetery?"

"Yes," replied the mayor. "The village has been talking about it for a few years. We need more space. We would like to use the waste ground beside the cemetery but there is a problem with the ownership of that patch of land. Never mind, we will sort it out. Please tell Beaky that I called. Perhaps she could phone me some time?"

"Yes, I'll certainly tell her."

I relaxed as I heard Pancho turning away, then froze in horror when I heard Joe's next words.

"Oh and before you go, come into the kitchen and I'll give you some eggs to take home."

What? Joe! How could you!

"Thank you, newly laid eggs are so fresh and tasty."

Their footsteps approached and I willed myself not to move, trying to regulate my breathing, praying Pancho wouldn't see me behind the kitchen door.

Joe seemed to take forever transferring the eggs into a paper bag. Divorce loomed large in my mind as they chatted. It was all I could think of when I heard what Joe had to say next.

"Can I offer you a coffee, Pancho?" he asked pleasantly. "Or a brandy, perhaps?"

To my profound relief, Pancho refused and left soon after.

"It's okay, he's gone," said Joe returning to the kitchen, grinning from ear to ear.

"I hope you've got a good solicitor," I said, coming out from behind the door. "You're going to need one."

※※※

Although Pancho brushed aside the subject of the land's ownership, we soon discovered that it was a bigger problem than he had admitted.

"Pah!" said Paco, thumping the kitchen table with his fist. "The village needs a bigger cemetery, there is no question about that!"

"So who owns the land next to it?" I asked.

"It's not clear," explained Carmen. "Some of the papers have gone missing. The village has always understood that it is land belonging to the council, but Alejandro has papers that seem to show that it belongs to his family."

"Alejandro Senior? Your friend the millionaire?"

"Yes, he insists the land is his."

"Perhaps he could sell the land to the council?"

"No, the council has no money to buy the land and Alejandro Senior refuses to sell it anyway. Alejandro Senior is a very generous man, but not

THE CEMETERY

when it comes to land. He will not part with land. It is the Spanish way."

I knew that was true. Village houses rarely came onto the market. Instead, they were passed down through the family from generation to generation. Even if houses were unused and had fallen into ruins, the owners wouldn't sell the land they stood on. We were lucky to be able to buy our own house.

"And what happens when Alejandro Senior dies?" ranted Paco. "If he doesn't give the village that land, there will be nowhere to bury *him*!"

"*Claro*," said Carmen, shaking her head until her chins wobbled.

In every house in the village, on every street corner, in the bar and in Marcia's shop, the question of the land was being discussed. We noticed that people took sides. Some were outraged that Alejandro Senior wouldn't give it up and others understood his traditional viewpoint. The land belonged to his family; it was their birthright.

A legal team was put on the case to determine to whom the land belonged. I quietly hoped it would find in favour of the council and the problem would be solved. An announcement was expected within a few weeks. In the meantime the subject of Alejandro Senior and the cemetery extension remained the hot topic.

Although the cemetery issue hadn't been resolved, the regular seasonal events came round with unerring regularity. Andalucía Day is celebrated in February and all the shops, schools and banks close for the day. Every Andalucía Day, the villagers made a procession up to the little shrine at the top of the mountain. Once there, they ate *churros* and drank hot chocolate.

But that year, things seemed different. Instead of an untidy column of people parading together up the mountain track, there were two distinct factions.

"This is more serious than I thought," I said to Joe as we watched from our roof terrace. "It looks as though the whole village has divided. The mayor and half the village are in the front group and Alejandro Senior and his friends and family are in the one behind."

"Can you see Paco and Carmen?"

I shaded my eyes from the glare. "Yes, they're in the mayor's group. What a pity! Paco and Alejandro have been friends since they were little boys. I hate to think they've fallen out."

Not only had the two old friends fallen out, but there was worse to come. We were to discover that the feud would affect even the younger members of the two families.

In early March the legal team responsible for investigating the ownership of the wasteland still hadn't announced its findings. Spring was already on the way and Paco and Uncle Felix arrived to prune our vine.

This time they were accompanied by

THE CEMETERY

Geronimo. I noticed that Uncle Felix now leaned on his mule for support, the mule slowing her pace to match his faltering steps. He tethered her to our window bars and Geronimo helped the old man through the house and to an outside seat where he could supervise the pruning.

When the vine had been sufficiently butchered and twigs and branches littered the ground, I invited them all in for coffee and brandy, as I always did.

Geronimo set his beer aside and accepted the brandy Joe offered him, refusing the coffee. Paco and Uncle Felix added a glug of brandy to their coffee and conversation began.

"It is good that you kept Veeky away from the vine this time," said Paco and Uncle Felix nodded in agreement. "A woman must never be allowed near a vine. It is man's work."

I bit my tongue. Fortunately, Joe had the sense to change the subject, probably fearing another mackerel supper.

"Will you be watching Real Madrid play Barcelona next weekend, Geronimo?" he asked innocently.

Geronimo almost spluttered his brandy and I smiled to myself. He set down the glass and gripped both ends of the Real Madrid scarf he wore around his neck.

"But of course! What a team! Never has a team played soccer like Real Madrid. Poetry. Every kick is poetry. Watching a team with skills like that is better than a night in bed with a beautiful woman."

He suddenly remembered me and flushed red.

"*Perdone, Señora* Twead."

Embarrassed, he took another swig from his brandy glass and my presence was forgotten again.

"When that ball glides across the pitch from one player to the next," he whispered, "it's like fingers moving up a woman's thigh."

Uncle Felix stared straight ahead, unblinking. Paco slapped the table, making the glasses dance.

"Geronimo! Enough! Remember Veeky is here. And don't forget," he lowered his voice, "Felix has never had a woman."

He clapped Uncle Felix on the shoulder, nearly knocking the old man off his chair.

I tried to steer the conversation to safer ground.

"How is your big new TV?" I asked Uncle Felix.

"He never misses that dating show!" shouted Paco. "Do you, Felix?"

Uncle Felix's expression didn't change, but his head nodded once in agreement.

"So, has anyone heard whether the waste ground alongside the cemetery belongs to Alejandro Senior or the council?" asked Joe.

Geronimo was still staring into the bottom of his glass, probably dreaming of Real Madrid goals, past and future.

THE CEMETERY

"Pah!" roared Paco, his face reddening. "No, we have heard nothing! It is a disgrace! El Hoyo needs that bit of land! I have known Alejandro and his father all my life and I cannot believe that they are being so difficult! Alejandro is a stubborn old fool and we are no longer friends. What does he need that land for? It is not good for olives and he would not be allowed to build on it. I have told our Sofía that I will not allow her to see young Alejandro until the whole stupid business is sorted out."

Joe and I gaped at him. Surely not? Not when his daughter had finally found The One? Alejandro Junior and Sofía seem so happy together, how tragic if they were forbidden to see each other!

"That's terrible," was all I could say.

"What does Sofía say?" asked Joe. "Will she obey you?"

"She must obey her father," said Paco, his eyes narrowing. "If she does not, she is no longer a daughter of mine."

After Paco, Geronimo and Uncle Felix had left, Joe and I mulled over the visit. Neither of us could believe Paco's decision.

"Was he serious?" I wanted to know. "Sofía is in her thirties, surely she can do as she pleases?"

"You know how close-knit Spanish families are and how the children, especially daughters, always obey their parents' wishes. I imagine she will do as her father orders."

"Well, it's a terrible shame. The sooner this mess gets sorted out, the better. Sofía and Alejandro Junior seemed made for each other. I really thought I could hear wedding bells."

Once again I prayed that the land would belong to the council. And I also put my thinking cap on, wondering if there was any way we could help.

BUTTERNUT SQUASH WITH GARLIC AND HERBS

A delicious vegetarian dish or side dish. Roasted butternut squash goes particularly well with roast chicken and also roast pork.

Preparation: 10 minutes

Cooking: 45 minutes

Serves 4

Ingredients

- 1 butternut squash
- 8 garlic cloves, crushed
- 1 tbsp fresh sage, chopped
- 1 tbsp fresh thyme, chopped
- Sea salt
- Cracked black peppercorns
- Extra virgin olive oil

Method

- Peel, halve and cut the squash into 1cm (½in)-thick strips.

- In a terracotta *cazuela* or oven dish, toss the squash with the garlic and herbs, adding a generous drizzle of olive oil.

- Season with salt and pepper and toss again ensuring all the squash is covered in the mixture.

- Arrange the squash in the cazuela or oven dish and bake for 45 minutes at 220°C (430°F) Gas Mark 7, or until golden brown.

24

PLUCKERS AND WILDFIRES

Our telephone rang and I picked up the receiver.

"Victoria? It's Alice here."

"Hello, Alice! How are you?"

"Oh, not too bad, thank you for asking."

"What's the weather like in England? We're hearing horrid things about it on the News."

"The weather's ghastly, floods and strong winds, but I am used to the British weather after all these years. I called because I've just recalled something else about Anna, your grandmother."

"Oh yes?"

"She was dog plucker, you know. Made quite a business out of it."

"A what?"

"At one time your grandmother plucked dogs for a living. She wrote an article about it for the

Tail-Wagger magazine. I'm having it sent over for you to see."

A stack of papers duly arrived with photocopies of Anna's articles and columns from various publications. Dated from the 1940s, they bore intriguing titles like *I Saw the Nazis March into Austria*, *I Stayed in the Same Hotel as Mussolini* and *Words and Phrases I Never Wish to Hear Again*.

Anna described Mussolini as 'a fat little man who looked as if he was still seated after he stood up'. The *Words and Phrases* were also fascinating. Anna must have been a list-maker like myself because she wrote in *The Countrywoman*:

Here is a short list of words and phrases I never wish to hear again: Coupons, black-out, spam, egg substitute, semi-fashioned stockings, black market, underneath the counter, make and mend, utility, purchase tax, fifth column, blitz, swastika, siren, direct hit, missing, gas mask, warden and concentration camp.

I shook my head. How little we knew about what the last generation had endured. I also wanted to know about my grandmother's dog plucking business. I found an article entitled '*I Pluck Dogs*' and I read on…

> *Most dogs cast their top coat at certain times of the year. With some of the terrier breeds, such as Scotties, Airedales, Lakelands, West Highland Whites, Irish Terriers and Wire Fox Terriers, this top coat is very loose when it is ready to fall*

PLUCKERS AND WILDFIRES

out and is easily removed with the help of a stripping comb or knife. This procedure leaves the undercoat exposed to light and air and enables the dog to grow a new warm coat in a few months.

The majority of my four-legged customers seem to enjoy the plucking operation, but a small number try and a still smaller number succeed in giving me a hearty nip.

I travel all over the country and know the bus and train timetables by heart and the conductors by sight. I pluck dogs in mansions and cottages, on sideboards and card tables, in stables and drawing rooms.
This variety of individualities, human and canine, prevents me from ever feeling bored with my work.

Fascinating stuff! I wondered how Anna disposed of the mountains of dog hair she must have collected. I read further and discovered that Anna used the hair to stuff pincushions, which she then sold to high-class stores in London. She also had another use for the dog hair.

Of course, combings from the coats of Samoyed dogs were woven into wool during the war and used for knitting comforts for troops. However, what else do I do with the hair I pull out? Well, at nesting time I put it into the hedges to let birds use it for their housing scheme.

A resourceful lady, my grandmother. I wish I had known her.

※※※

Although February is usually the coldest, wettest month of the year, February 2012 was glorious. Most days saw wall-to-wall blue skies, sunshine and not a single snowflake. I wasn't complaining but Paco shook his head.

"Weather like this is not good for the olives and grapes," he said. "You mark my words, the harvest will be poor this year. I cannot remember such a dry winter."

March was much the same, although the wind was still quite chilly and often blew with considerable force, bending the ancient trees that grew on the mountain slopes.

Another day in paradise, I thought as I climbed the staircase to our roof terrace.

I set down the heavy laundry basket, heaped with damp bed-linen. Perfect drying weather. Very windy, not a cloud in sight and the sun beating down. The washing would flap itself dry in no time.

I leaned on the terrace wall and looked around. Joe and I never wearied of the view over the village and around the mountains. I looked

PLUCKERS AND WILDFIRES

down at the cemetery, the cause of such controversy. It was empty and silent. I glanced at the rooftops and the few curls of smoke rising from the only occupied houses in the village. Puffs of smoke wafted from Uncle Felix's chimney and were immediately whipped away by the wind. I smiled to myself, imagining Uncle Felix cosy in his cottage, watching his dating show on his widescreen TV.

Clusters of almond trees dressed in white blossoms decorated the mountain slopes, the wind tugging at their petals. The green mountain tops undulated against endless blue sky.

I turned my head, then froze. To the west, on a nearby mountain slope, I could see a lot of black smoke. I squinted. Not just smoke but bright orange flames too. As I watched, they reared up and began to spread. I stared in horror. It was a wildfire and it was moving fast, whipped up by the high winds.

"Joe! Joe!" I yelled. "There's a wildfire on the mountain. Quick! Bring the binoculars!"

In the short time it took Joe to join me on the terrace, the fire had doubled in size. I estimated that the line of flames was now as wide as a football pitch. Trees and bushes burst into flame as the fire galloped up the mountain devouring the dry vegetation, fanned by the wind.

"I'm going to get Paco," I said and clattered back down the staircase at high speed.

I knew Paco would be next door as he always

took his annual leave during this time of year, spending it shooting quail and carousing with his friends. I shot out into the street, and, calling him, burst through his open front door.

Except for the dogs, Paco was alone in the little kitchen. He was busy skinning a rabbit for the pot on the fire. Yukky barked a greeting and Bianca wagged her tail in welcome. For once I ignored them.

"¿*Que pasa?*" asked Paco, alarmed.

"¡*Fuego! Fuego arriba!*" I explained breathlessly. (Fire! Fire above!)

"Where?"

I waved my arms and pointed. I knew that Paco would alert the authorities and he would describe it much more clearly than I could in my stumbling Spanish.

Paco wiped his hands on Carmen's best teacloth and followed me into the street. I pointed up the mountain and he stared, shading his eyes with his hand from the glare.

"I'll call the Fire Brigade," he said and disappeared back inside his house.

Joe and I watched from our roof terrace. The fire had crested the hill, travelling away from our village but heading towards the next out of sight over the mountain. Clumps of bushes on our side of the mountain were still alight, but the heart of the wildfire, judging by the columns of black smoke, was growing on the other side. El Hoyo was in no danger, unless the wind changed direction, but the next village was.

We couldn't hear the crackling of the flames as the wind whistled in our ears but then we caught a whirring sound growing louder. Helicopters arrived with giant bags of water. They buzzed overhead, hovering nose down like giant dragonflies. Having assessed the situation, they spilled their loads to douse the flames.

Next, little figures appeared on the hill. Each carried a tool like an elongated shovel and the last stray patches of flame were beaten into submission.

That evening, as the sun went down, Joe stoked the woodburner in our kitchen.

"I'd better bring the washing in," I said. "It'll be nice and dry by now."

I climbed the staircase yet again and looked at the scene of the fire. Although the mountainside was black and dotted with smoking tree skeletons, the fire was out.

It was then that I discovered that the laundry was not dry at all. Not in the slightest. In all the excitement of the fire, I had forgotten to peg it out and it still sat in a big wet heap in the washing basket.

But that was the good thing about living in Spain, tomorrow invariably brought another sunny day.

Before I went back down the stairs, I leaned on the terrace wall to watch the sunset. The sun was as orange as the flames we'd watched lick the mountain slopes earlier in the day. Shadows deepened and the whitewashed cottages of El Hoyo were bathed in a golden light.

A tiny movement caught my eye. There were two people in the little copse of fir trees just beyond the cemetery. I squinted and tried to identify the figures in the shadows, wondering what they were doing out so late on a chilly night.

The figures appeared to embrace each other, then settled on a fallen tree trunk, sitting very close to each other with their heads leaning together. I'd seen enough. I knew who they were. I collected my basket of wet washing and made my way back down the stairs.

"Very sad," I said to Joe.

"What? The fire? Or that you forgot to hang the washing out? It'll dry tomorrow."

"No, I just saw figures hiding in the copse."

"Did you? Who were they?"

"Sofía and Alejandro Junior."

🙍🙍🙍

I think it was around that time that yet another plague of miniature beasties appeared in our house. For a while, I'd heard funny little ticking sounds in the kitchen and it took me a long time to locate the source. We had a new fridge that made peculiar noises, sometimes like cows lowing in a distant meadow, so I blamed the fridge for a while.

Then, one evening, the tiny ticking seemed to be more insistent than usual. I tiptoed across the floor, listening carefully while following the noise. It seemed to be coming from a food cupboard, the one where I kept canned food and emergency supplies.

Even shining a torch into the back of the cupboard revealed nothing, so I resigned myself to taking out all the cans and packets. All seemed clear until I lifted a pack of pasta. It was tortellini, little circles stuffed with dried meat and designed to be emptied into boiling water.

The packet was riddled with tiny holes. Inside, the dried pasta was peppered with miniature gnawed-out tunnels, corridors and compartments. A thousand little round bugs, not much bigger than pin heads, were partying. The ticking noise was the sound of their munching through the plastic wrapping and once inside they feasted on the dried meat and pasta. It looked like a thriving, well-established community and I imagine that more bugs were created and born inside the sachet and were chewing their way out.

Whatever, I wasn't happy about their feasting and multiplying in my pantry, so I presented both pasta and bugs to the chickens. The chickens gobbled them up.

If only all bug infestations were so easy to eradicate.

Thankfully, (touch wood) Joe and I have yet to cross paths with a Mediterranean banded centipede.

Sounds pretty harmless, doesn't it, but don't be fooled. The banded centipede is a menace, a creature best avoided.

Mediterranean banded centipedes usually prey on crickets, worms, spiders and moths and sometimes each other. Apparently, if hungry enough, they'll even attack small rodents. Although venomous, they are not really dangerous to humans, but the bite is painful and affected parts often swell for a while before subsiding.

The biggest problem with banded centipedes is that they like the same kind of environment as humans do. When the weather turns colder, they often enter houses and their favourite place to hang out is the bedroom. Not on the bedroom walls, or under the nightstands, or dark corners.

No, Mediterranean banded centipedes love to snuggle in our beds. Reports show that they are often found under pillows or nestling under the duvet. Be warned. When disturbed, they will bite.

Hard.

※※※

At long last we heard that the legal team had finally delivered their verdict concerning the ownership of the cemetery. The news spread as fast as the wildfire on the mountain.

"Come to the square at six o'clock," said Marcia when we popped into the shop to collect our mail. "The mayor is going to make an announcement."

IBERIAN HAM WITH PEACHES AND OLIVE OIL

This is a light, satisfying dish with a beautiful combination of flavours and textures. Lovely served as a Mediterranean-style breakfast or supper.

Ingredients

- 3 – 4 thin slices of Jamón Iberico
- 1 medium-sized peach
- Olive oil

Method

Cut the peach into bite-sized pieces and arrange on a plate.

Place the ham on the plate with the fruit and add a drizzle of olive oil.

25

NEWS AND A PLAN

"I'm keeping my fingers crossed that the council legally owns that land," I said to Joe for the thousandth time. We were making our way down to the square, as were other villagers.

"We'll see," said Joe.

It was a Friday night and the square was already busy. Marcia sat in her shop doorway, her knitting needles clacking, the black cat sprawled under her chair. Uncle Felix and Geronimo sat on the stone bench, Geronimo's three dogs panting at their feet.

People chattered in groups, but it was clear that they had divided themselves and the atmosphere was more subdued than usual. Paco, Carmen and all their friends and relations stood on one side of the square while Alejandro's friends and family gathered on the other. Sofía stood near her parents, silent and pale. On the other side, Alejandro Junior stood a little apart from his parents, face expressionless, eyes staring down at his shoes.

"Let's stay here with Marcia," I muttered to Joe. "I don't want to be seen to be taking sides."

We waited and watched.

A car appeared high above us on the opposite side of the valley and began its descent into the village. It took five minutes or so to navigate down the twisting road, frequently disappearing from sight as trees briefly hid it from view. Every pair of eyes in the square was fixed on the vehicle, even Marcia's, although the clicking of her knitting needles never lost its rhythm. The car belonged to Pancho, the mayor, and the air was thick with anticipation.

He got out of the car and made his way across the square, where an upturned crate served as his stage.

"We have the legal results," he said, holding up a sheaf of papers. "I am here to announce that is has been ruled that the strip of land that runs along the cemetery from east to west…"

Pancho paused and one could have heard a pin drop as all present held their breaths.

"There is no doubt that this land belongs to the family of *Señor* Alejandro…"

The remainder of his sentence was drowned out as Alejandro Senior's side of the square erupted. Younger members punched the air in

NEWS AND A PLAN

triumph. Shock etched the faces of the other villagers. Marcia tutted, shook her head and stilled her knitting, her hands gnarled fists in her lap.

"Oh no," I said to Joe, "that's not good news."

I saw Sofía and Alejandro Junior steal the briefest of glances at each other, their eyes speaking volumes.

"There must be some mistake!" shouted someone.

"No mistake," bellowed Alejandro Senior. "I told you all, that land belongs to me and my family!"

The mayor climbed down from his box; there was nothing more to say. I imagined it was the shortest speech he had ever delivered. He made his way back through the crowd, ignoring the questions and protests hurled at him, climbed back into his car and drove out of the village.

The crowd soon dispersed, either to celebrate or to drown their sorrows, depending on which side they belonged. Joe and I walked home, absorbing the news. The only good thing about the meeting was that Pancho hadn't noticed me and had been too preoccupied to pester me for English lessons.

"There must be something that can be done," I protested. "It's a ridiculous situation. I hate the thought of Alejandro and Paco falling out. They've been friends for decades."

"All their lives, I think."

"Yes, and it's affecting both families as well. And what about poor Sofía and Alejandro Junior? It's so unfair to them."

"Stop worrying, there's nothing we can do."

But I couldn't stop worrying and I felt sure there must be a solution. I fretted for a week, annoying Joe by constantly resurrecting the subject.

And then it came to me. I had an idea.

We were on the roof terrace watching the sun go to bed and had yet again watched Sofía and Alejandro Junior keep a tryst in the copse. These clandestine meetings had become a regular occurrence, which both saddened and infuriated me.

"Joe, listen, I have an idea that might help."

"Oh, for goodness' sake! Stop trying to interfere! This is village politics and there's nothing we can do."

"Just listen," I said.

I explained my plan. Joe was quiet for a moment, then nodded his head reluctantly.

"Yes, that might just work…" he said at last.

The next day I began to put my plan into action.

I dialled Judith's number and waited for her to pick up her phone.

"Judith, are you at home this morning? We thought we'd pop round and see you," I shouted, trying to be heard above the baying of her hounds.

NEWS AND A PLAN

"Jolly good show, Vicky!" she yelled. "Sinbad, get DOWN! Tyson, if you don't leave Fluffy alone, I'm taking you to the vet, be warned!"

"Good, we'll see you in about half an hour," I yelled.

"Bring some eggs with you, m'dear. They're so fresh and tasty."

🐕🐕🐕

Sitting around Judith's kitchen table was always an experience. Getting to it was the first hurdle, forcing one's way through dogs and cats and stepping over food bowls. I patted one dog on the head while another offered me his paw. Two more were running round the table and the rest were barking, either at us or each other.

"DOGS!" bellowed Judith. "OUT!"

She opened the kitchen door and the pack careered outside, leaving us in peace. I sat back, noticing cats sleeping on various shelves. One black cat was curled up on the cooker, another had draped itself across a stack of cookbooks.

"How many dogs do you have now?" I asked Judith.

"Still only nine, m'dear," she chuckled. "Remember I always said I'd never have ten?"

"We remember," I said. "But then you adopted Half and then Invisible and then Ghost..."

"Exactly, so we only have nine and a Half, one that's Invisible and a Ghost..."

"And?"

"Well, m'dear, I caught a blasted farmer trying to drown this one."

She pointed to a basket in the corner that I hadn't noticed. A very young puppy squirmed on a blanket.

"Ah. So you rescued it and now you have ten?"

"Good lord, no! This one's called Undog, so he doesn't count," she chuckled. "So we still have only nine dogs."

Joe and I smiled.

"Ah, Joe, Victoria!" breathed Mother, drifting into the kitchen.

Joe and I rose and kissed her cheek. I caught the scent of Chanel N°5, which always accompanied her. She wore a pink, silky wraparound robe and could have stepped out of the pages of a film star magazine of the fifties. Tiny matching heeled slippers adorned her feet.

"I'm rather a late riser, I'm afraid," murmured Mother, joining us at the table.

"That's because you were out half the ruddy night!" exclaimed Judith, laughing and poured her a cup of tea. "Now, where did your fancy man take you last night? Restaurant? Dancing?"

Mother smiled to herself and sipped her tea. Joe and I exchanged glances. Mother was the reason we had made this visit. I still wasn't sure how I was going to broach the subject. I would have to bide my time.

NEWS AND A PLAN

For a while we chatted about this and that. Judith and Mother knew everybody in our village and asked after them by name.

"Our neighbours, Paco and Carmen, are very well," I said, in answer to Judith's question. "Their dog, Bianca, is managing perfectly well with three legs. It's their daughter, Sofía, who worries us."

"Why?" asked Judith. "What's wrong with the gal?"

At last, my opportunity had arrived. I waded in.

"Well, you know the problem with the strip of land by the cemetery?"

Judith nodded. Mother lit a herbal cigarette and placed it in a holder.

"Yes, that land belongs to Alejandro," said Judith. "He knew it belonged to him and his family all the time."

Mother blew smoke into the air.

"Yes, but Paco has forbidden Sofía and Alejandro Junior to see each other until Alejandro Senior gives the land to the village or something. Sofía and Alejandro Junior are devastated. I've never seen Sofía look so miserable."

"Frightful bloody shame!" said Judith. "Mother, can't you have a word in your fancy man's shell-like ear? You know he listens to you!"

This was going *exactly* as I had planned. I sat tight. Mother blew a smoke ring high into the air, then lowered her false eyelashes to study her crimson painted fingernails.

"I'll see what I can do," she said at last.

Back in the car, Joe and I headed home and discussed it further.

"Well, there's nothing else for it," I said, "except to hope that Mother has some influence over Alejandro Senior. If she can't persuade him, then I think that's the end of the story."

"Yes, we'll just have to wait and see. But no more interfering."

I promised.

※※※

As winter departed and gave way to spring, record keepers told us that it had been the driest winter in our region in living memory. The rivers and streams hadn't filled up as they usually did and the farmers' water storage tanks were low. Parts of Spain braced themselves for a serious water shortage.

With clear blue skies and scorching sun, we were fooled into thinking summer had arrived. I packed away our winter clothes.

Then came a patch of bad weather. Temperatures dropped, strong winds blew up and the clouds piled over the mountains in fifty shades of grey. Out came the winter clothes again and Joe lit the fire as the rain hammered down as though making up for lost time. The farmers

NEWS AND A PLAN

studied the sky with smiles on their faces, pleased that their tanks were filling up again.

Where water is concerned, people in our part of Andalucía are very fortunate. We never suffered from a water shortage as natural springs were plentiful. At the entrance of El Hoyo was a spring where locals filled their water containers. It was also the source of water for the entire village. In the next village was another spring, still surrounded by cement basins and washboards, where villagers once washed their laundry and exchanged news and views. Water flowed freely from both springs, day and night.

When we lived in southern England, our water was extremely hard and our pipes and kettles regularly clogged up with chalk. Moving to Spain, I looked forward to living in an area with natural water. I imagined that spring water, straight from the mountain, would be as close to perfection as possible. But it seemed I was mistaken. Mountain water might be clear, pure and untainted, but, unfortunately, it is not quite perfect.

The water around El Hoyo, although natural, was even harder than that in southern England. In fact it was the hardest, most chalk-filled water I had ever encountered. Our kettle became lined with a film of white limescale after only a few boilings. We knew it was harmless, but the water was cloudy and the heating element struggled against the caked chalk. I asked Carmen how she managed but she didn't own a kettle so she wasn't much help.

To combat the problem, I tried limescale remover, which I bought from the supermarket. It worked well enough, but it needed several hours to take effect and getting rid of the nasty smell was difficult. Neither Joe nor I wanted to wait around for our cups of coffee and we didn't enjoy coffee smelling of chemicals.

I searched the Internet and discovered that a mixture of white wine vinegar and water works very well. As a bonus, it was cheaper and much less smelly. The kettle still needed to stand for a couple of hours, to allow the vinegar to do its work, but the vinegar was a big improvement on the disgusting, expensive shop-bought limescale remover.

"What we need," I told Joe, "is two kettles. Then we can use one while the other is being cleaned."

The drive down the mountain was wonderful at that time of year. Crimson poppies nodded in the breeze and the grass and trees were lush with new growth. Silvery streams gurgled and meandered their way downhill after the recent rainfall. A snake slithered across the road in front of us and a green-headed, foot-long lizard watched us pass.

Like Carmen, Spanish people don't use electric kettles much, so there wasn't a great deal of choice, but we bought another kettle, identical to

NEWS AND A PLAN

our first, then finished our shopping. Back at home, I removed the new kettle from its box, rinsed it and plugged it in ready for use.

"You make the coffee and I'll finish putting the shopping away," I said.

Soon we were sitting at the kitchen table, coffee mugs and a slice each of almond cake in front of us. Joe took a big slurp of coffee. To my astonishment, his eyes bulged, then he spat it out, drenching me, the table and our almond cake.

"WHAT THE?" he spluttered, sprinting to the sink and rinsing out his mouth.

I gaped at him, then sniffed my coffee.

"Which kettle did you use?" I asked, mopping coffee off myself and the table.

"The one you'd already filled with water."

"I didn't fill the kettle," I said. "The old one had the vinegar and water solution in it... You didn't use that one, did you?"

Of course he had.

I highly recommend white wine vinegar for removing limescale, but please, not for coffee...

࿐࿐࿐

We had to wait until May before the news flew around the village. Pancho the mayor had another announcement to make.

"It has to be about the cemetery," I said to Joe excitedly.

"Well, we'll soon find out," he said.

SPANISH ALMOND CAKE

This delicious Spanish cake recipe was donated by a reader and has become a firm favourite with us.

Ingredients

- 125g (4½ oz) ground almonds
- 3 large eggs, separated
- 125g (4½ oz) sugar
- zest of lemon
- pinch of salt

Method

- Preheat oven to 350°F / 180°C / Gas Mark 4.
- Grease and flour a 7-inch (18cm) cake tin.
- Whip egg yolks in a bowl with sugar, salt and lemon zest.
- Add almonds and mix well until it becomes a very stiff paste.
- In another bowl, whip the egg whites to a soft peak and add one spoonful to the almond mix to loosen it.
- Carefully fold the rest of the almond mix into the whipped egg whites, but don't over-mix it.
- Place in the prepared cake tin, there is no need to level it too much.
- Bake in the oven for 30 to 35 mins or until it is golden brown. (A toothpick comes out clean when inserted in the centre.)
- Leave to cool on wire rack; it may sink a little in the middle.
- Dust with icing sugar and serve slightly warm with good quality ice cream.

Kindly donated by reader Jill Richardson, Derby, UK.

26

SORTING THINGS OUT

"Hello, Alice, nice to hear your voice. How are you?"

"Oh, not too bad. Getting old, of course. How is your family?"

"Oh, very well. Looking forward to my daughter, son-in-law and granddaughter coming over to visit us here in Spain later this year."

"Good! I called because I remembered something more about your grandmother, Anna."

"Oh yes?"

"Yes. Your grandmother, my aunt Anna, loved dogs, as I've already told you."

"Yes."

"When I was a little girl, I badly wanted a dog but my mother wouldn't allow me. Aunt Anna came to stay and said to my mother, 'For goodness' sake, let the child have a dog,' but my mother refused. When Anna left and went home, we received a telegram."

"What did it say?"

Alice chuckled, remembering what had happened a lifetime ago.

"It was addressed to my mother and said, *Urgent. Box arriving for Alice on the 6.00pm train. Please collect.*"

"Gosh!"

"I was so excited! At six o'clock my mother and I went to meet the train and were directed to a crate. Inside was a dachshund puppy. Well, of course, my mother wasn't pleased at all, but I loved it and my mother loved it, too, in the end. Your grandmother was a very kind woman."

𐂂𐂂𐂂

In May, I was thrilled to little pieces when *Two Old Fools on a Camel* hit the New York Times bestseller list. But I was just as excited to hear what announcement Pancho the mayor was going to make at the meeting he had called.

Overhead, the sun was beginning its descent and the sky stretched blue and vast as the villagers gathered in the square. Somehow the atmosphere was different. Alejandro Senior and his crowd stood tall and proud, as though they knew something the others didn't. Paco's side of the square looked curious, apprehensive.

The mayor approached the wooden box that

Geronimo had placed for him. He stepped up and the two distinct groups of villagers fell silent.

"Good evening," he said. "Today I come with good news for El Hoyo. Señor Alejandro Fernández Rodríguez has generously agreed that his land may be used for an extension to the cemetery. The land will remain legally in the hands of the Rodríguez family but the village has been given permission to use it indefinitely."

The crowd buzzed. Alejandro Senior stood with his arms folded, beaming benevolently.

"And that is not all," continued the mayor, holding his hand up for silence again. "I have another announcement. Señor Alejandro Fernández Rodríguez has also generously agreed to pay for the work himself, out of his own pocket. His team will draw the plans and take care of all the construction."

"Bravo! Bravo mi amigo!" shouted Paco, breaking the stunned silence and strode across the square to his old friend, clapping him on the back and pumping his hand.

As though Paco's shout was a signal, the village square became a mass of cheering, handshaking, hugging and kissing as families merged and congratulated each other and Alejandro Senior. Dogs barked. Geronimo took a huge swig of beer from his bottle and Marcia allowed herself a little smile. I saw Alejandro Junior make a beeline for Sofía and they stood, arms wrapped around each other, Sofía's head resting on his shoulder as the crowd seethed around them.

"Perfect!" I said to Joe. "The perfect solution! Alejandro Senior gets to keep his land, but lends it to the village. I wonder how Mother pulled that one off?"

"We'll have to ask her," he said, smiling.

So we did. We popped over to the next village, a few nice bottles of celebratory red in our hands and knocked on Judith and Mother's door.

"Come in, m'dears!" said Judith. "So you've heard the news? Top-hole, isn't it? Mother and I are sitting outside. Let's open those bottles and have a little drinky-poo."

The evening was still warm as the sun went down and stars began to pop out. When the dogs had calmed down sufficiently for us to talk, I asked the burning question.

"Mother, how on *earth* did you manage to change Alejandro Senior's mind? We've heard he can be very stubborn."

Mother smiled to herself and sipped from her glass, taking her time.

"I'll tell 'em!" said Judith. "You appealed to the silly old man's vanity, didn't you, Mother?"

Mother nodded and blew a smoke ring into the night air.

"Mother suggested he keep the land in his name, but let the village use it. Well, the old codger wouldn't agree to that at first. So Mother said, what about if he had the extension built himself so he could control it and designed some big fancy gates with his family name worked into them."

Mother smiled.

"He liked that," she whispered.

"Mother, that was inspired!" I said admiringly.

"Brilliant!" said Joe, then pulled a face. "I just hope in future generations that his family don't claim the land back. They'd have to dig up all the deceased and move them."

"Well, it's all sorted for the foreseeable future," I said. "A job well done, Mother! Thank you."

As a million stars flickered above us, we raised our glasses and drank a toast to Mother, Alejandro Senior, future generations and the new cemetery.

�☃☃☃

With our Australian family's visit drawing ever closer, Joe and I tried to spruce up the house a little. Naturally this was yet another opportunity for a domestic disaster.

I guess it was all my fault because there was nothing really wrong with our toilet seat. It was just old and I wanted a new one. Joe agreed. Although it was perfectly serviceable, we'd had it for nine years since we'd first built the bathroom back in 2004 when we moved to Spain.

The next time we went down the mountain, we visited our local DIY store. We headed straight for the bathroom section and gazed with awe at the dazzling display of toilet seats fixed to the wall. Such choice! Transparent ones, coloured ones, ones with seashells, zebra-print ones ... even one that glowed in the dark.

"Just a plain one, I think," I said at last.

Joe agreed and we picked out a handsome, black, wooden seat and carried it to the checkout. It cost 35 euros, which seemed rather a lot, but it was a good quality seat, heavy and polished.

"Are you sure it'll fit?" I asked Joe.

"Of course it will! Toilet seats have universal fixings. I'll fit it as soon as we get home."

True to his word, he removed the old toilet seat and attached the new one. He was right, the fixings were correct. At first sight, the seat looked good. It wasn't *exactly* the right shape, but only an obsessive toilet inspector would have noticed. Joe hurled the old seat, plus the packaging of the new one, into the village dumpster.

It was only after Joe had tested it that we discovered a fault. The seat, and lid, had a habit of slamming down without warning, especially during mid-flow, which he found most disconcerting. He put up with it for a few days, but after a few near-misses, he decided it had to go. The seat was threatening to inflict permanent anatomical damage.

"I'm going down the mountain to get another one," he said, "and this time I'm going to get the right shape."

"Don't you want to take some measurements?"

"No, I know now that we need a D-shaped one. Don't worry, I'll recognise the right thing when I see it."

He returned with a plain white seat, even more expensive than the black one. In case we needed to take it back, we unwrapped it carefully, tearing open the plastic wrappings but keeping the box intact. Joe tried it for size. Perfect.

He removed the black one, then howled with dismay. The new, white seat was the right size and shape, but the *fittings* were completely wrong.

Luckily, we'd kept the receipt and the box, so Joe repacked it and went back down the mountain. When he came back, he was empty-handed and shaking his head.

"It all went wrong," he said. "They wouldn't give me my money back because it was missing the inside plastic coverings. I just left it there, it's no good to us. And they didn't have any others that would fit our toilet, so we're stuck with the evil black one."

All in all, if one included the cost of petrol plus the price of the useless second purchase, we had spent nearly 100 euros on our new toilet seat.

There are times when I am very glad I am female.

"Mum, we were thinking that it might be nice to invite Luciano out to Spain at the same time as when we are there."

Luc (pronounced Looch) was one of my daughter's greatest friends from university. I'd met him for the first time at Karly and Cam's wedding in Australia. He'd travelled out from the UK and formed an important part of the bridal party as her 'bridesman'. Not to be outdone, Cam also had his old friend Hayley as a 'groomsmaid'.

At the time, bride, groom and many of the bridal party stayed in a house on the outskirts of Sydney, which had been rented for the wedding. Space had been scarce, so my niece Becky and I shared the bottom tier of a bunk bed, while Luc slept above us. Such intimacy in our living and sleeping arrangements meant we got to know each other well and I was delighted at Karly's suggestion that Luc should visit us in Spain.

Luc was duly invited and he accepted immediately. He had a passion for driving, so instead of flying straight into Almería airport, he decided to hire a car and drive from Málaga. It would be a trip of many hours, but a good opportunity to see something of Spain and compare it with his native Sicily.

Preparations were now in full swing and I was so excited to be seeing the little family again. Ten months had slipped by since I'd last seen Indy and I knew she would be a very different little person from the baby I'd left behind in

Melbourne. Those ten months of separation had been hard, but eased a little by the daily photos winging their way from Australia to El Hoyo. They showed Indy smiling, then crawling, then standing. I could not wait to cuddle her again.

We borrowed a highchair from a friend in the next village. We already had a stroller, a paddling pool and a travel cot.

When I'd finished cleaning the rooms, I fetched the cot and opened the box. It all came out in one piece and as *Simple Assembly, No Tools Needed* was written in big letters on the side of the box, I imagined erecting it would be a piece of *bizcocho* (cake).

It came out of the box as a single unit. Releasing a few clips, I was soon gazing at what looked like a disjointed tripod. I pulled. I pushed. I searched for hidden switches, buttons or levers. I turned it upside down and tried again. And then I admitted defeat.

"Joe! Come and give me a hand. I can't get this wretched travel cot up."

"Don't be ridiculous," said Joe, coming into the room. "Look, it says, *Simple Assembly, No Tools Needed* on the side. Here, give it to me, this'll take seconds."

I pushed it over to him and watched, arms folded, toe tapping, eyebrows raised.

He pulled.

He pushed.

He searched for hidden switches, buttons or levers. He turned it upside down and tried again.

He's going to blame the design now, I thought to myself.

"There's obviously a design fault," he said, scratching himself before he abandoned me.

So, for the third time I battled and failed again.

I went downstairs and typed in the travel cot brand on the Internet. Up popped a YouTube video entitled *'How to erect your travel cot in less than 30 seconds'*.

I watched in awe. So that was how it was done! *Pull out the end struts, pull up the base* and hey presto, it all snapped into place! I ran back upstairs and tried it. It worked!

"Joe, come here, I know how to do it!"

"Really? Show me..."

Joe entered the bedroom and watched my performance. *Pull out, pull up, snap!* I was even faster the second time.

"Well," he said, admiration in his voice. "I take my hat off to you. How did you work that out?"

"Oh, natural intelligence, of course. You know, a woman's intuition."

Not a mention of my friend Mr Google. My nose probably grew twelve inches.

I checked everything for the last time. I paid particular attention to Luc's room, remembering how clean and tidy he had been in Australia. I checked the jars of baby food, toys, towels, buckets and spades, the food in the fridge, special baby milk…

I also checked the pile of wrapped presents, birthday cake, balloons and bubble makers. Indy would be celebrating her first birthday in Spain.

STUFFED TOMATOES

Colourful and delicious. Experiment with other ingredients like black olives, mushrooms, bacon, spices, chillies, capers, etc.

Ingredients

- 4 medium to large tomatoes
- 3 - 4 slices of bread
- 1-2 cloves of garlic roughly chopped
- ½ onion roughly chopped
- A good handful of herbs (oregano, basil, thyme, parsley, etc)
- A good handful of Parmesan cheese (grated)
- Half a cup of any nuts (almonds, walnuts, etc) you may have, except peanuts
- Salt to taste
- Black pepper
- Oil (depending on type/thickness of bread, approx ¼ cup)

Method

- Cut the top off the tomatoes and scoop out the centre. Discard the pulp but keep the lid.

- In a food processor blend all the stuffing ingredients except the oil. I roughly chop the nuts first.

- Lastly drizzle in the oil. The mixture should be crumbly but firm when squeezed by hand.

- Spoon the mixture into each tomato and place the lids on top.

- Bake in a moderate oven for 20 – 30 mins. To keep them upright I set them on a tray and bunch some tinfoil around them.

Recipe and photo kindly donated by reader Louise Lamb.

27

HIGHS AND LOWS

Before our visitors arrived in Spain, they had spent a week in England catching up with other family members and introducing Indy to a host of friends who hadn't yet met her or Cam.

Their flight from Australia had been horrendous. A couple of weeks before their journey, Indy had suffered from an ear infection. The doctor had pronounced her fit to travel, but he was wrong. The poor little mite screamed for 15 solid hours on the flight. It can't have been much fun for Mum and Dad or their fellow passengers. Karly and Cam were reduced to walking up and down the aisle trying to pacify her.

After a week in the UK, Indy was back to her usual sunny self. At last the day came for their arrival in Spain.

"Time to drive to the airport," said Joe.

And then suddenly, there she was, bouncing in her mother's arms.

I held her, stroked her soft, baby skin, played with her curls and drank in the scent of her, making up for lost time.

Our house came to life, ringing with Indy's giggles. Floors, once clean and tidy, were strewn with toys and smeared with baby food. Books were pulled out of the bookcase and papers scattered across the floor. Baby bottles appeared on the draining-board and baby paraphernalia covered every surface. After 24 hours it seemed as though they'd always been there. We loved it.

We discussed their forthcoming move from Melbourne back to Sydney and how they planned to buy a new house with a garden and plenty of space for grandparents to stay. Life was wonderful.

Luc arrived in the tiniest car, sending us into peals of laughter. It looked like a Noddy car and he looked exactly like Enid Blyton's Noddy sitting behind the wheel.

But it was useful having another vehicle. There were so many of us and Indy's car seat took up a lot of space in our car.

One night, we went to Judith's village and had a meal at the outdoor restaurant there. It opened at 9 in the evening, which was far too late for Indy to be up. Joe kindly offered to stay home and

HIGHS AND LOWS

babysit. We all enjoyed sitting under the almond trees and the food was good.

"Was Indy okay?" Karly asked when we arrived home after midnight.

"Never heard a peep," said Joe. "She never woke at all."

Unfortunately, Indy woke up as soon as her parents entered the room. She howled, rather spoiling poor Karly and Cam's night and it took several hours before she settled again. She was teething, so easily forgiven as most of the time she was a happy baby.

The Spanish are extremely family-oriented. Carmen wondered at how we lived so far from our families as her family had never ventured out of Andalucía and had no wish to. In the village, every new baby was proudly shown off and now I had a baby to show off too. I knew that Carmen and Paco wanted to see Indy and visiting them would be a good opportunity for Cam to see the interior of a typical village cottage. This was his first visit to Spain and, being Australian, he was fascinated by village life, which was so different from his own back home.

"*Guapa!*" shouted Paco.

"*Guapa!*" exclaimed Carmen, stroking Indy's hair.

Indy beamed at her.

"Is she walking yet?"

"No," I said, "but she crawls really fast."

To demonstrate, I set her down on Carmen's

floor. Indy shot off at a rate of knots, closely followed by a snuffling Yukky.

I caught Cam looking around the neat little house with its host of family photographs crowding its white walls. No doubt he was comparing the tiny interior with the large, airy, spacious houses of his native Australia.

Our next stop was the village shop. Uncle Felix sat outside and forgot his reticence long enough to touch Indy's cheek with his ancient, horned finger.

We entered the shop and Cam stared around in disbelief. There was nothing in the shop apart from a counter, cobwebs hanging from the ceiling and a yellowed portrait of the village saint. No shelves of merchandise, no freezers full of food, no fresh produce. Not remotely like the supermarkets he was accustomed to in Australia.

"*Guapa!*" said Marcia and offered Indy a lollypop from under the counter.

Karly thanked her and slipped the lollypop into her own pocket. She didn't want to start rotting Indy's teeth before they had even grown. Indy cooed at Marcia's black cat as it wound itself round the old lady's ankles.

On the evening before Indy's birthday, Joe and I inflated fifty balloons and hung them everywhere to surprise her when she came down next day. I couldn't wait for her to open her presents.

The balloons were a great success and

entertained Indy (and us) no end as she chased after and caught them. Of course she was far more interested in tasting the tinsel and eating the paper than the gifts themselves. Eventually each present was opened and then it was time to move outside so she could enjoy her birthday cake.

We put the cake on the ground, in the middle of a large plastic tablecloth decorated with birthday greetings.

The idea was that she could dive in, making as much of a mess of herself as she pleased. Unfortunately it backfired a little because Indy was uncertain about the strange looking thing in front of her. Instead of heading for the cake, she turned and headed for her mum. However, after a little encouragement, she got the idea and managed to cover almost every part of herself and the sheet with the cake.

A splash in the paddling pool washed off any excess cake. She cooed and gurgled as bits of cake, plastic frogs and ducks floated around her, while she made every effort to empty the pool using a plastic bucket.

Cleaning the cake off the plastic birthday sheet had an unexpected consequence. We hosed it down and left it on a glass table to dry out in the sun. The next morning we found the tabletop had shattered, much like a car windscreen does during an impact. Initially, we thought somebody had thrown something heavy over the wall and it had struck the table. Highly unlikely and no missiles were lying on the ground so we dismissed that theory. We could only surmise that water trapped under the plastic cloth had been heated by the sun during the day and then cooled overnight, causing the table to shatter. Sweeping the garden took forever as the bits of glass had flown far and wide.

Apart from that small mishap, the days were filled with banter and laughter and we loved it. Indy enjoyed sampling the Spanish fruit and soon became a big fan of peaches and watermelon.

We never tired of teasing Luc about his toy car, but he was a good sport and took it in his stride.

Evenings were spent eating and drinking outside under the vine. We shared cooking duties and one night Luc cooked us a delicious Italian dish.

All too soon the visit came to an end.

"We're going to try really hard to come over to Australia this winter," I told Karly and Cam.

"We've contacted our builders," said Joe. "We want to make sure this house is totally secure so we can come over for a few months."

"We should be in our new house by then," said Karly, excitedly. "We should have loads of room."

"So we'll probably see you in a few months," I repeated, trying hard to look on the bright side.

"Time to drive to the airport," said Joe.

With leaden hearts, we waved our family goodbye.

I tidied away the books and toys, packed away

the cot and stroller, washed the sticky fingerprints off the walls and emptied the paddling-pool. A few balloons still remained, drifting aimlessly across the floor. I knew I should pop them and throw them away, but I didn't. The balloons reminded me too much of Indy giving chase, scuttling across the floor on all-fours at great speed and squealing with delight when she caught one.

⁂

As another summer began to die, so did the leaves on our vine. Our garden needed tidying constantly and we always had rubbish to dispose of.

Since moving to El Hoyo, we'd discovered that the Spanish are extremely resourceful and find ingenious ways to use items that Brits happily throw away. The previous owner of our house used an old upside-down frying pan to cap one of the chimneys to stop the rain coming in and sparks flying out. It was a little quirky but worked perfectly well. So we kept it, giving it a new coat of black paint every now and then.

Any person walking in the Spanish countryside will soon encounter gates barring entry to private property. Closer inspection will reveal that these gates are often homemade and can be quite elaborate. One such existed close to our village, halfway up the mountain. The owner had fixed two metal bed frames, with springs and all, to posts. The frames met in the middle and were padlocked together, making a very serviceable portal. Topped with an old bed-head and a weather vane, it was almost a work of art.

We learned all kinds of tips from the villagers. For instance, we kept and dried the annual prunings from our grapevine as they made excellent fire-starters in the wood stove.

However, El Hoyo hadn't yet embraced the ethic of recycling daily household waste. We had no bins of different colours for different types of trash. All rubbish, whether glass, paper or general waste, was hurled unsorted into the same bin. People often left the lid open and village cats dived in to search for scraps. As the sun beat down, unpleasant odours of rotting food wafted out. Then, at six o'clock every morning, the refuse collection men arrived to take it all away.

When we first came to the village, communal bins were conveniently placed at most street corners. But times changed and since the economic crisis, cutbacks were made.

"It's gone," said Joe one day, coming back into the house still carrying a bag of trash.

"What's gone?"

"The garbage bin. The one next to the cemetery."

"Really? I expect they've just moved it. They are planning to begin work on the extension soon, perhaps they wanted it out of the way."

HIGHS AND LOWS

"Well, I can't find it."

We traipsed round the streets looking for a skip and finally located one near the square. For the next few weeks, throwing rubbish away became a game of hide-and-seek as the bins never remained in the same place twice. Good exercise, but slightly annoying and Joe constantly complained.

Then, one day, a massive, shiny new bin appeared in its original place beside the cemetery. It gleamed with newness and around the base was a metal bar. For a while, Joe wrestled to open the lid, sweating and cursing, then discovered that if he stood on the bar, the lid magically snapped open. His good temper was restored.

No longer would the village cats be able to sneak in and ferret out the wonderful delicacies a communal garbage bin had to offer. But Joe was happy.

Until a rather unfortunate incident occurred.

LUC'S ITALIAN PASTA WITH FRESH TOMATO SAUCE

In the classic Italian tomato sauce you would normally start with the *soffritto*, onion and garlic finely chopped and fried in olive oil until blond, then you add the tomatoes, but with this version you cook all at once, hence the 'all fresh' thing… All quantities can be modified.

Serves 4

Ingredients

- 1kg (2.2lb) of ripe, juicy tomatoes
- 1 onion
- 1 or 2 cloves of garlic
- 3 or 4 tablespoons of olive oil
- 1 bunch basil leaves
- 1 teaspoon sea salt (for the sauce)
- 1 tablespoon sea salt (for the pasta)
- 500g (18oz) pasta (dry or fresh, any variety you like)

- 100g (3½oz) grated Parmesan cheese (or 1 mozzarella ball)

Method

- Chop the onion and the garlic, as fine or thick as you like, then chop the tomatoes. Put all together in a pan.

- Add olive oil and salt, give it a nice stir and put it on the stove on a nice lively flame.

- When it starts bubbling, lower the flame and keep cooking for 10-15 minutes, until the tomatoes lose identity and the sauce starts thickening. Make sure it doesn't thicken too much though as you still need it fairly fluid to use on the pasta. When the sauce reaches this stage, turn off the flame and stir in the basil leaves. Your sauce is ready!

- As for the pasta, you can start cooking this as soon as the sauce goes on the stove. You will need a tall pan, three quarters full with water. Add the salt and as soon as the water starts boiling add in the pasta.

- Cook for just over 10 minutes (or follow the timing advised on the package), then drain thoroughly (nothing worse than a waterlogged pasta).

- At this point add the sauce to the pasta, liberally sprinkle with Parmesan cheese, or alternatively chop the mozzarella and add it instead of the Parmesan... Enjoy and don't forget to have some fresh crispy bread at hand to scoop up the sauce left in the plate at the end.

Recipe kindly donated by Luciano Balloi.

28

PREPARATIONS

Joe stepped on the bar, watched the lid jump open, then absent-mindedly threw the car keys into the dumpster instead of the bag of rubbish he was holding in his other hand. He stared in disbelief into the depths of the vast bin before turning the air blue with Anglo-Saxon profanities.

The bin was empty and the car keys lay at the bottom, winking at him. He leaned down into the bin, reaching for the keys, but they were tantalisingly just out of reach. He stretched further, until the keys were only inches from his fingertips. With one last effort, he tried again. And that's when catastrophe struck.

As he reached down, his feet left the rail and the dumpster's lid snapped shut.

"Hey!" he shouted into the bin's dark interior,

his legs flailing as he tried to push the lid back up and slide his body out.

But the bin was not letting go its hold. He couldn't push the lid up and his feet couldn't reach the rail. He was afraid to squirm too much in case he overbalanced completely and fell into the bin.

"Hey! Help! ¡Ayúdeme!"

As luck would have it, he had to wait only a few minutes for rescue, although he later told me that each minute felt like a lifetime.

Fortunately, Pancho the mayor happened to walk round the corner, no doubt to check some detail at the cemetery. He quickly stepped on the foot rail and the lid flew up, releasing its hold on Joe.

"Ah, good, I was hoping to see you or Beaky," he said, as Joe brushed himself down.

He didn't seem at all surprised at Joe's predicament and didn't even question why Joe was headfirst in the village dumpster.

"In case you were wondering, I dropped my car keys in the bin," explained Joe. "Would you mind standing on the rail so I can get them out?"

So the mayor stood on the rail again and Joe managed to reach the keys successfully without the lid descending on him again. Pancho carried on talking.

"I was going to ask Beaky to arrange our first session of English lessons," he said. "Could you ask her to get in touch with me, please?"

Joe assured him he would, stopped rubbing his bruises and made his way home.

"Well, I'm certainly not going to get in touch with him," I said firmly, having heard Joe's tale of woe, finishing with the mayor's request.

"I'm going to take a shower," said Joe. "Wash the bin smell off me."

"One question... When it happened, why didn't you find a stick and fish the keys out?" I asked. "Or call me to stand on the rail to keep the lid open?"

"Oh," said Joe, a highly educated man with a string of letters after his name. "I didn't think of that."

⚜⚜⚜

"I think we should chase the builders again," I said to Joe that autumn. "If we're going to Australia in the New Year, we must have our new window bars finished. Especially if we're going to be away for a couple of months or so."

It wasn't just the security of the house that worried us. The upstairs door that led onto the roof terrace had become warped and was letting in water. Whenever it rained, water poured under the door and flooded the floor so badly that water ran down the walls into our dining room below. We needed the house to be both secure and watertight before we left for Australia.

PREPARATIONS

We'd first contacted the builders back in March.

"We'll come and look at the job next week," Julio had said at the time. He was the boss, Romanian and fluent in English and Spanish.

The builders had arrived in June to take measurements. We chose the doors and burglar-bar designs and were excited about getting the work done. A week later we received an estimate and agreed on the price.

"It'll be nice to get it all done before Karly, Cam and Indy come in August," I had said to Joe.

"Pigs might fly," he snorted.

He was right. Nothing happened. Our family and granddaughter arrived and the summer was now making way for autumn. The sun still blazed and there hadn't been a drop of rain, so replacing the leaky door wasn't essential. Winter still seemed a long way off.

In September we phoned the builders again.

"Your new doors and bars are ready," said Julio. "We will start work next week."

"Pigs might fly," snorted Joe.

The builders arrived early in October. They brought the new doors and laid them out on the roof terrace and in the garden. They tapped the walls with a hammer and left a few pencil marks. I was delighted that work had begun.

"That's good!" I said. "It'll all be finished before the fiesta and the Gin Twins' visit at the end of the month."

"Hurrumph!" snorted Joe. "Pigs might fly."

Summer stretched long that year and the village fiesta weekend approached. The builders didn't turn up, but as the village was so busy, it was probably just as well.

It was around that time that I developed big red splotches all over my body. They appeared on my arms, hands, legs, elbows and even my face. I wondered if it was some kind of allergy. I felt fine and they didn't itch but the look of the spots made me self-conscious and I avoided mirrors. For the first time, I didn't go to any of the fiesta events.

Luckily, our roof terrace commanded a perfect view of the village, so at least I could be a spectator. I watched as all the villagers arrived with their friends and families. I saw Geronimo let off the fireworks that marked the beginning of the festivities. Unseen, I saw all of Alejandro Senior's family pile into Paco's house for a few drinks and tapas before ambling down to the square. It was good to see them all firm friends again.

Over the weekend, Joe and I watched the processions, the marches and the games. We saw the band strike up in the square and watched the dancing.

We watched the village ladies carefully carry their dishes to the square for the Pudding Contest and the men take their bottles of wine for judging. Paco never entered the Wine Contest. He always said there was no point as everybody knew his

PREPARATIONS

grapes made the best wine. It wouldn't be fair to the other contestants if he won year after year.

We saw groups of visitors making their way to the cemetery. Villagers pointed out the progress of the enlargement, although at the moment there wasn't much to see except marker stakes.

I loved watching it all, but there was one particular little scenario that filled my heart with hope.

The Ufarte house had remained empty and locked up after Lola and her seedy-looking partner had left. But on the Saturday afternoon of the fiesta, I saw two people unlock the front door of the little house and enter. It was Papa and Mama Ufarte.

Were they back together? I tried to read their body language. The children weren't with them and Maribel had regained her lithe figure after her latest pregnancy. She looked well and her hair shone with health. Papa Ufarte looked more relaxed than I had seen him for a long time.

Their visit was short but it was a good sign and gave me hope. Perhaps Maribel had forgiven her foolish husband. But until they returned with all the children and the old grandmother, until Papa Ufarte strummed his guitar and Maribel danced in the street, I couldn't count on it.

On Sunday evening, the village emptied again as the cars followed each other, nose to tail, up the winding road and out of the valley.

The weather stayed beautiful for the Gin

Twins' stay. The swallows hung around for longer than usual but there was still no sign of the builders. The Gin Twins had to share their roof terrace space with the new doors, laid out and ready to be fitted. In the garden below, the burglar-bars leaned against a wall awaiting installation. The sun soon turned the Gin Twins' pale skin the same colour as the rusting burglar-bars.

November came and the days shortened. After a couple of wild nights of driving rain, water leaked under the old door upstairs. We mopped up as fast as we could, but water still seeped through the floor and streamed down the dining room walls. Getting the builders in was becoming decidedly urgent. I called them on the phone and emailed, but couldn't make contact.

One evening after dark, Joe was in the city taking a short-cut through some waste ground to get back to the car. In Spain, many shops don't close until 10:00pm. A huge figure suddenly loomed out of the shadows. Joe clutched his purchases and car keys tighter and quickened his pace.

"Joe! Joe! It is I, Mario!" boomed a voice from the darkness. "My boss is Julio! We are your builders. We come next week."

"Oh! Hello Mario," Joe said, greatly relieved. "Fancy seeing you here!"

"Yes, I saw you in the shop and followed you."

PREPARATIONS

"Oh I see. Well, we are really looking forward to seeing you next week."

However, Joe wasn't totally convinced.

"Did you see that pink thing flying past our window?" Joe asked me a week later.

But this time he was wrong. Our builders did arrive. But in our village things rarely go smoothly. Unfortunately they picked the week when the cemetery works began in earnest. Their arrival also coincided with a major overhaul of El Hoyo's sewage system and a resurfacing of the main street. Unable to bring their equipment to our house, the builders shrugged and disappeared once again.

"Well, there's nothing more we can do," I said to Joe. "We'll just have to be patient. This is Spain, after all. In the meantime, perhaps we should dig out and check our passports. Then we can book flights as soon as the building work is done."

It felt good preparing for the trip to Australia. Cam, Karly and Indy would soon move to their new house. Humming to myself, I found and opened our passports.

Valid until 2014? To my horror I discovered that our passports would expire in January. We wouldn't be travelling anywhere unless we renewed them immediately.

Nothing is ever simple. Living in Spain, we couldn't just pop to the post office and get them renewed.

I hurriedly researched the renewal process for overseas residents. I found the relevant government website and read it carefully. The fee was hefty, £295.72 ($500). Ouch! They also required a signed declaration form and two passport photos. That seemed simple enough.

I began with the forms, which I could download and print off. Of course, the ink had dried in our home printer, which infuriated Joe. He always maintained it would be cheaper to buy a new printer every time we needed to print something rather than pay for yet another cartridge of printer ink.

We bought more ink and completed the forms successfully. The next hurdle was the passport photographs.

"Have you ever seen a photo booth anywhere?" I asked Joe.

He thought hard. "Nope, I don't think I have. I guess we'll have to go to a photographer's shop?"

Carmen and Paco, having never been out of Spain, had no need of passports and no idea where we might find a booth or a shop that produced passport photos. So we went in search of a professional photographer.

Surprisingly, we found one quite easily and entered his shop, full of hope.

"Passport photos? No, we only do weddings, family portraits and fiestas," said the assistant, surrounded by galleries of arty photos showing smiling brides, babies and happy families.

PREPARATIONS

"Can you suggest anywhere we can go to get them done?" asked Joe.

The man was very helpful, even drawing us a little street map. We eventually tracked down the little shop he recommended. We'd passed it a thousand times and had never noticed it before. Other than seeing a few photo frames in the window display, we weren't very hopeful. We pushed the door open and entered.

The shop was filled with all sorts of strange paraphernalia: flower vases, snow-globes, luggage straps and calendars. The walls were plastered with posters and, to our astonishment, one showed an array of passport photos.

"We'd each like a set of passport photos," Joe said to the smiling young assistant behind the counter. "Like those," he said, pointing at the poster.

"Of course," said the girl. "Follow me."

She led us into a small back room where a stool had been placed in front of a white screen. Gleefully we each had a set of photos taken and the assistant waited for a machine to spit them out. Then, using a special clipper tool, she helpfully cut them to size.

"I can't believe it was so easy!" I said to Joe as we left the shop with our precious photos.

My smugness, however, was short-lived. Did you know that Spanish and British passport photo sizes are different? I didn't know that until I checked the passport website again. Back we went to have another set taken and this time the girl cut them to the UK size.

I was on the point of sealing the envelope addressed to the Passport Office when I noticed something else. Not only is the size of the photo important, but the *dimensions of the head* are significant too. Our latest photos were still wrong. We needed to have them taken again. By now we were on first-name terms with the girl in the shop.

Third time lucky, we hoped. We posted the photos and forms to England, hoping everything was in order. We were told that the Passport Office would need at least 4 weeks to process our applications and allowing for the Christmas holiday period, we doubted if we'd get them until well into the New Year.

Then, wonder of wonders, the week before Christmas, our builders returned. They did such a fantastic job replacing the door and fitting the burglar-bars that we kept thinking of more jobs for them to do before they disappeared again. They replaced all our windows and we were delighted with their work. All the winter draughts vanished and at last our house was watertight and secure.

We waited for news of our passports and hoped that the UK Passport Office would find our applications satisfactory. If it did, we'd soon be on our way to Australia.

Christmas passed without incident and Joe

PREPARATIONS

and I were presented with hand-knitted hats by Marcia. Neither of us ever wore hats but we were touched by the thought.

We also received a phone call from Karly in Australia.

ANA'S LEMON LEAVES

"Ana is my Spanish neighbour and she makes these for all the kids (and me). Ana cannot read or write and brought up her brothers and sisters while her dad worked in French vineyards and her mum worked on the land. Ana says her mum used to make this during the Civil War as a treat for her 8 children as she had no money. Honestly, they're dead yummy!"

Frankie Knight

Method

- Pick some very large lemon leaves. Wash thoroughly.

- Mix up some batter (egg, milk, flour) and dip the leaves, holding by the stalk, in the batter, making sure they are totally covered.

- Drop the whole sprig into very hot, deep fat and fry for a few minutes. When you see the batter start to separate from the leaf, remove carefully with a large kitchen spoon onto kitchen paper.

- Then place on a plate of sugar, turning to coat all the batter.

- Carefully remove the leaf from inside batter (it should come out easily).

- Discard leaf and eat batter immediately! It will be crunchy and taste of lemon.

29

WINTER

"Merry Christmas, Mum!"

"Merry Christmas! How has your day been?"

"Lovely, we had a *brilliant* day. We *love* the new house and I cooked Christmas dinner for twelve! Cam's parents and grandparents came and it was really good. Indy was spoilt rotten of course."

"Oh, good! So how do you like having Christmas in midsummer?"

"Well, I'm pretty used to Aussie Christmases now. Doesn't feel that strange anymore. We've filled the swimming pool and we use it every day. Are you still coming over, do you think? Escape your winter and enjoy our summer? Time's running out now."

"Well, I don't know... Our passports still haven't arrived. We've been watching the news and the weather in the UK has been awful.

Terrible floods, worst on record. What with Christmas and trains and planes being cancelled by bad weather, who knows when we'll get our passports? All we can do is wait."

※※※

Joe had gone out shopping and I was on my own when somebody knocked on the door. I knew who it was because I had seen him passing the window. It was Pancho the mayor.

My mind raced. *No way* was I letting him in, especially as Joe wasn't there to protect me from his unwelcome attentions.

Lightning fast, I grabbed my jacket and Marcia's woolly hat. Pulling them on, I opened the door.

"Beaky, I…"

"Oh hello, Pancho!" I said breathlessly and slammed the front door behind me. "I'm so sorry but I'm in a tearing hurry. I can't stop, I'm late for a very important appointment."

I pushed past him and jogged down the street, leaving him gaping after me.

Where to go? Joe had taken the car so there was no point unlocking the garage. I scooted round the corner and up the next street. I had the house keys in my hand. My aim was to re-enter the house through the seldom-used upstairs door that opened onto that street. Swiftly, I unlocked it and let myself in.

Panting, I waited to catch my breath. I didn't immediately go downstairs because Pancho might still be lurking outside. I wouldn't put it past him to make an effort to peer through the high living-room window.

Thank goodness, I heard Joe returning and it sounded as though he was alone. I went downstairs.

"Oh, I wondered where you were," said Joe. "Why were you upstairs in the flat? And why are you wearing outdoor clothes?"

I explained about Pancho knocking on the door and my cunning escape.

"Quick thinking," said Joe. "but why Marcia's hat?"

"I just wanted it to look as though I was going out."

"Look in the mirror," said Joe, beginning to laugh.

"Why?"

"Just look."

Puzzled, I did so. The woolly hat looked ridiculous, but that wasn't the reason Joe was laughing. Because we had been on our own that Christmas, I had pinned cardboard reindeer antlers to both our hats and we had worn them all day, making each other laugh every time we caught sight of them. I hadn't removed the antlers. No wonder Pancho had gaped at me.

"I have a question," said Joe when he'd stopped laughing. "Why didn't you just *not* answer the door when Pancho knocked and pretend nobody was in?"

"Oh," I said, "I never thought of that."

※※※

It was an uncomfortable feeling being without our passports. We felt trapped without them and wondered what we would do in the event of an emergency. It had been over a month since we applied for them and we had even paid extra to have them delivered by courier.

I couldn't stop worrying. The chance of their arriving in time for us to make our trip to Australia was becoming slimmer. Had we filled out the forms correctly? Were our photographs acceptable? Had the passports been lost in the Christmas mail? Had they been destroyed in the terrible floods that the UK had recently suffered from?

"Even if they do arrive now," said Joe, "we've spent so much on house renovations recently, it might be best to wait until next winter and go to Australia then."

I was deeply disappointed, but Joe was right. I sighed.

"Yes, I suppose that's sensible. We could go over for the whole of next winter, perhaps."

One cold but sunny morning, we heard a commotion in the village. There were shouts and a large engine revving.

"What's going on?" asked Joe.

"I've no idea," I said, shaking my head. "Perhaps it's work going on at the cemetery? Excavations? Levelling the ground or something?"

Curious, we went outside to investigate. No, the commotion wasn't coming from the cemetery. We headed for what sounded like the source of the noise, which was coming from the direction of the square. The problem was soon obvious.

El Hoyo's streets are extremely narrow and the corners are all sharp right angles. Cars negotiated them with difficulty. Only pedestrians, Uncle Felix's mule and motorcycles sailed around them with ease.

A massive yellow lorry had tried to negotiate a corner and was stuck. The driver was standing beside the truck, scratching his head. Being January, there weren't many villagers around, but those that were had congregated at the scene.

Geronimo was gesticulating, pointing this way and that and shouting suggestions over the noise of the engine. Paco was there, firing off alternative suggestions, thumping the side of the enormous truck with his fist. Even ancient Marcia had left her shop and was leaning on her walking stick, shaking her head and muttering *madre mía* at regular intervals. Geronimo's three dogs barked with excitement, while Yukky cocked his leg enthusiastically on the truck's yellow paintwork. Only Uncle Felix stood back, leaning on his mule for support, his gnarled hand holding her rope halter. The mule stood quietly, occasionally shuffling her hooves.

The truck blocked the street entirely; it was going to take a lot of manoeuvring to get out of this jam. The driver climbed back into his cab and Paco, Geronimo and Joe took up their stations, shouting, waving and beckoning to the driver who leant out of the cab window, following their instructions. With much crunching of gears and squealing of brakes, the truck inched forward and back, forward and back, then reversed slowly back to the square.

The driver jumped out and all the men clapped each other on the back. Success. The truck's paintwork had been scraped only a little, leaving a telltale yellow stripe on a house wall. It could have been much worse. Geronimo drew a bottle of beer from his pocket and took a celebratory swig.

It was only then that I really noticed the writing on the side of the truck. 'DHL'.

The driver looked at his watch. "Does anyone know *Señor* and *Señora* Twead?" he asked.

All eyes turned to Joe and me.

"That's us," I squeaked.

The driver unlocked the enormous doors at the rear of his truck, revealing stacks of boxes and parcels ready to be delivered. He climbed in and disappeared into the dark, cavernous depths. We heard rummaging, then he reappeared clutching two small envelopes.

"For you," he said. "Please sign for them here."

I took the pen and signed, my face red. A truck the size of a house and all that fuss to deliver two small envelopes to us?

Back at home, we tore the envelopes open, but we already knew what they contained. In spite of Christmas, British floods and El Hoyo's tight corners, our passports had safely arrived, if rather dramatically...

※※※

The building of the cemetery extension was coming along well. We watched with interest as excavators and diggers arrived to gouge out the rocks and level the ground. The surrounding walls were built up and painted white. Gravel had been laid. The old entrance to the cemetery was taken down and a huge new one was built, with a paved path leading to it from the street. As yet unfinished, the entrance was just a gap, awaiting the arrival of the gates.

From our perch on the roof terrace, we watched a flatbed truck arrive with the gates strapped on. Then the mayor swept up in his car, swiftly followed by the three Alejandros in their flashy Mercedes.

Eight workmen lifted the gates from the truck

WINTER

and laid them on the ground. They carefully lifted them again and slotted them into place. It was not an easy task as the gates must have been nine feet high and were clearly very heavy. Then they tore off the protective covering, revealing the new entrance in all its glory.

"Bravo!" shouted Alejandro Junior and clapped his hands as his father, grandfather and Pancho stood back to admire the gates.

"Good gracious," said Joe. "Talk about a statement!"

Joe had a point. Even from our terrace we could read the inscription. Set into the elaborate design were the gilded words, *El Hoyo* and beneath, *El Cementerio de Rodríguez*. But the gates were magnificent. Painted glossy black, the wrought ironwork was a mass of intricate, sweeping curlicues.

"Have you seen the new cemetery gates?" Paco asked us that weekend.

"Yes," we said, "they are very handsome. Are all the villagers pleased with them?"

"*¡Claro!* On Andalucía Day El Hoyo will celebrate. At four o'clock, the mayor will give a speech and Alejandro will cut a ribbon and declare the new cemetery open. Then we will all walk up to the shrine for hot chocolate and *churros*."

And so it was.

On Andalucía Day, *everybody* turned up. A large crowd surrounded Pancho as he delivered his speech and all eyes were on Alejandro Senior as he cut the ribbon with a flourish and declared the cemetery open. The gates swung open and everybody cheered and clapped.

Then, united and chattering, the villagers swung round and began to walk up the steep path to the little shrine at the top of the mountain. The children and dogs galloped ahead while the adults straggled behind in knots. I concentrated on putting one foot in front of the other, wishing I wasn't so unfit. Even the very elderly folk were climbing faster than I was.

"*Tía* Veeky," piped a little voice and a small hand touched my arm. "Can we come and help you do some baking soon?"

I stopped, glad to catch my breath and looked down at two identical upturned faces.

"How lovely to see you both!" I said in surprise and gave the pair of them a hug. "How tall you've grown! Look, Joe! The Ufarte twins are back!"

"*Tío* Joe, can we go looking for those sabre toothed tigers you said live in the woods?"

"We're big now, so we know they don't really exist."

"But we could go and look, just in case."

"Of course we can!" said Joe.

"Is your whole family here?" I asked.

"Yes, Mama and Papa are up ahead."

"And our brothers are kicking their silly ball. Look, they have reached the shrine already."

"And your *tía*, Lola?"

"*Tía* Lola has gone away."

"Mama says *tía* Lola is catching fish in another country."

"And she won't be back for a very long time."

"And Fifi?" asked Joe casually.

I smiled to myself. We may have missed the Ufarte family, but Joe certainly hadn't missed being a target of Fifi's nips.

"Fifi is down below in our house."

"With our *abuela*."

Joe relaxed a little. His ankles were safe for the moment.

The twins raced away to renew other acquaintances and we carried on climbing the path to the shrine.

It had been a good day. The village was reunited and it certainly looked as though the Ufartes were back together again. All was well in El Hoyo and with the world.

But time doesn't stand still and the next month would bring many surprises, both good and bad.

LAMB STEAKS WITH HAZELNUTS AND PAPRIKA

If you are lucky enough to live in Spain where hazelnuts are plentiful, this sauce is a delicious, unusual way to use them.

Ingredients

- 8 lamb steaks
- 800g (28oz) chickpeas
- Salt
- Paprika
- Olive oil

Method (sauce)

- 4 garlic cloves, chopped
- 2 tinned *piquillo* peppers, diced
- 300g (10½oz) tomatoes, chopped
- 60g (2oz) hazelnuts, crushed

- ½ teaspoon hot smoked paprika
- 4 sprigs oregano, leaves removed and sliced
- 2 teaspoons sherry vinegar
- Olive oil

Method

- Preheat your oven to 200°C/400°F/Gas Mark 6.

- Season the lamb steaks with salt and smoked paprika then fry in a frying pan for 1 minute each side until brown.

- Drain the chickpeas, transfer the lamb to a plate then add the chickpeas to the frying pan, season and fry for 2 minutes.

- Place the chickpeas in a *cazuela* or oven dish and arrange the lamb steaks on top. Bake in the oven for 10 minutes.

- While the lamb steaks are cooking, make the sauce. Pour some olive oil in the frying pan and sauté the garlic, pepper and hazelnuts.

- Add vinegar and bring to the boil, then add tomatoes and paprika and simmer for 1 minute. Lastly add the oregano and season the mixture with pepper.

- When the lamb is done, serve on top of the chickpeas and spoon the salsa over.

- Serve with vegetables and fresh crusty bread.

30

UPS AND DOWNS

Whenever the phone shrilled very early in the morning, it was almost always Karly ringing from Australia. As she was finishing her day, we were beginning ours.

"Mum, you'll never guess what... I'm pregnant again! Indy's going to have a new baby brother or sister!"

"Oh my, oh my, oh my!"

I shrieked the news to Joe.

"Karly, are you quite sure?"

"Yes, positive. It's really, really, really early days yet, but I've done the test three times and they all showed positive."

"Oh, that's just fantastic!"

"And you know what that means? When you come over next winter, you'll be here when the baby's born! Perfect timing!"

"Have you told everybody?"

"No, you're the first. We're going to wait just a little longer in case anything goes wrong. We'll just tell close family for the moment."

When we had something to celebrate, Joe and I would often take an evening drink up to the roof terrace. Nights were still cold, but it was a pleasure to survey the village and valley and watch the stars come out. Smoke curled from our chimney and from a couple of others.

"Looks like Uncle Felix hasn't got his fire lit," I observed. "But I can see Geronimo's and Marcia's."

"And the Ufartes are in, that's good."

"So, there will be *two* babies when we go over to Australia in November."

I had to keep saying the news aloud to myself, to help me absorb it.

"And we'll have Christmas in the sun and swim on Christmas Day," remarked Joe.

We finished our drinks and went back inside our warm house, still making plans for the following winter. Nothing would stop us this time.

The next day, somebody knocked on our door. It wasn't a familiar knock. We would have recognised Marcia's walking stick tap, or Geronimo's distinctive knock. It certainly couldn't be Paco who always pounded with his fist and shouted "English!" at the same time. My heart sank. I was convinced it was

Pancho, intent on pursuing his English lessons.

But it wasn't Pancho, it was our neighbour, Paco. I'd never heard him knock so lightly and I knew immediately that something was wrong.

"Paco? ¿Qué pasa?"

This wasn't the Paco that we knew and loved. His usual exuberance had disappeared and his expression was solemn. There was no sign of the customary twinkle in his eye. He walked slowly into our house and sat heavily on one of our kitchen chairs.

"Paco? Is something the matter?"

"I thought you would want to know. Uncle Felix passed away yesterday."

"Oh no!"

"He was an old man. It was expected."

Joe and I stared at Paco in silence.

That explains why there was no smoke curling from Uncle Felix's chimney, I thought.

"That's very sad news," I said at last, as Joe poured us all a brandy. "Was he sick? How did it happen?"

"No, he was not sick. He died peacefully in his cottage. Geronimo found him. Felix was sitting in his armchair watching his big TV." A smile flickered on Paco's lips. "He was probably watching his favourite matchmaking show."

"Poor Uncle Felix," I said.

Fond memories of the old man crowded my mind.

"He never had a woman," said Paco and pulled a rueful face.

Would Uncle Felix never again sit in the shade outside Marcia's shop? Never again supervise the pruning of our vine? Would we never see him and his beloved mule passing the house, or in the distance as he tethered her on the lush mountainside to graze? A thousand memories played in my head. A lump was forming in my throat and I was finding it difficult to swallow. El Hoyo without Uncle Felix? It was unthinkable.

"What about his mule?" asked Joe, voicing the question at the forefront of my own mind.

"Geronimo has taken her. She will be fine."

But Uncle Felix's mule wasn't fine. Geronimo did his best but the mule was pining and inconsolable. As fast as he tethered her, she'd pull the stake out of the ground and trot back into the village, searching for her master. And when she didn't find him, she would stand quietly outside Marcia's shop, her head hung low, looking up only when she heard footsteps, always hoping her beloved master had returned. She stopped eating and lost weight.

"Poor old girl," I said, as I patted her head. "I wish I could bring him back to you."

The mule's large, liquid brown eyes just stared at the ground. I doubt if she even noticed me.

The month had started well with Karly and Cam's baby news, but the loss of Uncle Felix was a blow and hard for the village to bear. The funeral was a sad one and Felix was the first villager to be laid to rest in the new part of the cemetery.

※※※

Uncle Felix's death seemed to herald a string of unhappy events, both minor and major. I was already sad at the old man's passing and the fact that we hadn't travelled to Australia that winter.

We should have seen the next domestic catastrophe coming; we'd been warned after all, but I don't think anybody really believed it was going to happen. But it did.

When we arrived in Spain 10 years earlier, we were delighted that, with the correct viewing equipment, we could watch all the British terrestrial channels on TV.

Then, one day all the BBC channels simply vanished from our TV screens. One could almost hear the howls of anguish from expats across Europe and Joe's was probably the loudest.

"No BBC1 or BBC2?" asked Joe, desperately punching the buttons on the remote control, scrolling through the channels. "No BBC3? Or 4?"

NO SATELLITE SIGNAL IS BEING RECEIVED advised the message on the otherwise blank screen.

"No news? No *Match of the Day*? No golf? No rugby? No *Pointless*?"

"All gone," I sighed. "I understand they've replaced the old Astra satellite, which means UK residents will get a better picture, but the footprint is smaller. Viewers in Spain and the rest of Europe won't get anything."

"No darts, no tennis? No World Cup soccer?" Joe slumped back on the cushions in despair.

"Well, at least we have all the ITV channels," I said. "And maybe it'll force us to watch more Spanish TV, we've always meant to. It'll help improve our Spanish."

I won't reproduce Joe's reply here, it might offend. The independent channels were awash with advertisements, which Joe hated. But even he agreed that ITV was better than nothing, despite the adverts. But the loss of all his favourite sports channels didn't do his blood pressure any good.

I was already aware of Joe's high blood pressure. We discovered the problem in Bahrain but now, back in Spain, he refused to do anything about it even though the health system was excellent. However, to my relief and after constant nagging, I finally managed to steer him to a doctor to have it checked.

It was an evening appointment and Joe had the doctor's address scribbled on a piece of paper. Eventually, he located it. The surgery was on the ground floor of a large block of apartments.

He rang the bell and the building's main entrance buzzed open. He stepped inside and the door snapped shut behind him. He found himself in a large foyer with a communal table set against one wall and a fake potted plant alongside another. Four doors led to ground-floor apartments.

Before he had time to discover which was the doctor's door, the lights suddenly switched off leaving him standing in pitch darkness. The lights were the energy-saving kind and designed to switch on for a few moments when the main entrance was opened. He fumbled up and down the nearest wall, feeling for a light switch but found nothing. So he opened the main door and the lights came on again. He spotted the light switch on the wall opposite and reached it just before the lights switched off again. But the light switch didn't work.

Well, I'll just have to feel my way around, he thought.

Joe had no idea which door belonged to the doctor. He walked around the wall, feeling his way.

"Ouch!" he exclaimed as he tripped over the communal side table. And, "Oh, for goodness' sake!" when he stubbed his toe and became entangled with the large fake potted plant.

Having reached a door, he listened carefully. He could hear children's voices and a distant TV, so he was pretty sure that this wasn't the doctor's surgery.

He felt his way to the next door and laid his ear on it, listening intently. He could hear nothing, so he crouched down to peer through the key hole.

To his embarrassment the door swung open to reveal a nurse. Joe quickly straightened and stepped back.

"*Señor* Twead?" she asked.

"Yes, I was just checking to see if I had found the right place," he explained. "The lights in the hallway don't work."

"I know," she smiled. "They never have. The doctor is expecting you."

The doctor examined him thoroughly. Of course by now, Joe's blood pressure was through the roof.

"Your blood pressure is very high," said the doctor.

He made copious notes, then presented Joe with two huge plastic containers.

"What are they for?" asked Joe.

"You must collect all your urine for 24 hours. Then you must take it to the hospital for testing."

"Really? Well, I won't need both of these containers, will I?"

But he did.

On his next visit to the doctor the lights in the hallway still didn't work, but he remembered which direction to head for and fumbled his way to the correct door quite quickly. The nurse, who turned out to be the doctor's wife, let him in and the doctor examined him again.

"I have something I want you to wear," said the doctor, unpacking a box.

This time Joe had to wear a 'halter' for 24 hours. A band was wrapped around his upper arm and attached to a little machine at his waist. At half-hour intervals the machine beeped shrilly, the band inflated and his blood pressure reading was recorded.

"I have to do some shopping on my way home," said Joe.

"That is okay, you must carry on with your life as normal for 24 hours."

As Joe stood in line at the supermarket checkout, the machine beeped and his fellow customers looked around, wondering where the beeping was coming from.

"*Madre mía*," said the cashier and checked her till, convinced it was malfunctioning.

It was an uncomfortable day and a bad night for Joe. He tried hanging the machine over the bedpost but ended up tying himself in knots. It was a great relief to both of us when the 24 hours were over.

He returned to the doctor, who analysed the readings and prescribed tablets. A couple of weeks later he measured Joe's blood pressure again and was pleased with the results.

"The doctor said I need to keep taking the

tablets, but he said they are working well and my blood pressure is nearly normal."

Of course I was delighted.

※※※

One might think that our lifestyle wasn't very stressful. After all, we were retired and no longer went to work. But there was always something to sky-rocket Joe's blood pressure to dizzying heights. And sure enough, he was about to be dealt another blow.

Ten days after losing all our BBC channels, Joe switched on the TV to watch the early evening news. We'd adjusted ourselves to watching the independent channel, ITV. Joe hated the advertisements with a passion but he'd accepted them as a necessary evil and at least he could watch the British news and some sports events. Now he stared at the screen in disbelief.

NO SATELLITE SIGNAL IS BEING RECEIVED.

Joe's roar could be heard several villages away. "WHAT? Have they taken away ITV too?"

Sadly, it was true.

I was very pleased that Joe's blood pressure had been stabilised with medication. Without the tablets, I think that final blow may have sent it over the edge.

Although the loss of all our TV channels was lamentable, that paled into insignificance when compared with the next loss. Early in the morning the telephone rang again. It was Karly and her voice was small and sad.

"Mum, we've just come back from the hospital. Bad news, I'm afraid. They couldn't detect a heartbeat. The baby died."

SPANISH EASTER BISCUITS

Melt in the mouth seasonal treats. Less than 30 minutes preparation and will make about 40 biscuits depending on your cutter shape and size.

Ingredients

- 180g (6.3oz) softened butter
- 200g (7oz) caster sugar
- 2 eggs
- 1 tsp vanilla extract
- 400g (14oz) plain flour
- 1 tsp vanilla extract
- 1 tsp baking powder
- 1 tsp mixed spice
- 1 tsp ground cinnamon, plus extra for dusting
- Icing sugar for dusting

Method

- Preheat the oven to 180°C/350°F/Gas 4 and line two baking trays with baking paper.
- In a large bowl, beat together the butter and sugar until pale and fluffy.
- Beat in the eggs and the vanilla. If the mixture starts to separate, add a little flour and beat again.
- Add the dry ingredients and mix together gently until all the ingredients are incorporated and you have a soft dough.
- Take half of the mixture and roll out onto a floured surface. The dough should be between ½ and 1cm (about ¼ inch) thick. Stamp out the biscuits with a cutter.
- Place onto the baking sheet, not too close together as they will spread out a little, then bake in batches for 10-15 minutes until the biscuits are lightly golden. Cut out the second lot while the first batch is cooking.
- Remove from the oven and place biscuits onto a wire rack to cool, then dust with icing sugar.

31

EPILOGUE

It's May now and summer is already in full swing. Giant carpenter bees bumble around the garden searching for rotten wood to excavate and lay their eggs in. The exotically coloured bee-eaters have returned from wintering in Africa, filling the valley with their distinctive trills. A cuckoo is calling and I know the swallows will arrive any day now.

Our vine has sprung back into life, providing us with a canopy and a hiding place for fledglings. Tiny grapes are already forming.

Our chickens are not looking their most beautiful. They are moulting and Joe still says they look more like roadkill than hens.

Easter has come and gone in a clamour of church-bells and processions. As always, Marcia made us a delicious rice pudding, which her youngest son, now well into his forties, delivered to us. It was still warm and scented with lemon and cinnamon. When we take the plate back, we'll give her a dozen eggs.

Marcia still lives alone behind the shop with only her black cat for company. Sometimes Geronimo sits with her outside the shop, his three dogs at his feet and the black cat tucked safely under Marcia's chair or high on the windowsill. They don't talk much, but Marcia's knitting needles clack with disapproval when Geronimo swigs from his beer bottle.

Judith is fine, kept busy by her ever-growing pack of rescued dogs and cats. Mother is often seen in the passenger seat of Alejandro Senior's flashy Mercedes as they sweep off together to enjoy evenings in the city.

Alice celebrated her 95th birthday this January. My brother and sister have been to visit her, but Alice and I have yet to meet. I chat with her on the phone every two or three weeks and she often passes on new nuggets of information she has remembered about my grandmother, Anna.

Since the Ufartes returned, the Boys no longer need us to babysit. Little Emilia is growing tall and has become firm friends with the Ufarte children. The Ufarte house is always bursting with children and one more makes no difference.

We haven't seen Lola again, or her partner. She

EPILOGUE

is rarely mentioned in the village and we assume she has settled elsewhere, no doubt to wreak havoc in her own special way.

I continue to avoid Pancho the mayor. So far successfully. I have absolutely no intention of giving him English lessons.

Ever.

Evenings are warm and Grandmother Ufarte sits dozing in her armchair, placed in the street. Papa Ufarte often sits on his doorstep, like old times.

Papa Ufarte's handsome head is bowed over his guitar, concentrating on his fingers plucking at the strings. At first he strums odd notes, then gradually, the notes join together and become phrases which increase in urgency and volume. Flamenco music is infectious and soon Grandmother Ufarte's toe is tapping. Then the full-blooded flamenco floods from his fingertips, the urgent, explosive gypsy melodies filling the street.

Maribel emerges to sit beside her husband. Before long, her foot is tapping and her body begins to sway. If they have friends and relations visiting, everybody spills out into the street and the dancing begins. Sometimes the twins join in, but more often they break away to run wild with the other village kids, while their brothers play a never-ending game of soccer in the square.

Felicity still likes to sit on the kitchen

windowsill and peer inside, just like her mother Sylvia did and her grandmother, Little Tabs, years ago. If we open the window, she disappears in a flash. But with the glass between us, I guess she feels safe. Sometimes we catch a glimpse of her offspring from last year, crowding round the fish van waiting for scraps. By now they have found territories of their own to patrol in the village.

This week, Felicity surprised us. She sat tall and proud on our windowsill and playing between her front paws was a tiny black kitten. We admired the baby, which stared at us wide-eyed.

"Well, I think we can guess who the father is," I said to Joe. "It's old Black Balls ... I mean Blackie."

The next day, there was no sign of Felicity or her kitten. That is, until the evening, when I happened to look out of the window into the garden and saw her washing one black kitten while another played with her tail. A third pranced around, pouncing on nothing in particular.

"Another generation," said Joe and I knew he was also thinking of the baby in Australia that would never be born.

The good news is that it was such early days and the baby was so unformed that they could just give Karly a 'D and C', or scrape.

"It's nature's way," I said. "There must have

EPILOGUE

been a reason for her to lose the baby. Anyway, the obstetrician told her that everything looks great and there's no reason to wait to start trying again. Apparently she'll be even more fertile for the first three months after the D and C."

"We'll keep our fingers crossed."

"It's awful, I'm so sad for them, but at least it was no bigger than a grape. It could have been so much worse."

Last week we were invited next door for drinks. Paco and Carmen's house was stuffed full of people. All Paco's cousins, nieces and nephews were there and all three Alejandros and their families. Yukky pushed his way through legs, thrusting his cold, wet nose into people's hands, while Bianca sat under the table.

Little Paco is nearly nineteen now and much taller than his mother. He had his arm draped around a pretty girl and introduced her as his girlfriend. My mind backtracked ten years to when we first moved into the village and Little Paco had burst in and placed a huge, green cricket on the table. I smiled, remembering how Paco had moved like lightning, seizing the cricket in one capable hand and his son's ear in the other and had evicted both small boy and cricket into the street.

Little Paco's big sister, Sofía, sat at the table, her hands in her lap.

"English! You must have a glass of wine," said

Paco. "Here, taste this. Made with my grapes and the grapes of my good friend Alejandro. It is excellent wine."

We sipped and agreed with him.

"Beautiful taste," I said, "very clear with a wonderful rich colour."

Paco nodded. "Everybody knows I make the best wine in the village, no, the best in Andalucía and I think this is the best year yet!"

He turned away to fill other guests' glasses.

"What's all this about?" Joe whispered to me in English. "Are we celebrating something?"

I shook my head, but I had a suspicion. I caught sight of Carmen and she was smiling so broadly I thought the top of her head might come off.

Everybody was talking at once and the level of noise was high. Paco put the wine bottle down and thumped the table with his balled fist. The voices fell silent.

"We have brought you here to celebrate a great event," he roared. "I am happy to announce the engagement of my daughter Sofía and Alejandro, son of my old friend Alejandro. Please raise your glasses and drink a toast to the happy couple! Sofía, show everybody your engagement ring!"

Alejandro Junior moved through the crowd and stood behind Sofía's chair, his hands resting on her shoulders. Blushing, Sofía spread her hand on the table, revealing a diamond ring with a sparkle almost as bright as the one in her eyes.

EPILOGUE

"Pah! Hold your hand up, girl! Show everybody!" shouted Paco.

Sofía obediently lifted her hand and waved it for all to see. As glasses clinked and congratulations were shouted, I thought Carmen might burst with pride.

Sofía had finally found The One.

How Uncle Felix would have enjoyed that gathering! Never a man of many words, he would have sat quietly in the corner, watching from under his flat cap. I hoped he was watching from up above.

I often think of him. He never learned to read, write or count, but Paco said Felix instantly knew when one of his sheep or goats was missing. He was recognised as the village authority on vine pruning. Uncle Felix was the first villager we saw when we returned from the Middle East and his mule carried our suitcases down the mountain.

As for Uncle Felix's mule, well, I can see her from where I'm sitting now. The whole village was convinced she would pine away when her beloved master died. Nothing Geronimo did had any effect and the old mule hardly ate. She stood with her head hung low, utterly dejected, the bones beginning to show through her grey coat. Geronimo was at a loss what to do.

"Bring her over to my place," said Alejandro, Alejandro Senior's son. "She can live with my young horse. She might teach him some manners."

So Geronimo led her through the gates of Alejandro's property, past the three giant snarling dogs and to the smallholding at the side. The mule never lifted her head and dragged her hooves as he urged her along.

Geronimo brought her slowly up to Alejandro's young horse and then something extraordinary, something magical happened. Felix's mule lifted her head, perked up her ears and snickered. The horse whinnied softly and the two touched noses. Suddenly, the old mule stood more upright and there was a gleam of interest in her eyes.

The friendship blossomed. The old mule began to eat again and developed a spring in her step. The two became inseparable, grazing together and grooming each other.

I can see them now, standing close together high on the mountain slope, hoof-deep in wildflowers, cropping the lush green grass. As one moves on, so does the other.

Life is full of ups and downs, losses and gains. I've learned that however bad things seem, something wonderful always awaits just around the next corner.

Our plan is still to visit Australia this year, probably in November, for several months. We can't wait to see Indy and who knows, there just may be another little one on the way by then.

And as much as I love Spain and our

EPILOGUE

wonderful little village of El Hoyo, I'm finding it harder and harder to leave my family behind.

Victoria Twead
    May 2014

A REQUEST...

We authors absolutely rely on our readers' reviews. We love them even more than a glass of chilled wine on a summer's night beneath the stars.

Even more than chocolate.

If you enjoyed this book, I'd be so grateful if you left a review, even if it's simply one sentence.

THANK YOU!

SO WHAT HAPPENED NEXT?
A PREVIEW OF THE NEXT BOOK IN THE SERIES

Two Old Fools in Turmoil

When dark clouds loom, Victoria and Joe find themselves facing life-changing decisions. Happily, silver linings also abound in this, the fifth Old Fools chronicle.

A fresh new face joins the cast of well-known characters but the return of a bad penny may be more than some can handle.

What does the future hold for the Spanish village of El Hoyo and the two old fools?

Chapter 1
The Enchanted Pool

When the phone rang very late in the evening or early in the morning, it was usually my daughter, Karly, ringing from Australia.

"Hi Mum! How are you both? What's the weather like in El Hoyo?"

"Karly! Lovely to hear from you! Joe's fine and you know what Spanish summers are like, sunshine every day. How are you? How's Cam? How's my gorgeous granddaughter?"

"Indy's fine. We're all fine. Actually, we were thinking of getting a pet to join the family."

"Lovely! Like a guinea pig or rabbit?"

"Well, no…"

"Oh, a cat. Dog?"

"No…"

"What then?"

"We thought it might be nice to get a pig."

"Wow! Do you have enough space in your new garden?"

"Yes. Plenty. Pigs are very intelligent and affectionate, apparently. Anyway, this weekend we're going to visit the farm where they're for sale."

"Keep me posted! I wish Australia wasn't so far away!"

"I will. Can't wait for you both to come out to Aus this Christmas. You won't believe how Indy's grown, and I can't wait to show you our new house. We love it!"

"We can't wait either!"

♀♀♀

It was the summer of 2014 and life was almost perfect. I say 'almost' because one thing was bothering me. I couldn't talk to Joe about it. He wouldn't let me.

But for now we were soaking up the Spanish summer. We hoped to spend Christmas in Australia but that seemed a long way off.

As a child, I used to love the feeling I had on the first day of the school holidays, when I knew I had six whole weeks stretching out ahead of me. It was the same in El Hoyo in June. Hot weather was guaranteed. Barbecues would never be rained off. The Spanish sun was so big, hot and heavy that it barely managed to heave itself over the mountain range. But it did, and as the day progressed, it rolled in a giant arc across the sky until it hung high, burning all within its reach.

While the villagers hid from the sun, Joe and I drove out of the valley to a neighbouring small town where a cool, sparkling, public pool awaited us. We loved it. Only mad dogs and Englishmen go out in the midday sun so we often had the pool to ourselves until later in the afternoon.

A waterfall cascaded down the mountain slope

above the pool, fed by warm natural springs. Sometimes we saw wild goats cropping the dry grass on the crags above us. As they grazed, they stood silhouetted against the gigantic blue sky. Bright red dragonflies whizzed to and fro, often settling on the edge of the pool to rest.

To us, the pool was enchanted.

"Pah!" said Paco, our next door neighbor. "You go to that pool so much, you should get yourselves an *abono*."

Joe nodded sagely. I had no idea what an *abono* was and made a mental note to ask Mr Know-It-All later.

"Have you heard about the King of Spain?" asked Carmen, her eyes wide with disbelief. "I can hardly believe it!"

"Yes, we watched the news last night."

I didn't know a great deal about Spanish history, but I knew that Juan Carlos became King on the 22nd of November, 1975, two days after the loathed dictator, Franco, died. Juan Carlos introduced reforms and gently guided Spain back to democracy. Ordinary people like our neighbours, Paco and Carmen, adored their King who they believed to have delivered them from evil.

"¡Madre mía!" exclaimed Carmen, her double chins shaking. "When Prime Minister Rajoy called that emergency press conference, we didn't expect King Juan Carlos to step down."

"Pah!" shouted Paco. "He was a good king!

Exactly what we needed after that *bastardo* Franco."

"Paco!" chided his wife. "We have company."

"Pah, Joe and Veeky know what kind of a man Franco was. But Juan Carlos is only 76 years old, he did not need to step down!"

"It's a shock," agreed Carmen, "but perhaps it's time the young ones took over. Soon Spain will have a new king and queen in Felipe and Letizia."

Carmen was right. Less than three weeks later, Spain had a new king and queen.

"What's an *abono*, then?" I asked Joe when we were back home.

He looked at me blankly.

"You know, the thing Paco suggested we take to the pool. You nodded as though you knew exactly what it was."

"I have no idea. I guess it's some kind of inflatable or a sun lounger or something."

I sighed and settled in front of the computer. I didn't know it at the time, but the *abono* quest had just begun.

I typed *abono* into Google Translate and read the results.

"Fertiliser? Manure? Why *on earth* would Paco suggest taking fertiliser or manure to the pool?"

Joe looked blank.

"Oh, wait. There's more. It also means season ticket."

"Ah."

"Now that would make more sense. We'll ask about that."

The next day we arrived at the pool. Apart from the life guard, nobody was there.

We were familiar with all the life guards who worked at the pool. Lorenzo was our favourite and we'd already decided he should get the EPLGY, or Enchanted Pool Life Guard of the Year award. Lorenzo was almost square-shaped, and although he didn't look the athletic type, he took his job very seriously.

He never stopped working. Even if there were no swimmers or sunbathers, Lorenzo busied himself. Using his net, he skimmed off invisible floating leaves, or polished the sun loungers with a soft cloth. When children arrived, he watched them with narrowed eyes. Woe betide them if they were over-excited, too boisterous, or threatened to endanger themselves or others. Picnickers were welcomed, but firmly instructed where to find the garbage bins and where to set out their meals.

Our least favourite life guard was Alberto. Alberto was tall, handsome and bronzed by the Spanish sun. He rarely wore a shirt and his oiled six-pack and biceps gleamed. Girls stuttered when they spoke to him, and, believe me, even grandmothers found themselves staring in his direction.

We would have awarded the WEPLGY (Worst Enchanted Pool Life Guard of the Year) to Alberto without hesitation because he did almost nothing. Alberto sat on a folding chair under a parasol, tapping out texts or playing games on his mobile phone. This took all his attention, and he rarely looked up from the task. New arrivals were forced to wait at the gate until he was ready and dozens of small children might have drowned before he had even noticed.

Occasionally he would put his phone aside and stretch theatrically, thus attracting maximum female attention. He then strolled to the edge of the pool, poised and dived in like a harpoon, cutting through the water with hardly a ripple. After several lengths, he climbed out, water streaming from his muscular torso. Girls averted their eyes, trying not to stare. He would then resume his seat and take up his mobile phone again.

Alberto was on duty that day, in the loosest sense of the word.

"Ahem."

No response. Joe tried again.

"¡Buenos días!"

The game Alberto was playing on his mobile must have been enthralling. At last his eyes flicked up at us.

"Four euros," he said, resuming his game.

"Thank you," said Joe, placing the coins in a tidy little pile on the table. "Um, we were wondering if we could buy *abonos*, please."

"Not here," said Alberto. "You can buy them at the bank."

Joe and I looked at each other. *The bank? Really?*

Alberto's dark head was bowed as he tapped away at the little screen on his phone. Unwilling to continue talking to the top of his head, we walked away.

We'd been given the clue, and the second phase of the *abono* quest had begun.

"Honestly! Alberto doesn't deserve that job! How can anyone be so unhelpful?"

"Never mind," I said. "Let's not bother today, it's too hot. Tomorrow we can come earlier and go to the bank first."

We shrugged off our outer clothes and slipped gratefully into the cool waters of the pool. Bliss.

The next day, we parked the car at the far end of the town, near the bank. It was late morning and the bank was busy with queues at every counter. My heart sank, and I remembered why I avoided shopping with Joe at all costs.

Running errands and getting groceries was Joe's task. Curious friends often asked me why I didn't accompany him, and the answer came easily. I didn't go with him because I valued my sanity. In fact, I'd rather have my brains pulled out through my nose than go shopping with Joe.

Nobody *enjoys* queuing, although most of us accept it as a necessary evil. However, queuing and Joe are like cats and water; he *detests* it. At first he just grumbles loudly, and scratches himself, which is bad enough. If things don't improve, he will begin to heckle, making me shrivel with embarrassment as people turn to stare. It amazes me that no stores have banned him from entering their premises.

"I'll sort this, why don't you wait outside?" I suggest sweetly, but he ignores me, preferring to stand with me and complain at the top of his voice.

I have to admit that I prefer the polite British attitude to queuing. You know exactly where you are, who is in front and who is behind. This concept is usually ignored in Spain and the person with the sharpest elbows gets served first.

Our local chemist, or *farmacia*, had recently adopted the ticket system. Simple, take a ticket from the machine and wait for your number to show on the screen. Even Joe was pleased.

"How did you get on at the chemist?" I once asked, when Joe returned from a shopping trip.

"It was frightful, you won't believe what happened."

I groaned. What had annoyed him this time?

"Go on, what happened?"

"I pulled ticket #63, and when it was my turn, this dreadful old goat pushed in front of me. I jumped forward, showed her and the assistant my ticket, but the old goat still got served before me! Can you believe it? So I stood back and waited. By the time she's finished, #64 is being called and *another* old goat barges past me."

"Oh dear."

"This one flashes me her #64 ticket, and points to the screen showing #64, so the assistant serves her!"

"So what did you do?"

"Do? DO? I exploded!"

What a surprise.

"I went up and down the queue and showed everybody my ticket and told them what I thought of their queuing system. When the number changed again, I marched up to the counter, but so does another customer! The assistant looked at both of us, from one to the other."

I winced, imagining the scene.

"Everybody is watching now. I waved my ticket at the crowd, pointing at the number: ticket #63. The assistant looks again at the screen, and the other man's ticket. Then she raised her eyebrows, not sure who to serve. So she looked at the other waiting customers in question. "Who's next?" she asks."

"And?"

"All the other customers swung around. "Serve him! Serve him!" they said, pointing at me, knowing I would erupt again."

I had to laugh at the story, but I was very glad I hadn't been there.

No, Joe is not at his best shopping, or waiting

in queues, but he behaved himself quite well as we made our way closer to the bank teller that day. When it was our turn, I did the talking.

"Good day," I said, in Spanish. "We would like to buy two *abonos* for the public swimming pool, please."

The girl behind the counter smiled and ignored my Spanish.

"Good morning! I speak English very nice."

"Oh, thank you!" I said brightly. "We'd like two season tickets for the public swimming pool, please."

"I have no problem."

"Oh, that's good news. You sell *abonos* here at the bank?"

"Yes. How much you want pay?"

"Pardon?"

"You must say to me how much you want pay."

Was this a game? A strange Spanish tradition? Was she trying to catch me out?

"But we don't know! We don't know how much a season ticket costs. Don't *you* know how much it is?"

Joe's foot was starting to tap the floor dangerously. Other bank customers were beginning to stare.

"No, I do not know how much euros. You must go and find out, then come back and say me and give me money."

"But who will know? Where do we go?"

"This is like some stupid treasure hunt," growled Joe at my side. "Let's go and find a gypsy. I'm sure she'll tell us if we cross her palm with silver."

Read more in *Two Old Fools in Turmoil*

THE OLD FOOLS SERIES
SEVEN OLD FOOLS BOOKS, PLUS TWO YOUNG FOOL PREQUELS, A COOKBOOK AND STILL COUNTING!

Book #1 Chickens, Mules and Two Old Fools
If Joe and Vicky had known what relocating to a tiny Spanish mountain village would REALLY be like, they might have hesitated...

Book #2 Two Old Fools - Olé!
Vicky and Joe have finished fixing up their house and look forward to peaceful days enjoying their retirement. Then the fish van arrives, and instead of delivering fresh fish, disgorges the Ufarte family.

Book #3 Two Old Fools on a Camel

Reluctantly, Vicky and Joe leave Spain to work for a year in the Middle East. Incredibly, the Arab revolution erupted, throwing them into violent events that made world headlines.
New York Times bestseller three times

Book #4 Two Old Fools in Spain Again

Life refuses to stand still in tiny El Hoyo. Lola Ufarte's behaviour surprises nobody, but when a millionaire becomes a neighbour, the village turns into a battleground.

Book #5 Two Old Fools in Turmoil

When dark, sinister clouds loom, Victoria and Joe find themselves facing life-changing decisions. Happily, silver linings also abound. A fresh new face joins the cast of well-known characters but the return of a bad penny may be more than some can handle.

Book #6 **Two Old Fools Down Under**
When Vicky and Joe wave goodbye to their beloved Spanish village, they face their future in Australia with some trepidation. Now they must build a new life amongst strangers, snakes and spiders the size of saucers. Accompanied by their enthusiastic new puppy, Lola, adventures abound, both heartwarming and terrifying.

Book #7 **Two Old Fools Fair Dinkum (coming)**
Subscribe to the Old Fools Updates for advance news, free books and recipes. https://www.victoriatwead.com/free-stuff/

Two Old Fools in the Kitchen, Part 1 (Cookbook)
The *Old Fools' Kitchen* cookbooks were created in response to frequent requests from readers of the *Old Fools series* asking to see all the recipes collected together in one place.

One Young Fool in Dorset (PREQUEL)
This light and charming story is the delightful prequel to Victoria Twead's Old Fools series. Her childhood memories are vividly portrayed, leaving the reader chuckling and enjoying a warm sense of comfortable nostalgia.

One Young Fool in South Africa (PREQUEL)
Who is Joe Twead? What happened before Joe met Victoria and they moved to a crazy Spanish mountain village? Joe vividly paints his childhood memories despite constant heckling from Victoria at his elbow.

THE SIXPENNY CROSS SERIES
SHORT FICTION, INSPIRED BY LIFE

A is for Abigail

Abigail Martin has everything: beauty, money, a loving husband, and a fabulous house in the village of Sixpenny Cross. But Abigail is denied the one thing she craves... A baby.

B is for Bella

When two babies are born within weeks of each other in the village of Sixpenny Cross, one would expect the pair to become friends as they grow up. But nothing could be further from the truth.

C is for the Captain

Everyone knows ageing bachelors, the Captain and Sixpence, are inseparable. But when new barmaid, Babs, begins work at the Dew Drop Inn, will she enhance their twilight years, or will the consequences be catastrophic?

D is for Dexter (coming soon)

Subscribe to the Old Fools Updates for advance news, free books and recipes. https://www.victoriatwead.com/free-stuff/

MORE BOOKS BY VICTORIA TWEAD...

Dear Fran, Love Dulcie (letters collated by Victoria Twead)

An unforgettable glimpse of life and death in the hills and hollows of bygone Australia through the letters of two newly-weds.

How to Write a Bestselling Memoir

How does one write, publish and promote a memoir? How does one become a bestselling author?

Morgan and the Martians - A COMEDY PLAY FOR KIDS

Morgan is a bad boy. A VERY bad boy. When a bunch of Martians gives him a Shimmer Suit that makes him invisible, he wastes no time in wearing it to school and creating havoc. Well, wouldn't you?

Two Old Fools in the Kitchen, Part 1 (COOKBOOK)

The *Old Fools' Kitchen* cookbooks were created in response to frequent requests from readers of the *Old Fools series* asking to see all the recipes collected together in one place.

ABOUT THE AUTHOR

Victoria Twead is the New York Times bestselling author of *Chickens, Mules and Two Old Fools* and the subsequent books in the Old Fools series.

After living in a remote mountain village in Spain for eleven years, and owning probably the most dangerous cockerel in Europe, Victoria and Joe retired to Australia.

Another joyous life-chapter has begun.

For photographs and additional unpublished material to accompany this book, download the **Free Photo Book** from
www.victoriatwead.com/free-stuff

CONTACTS AND LINKS
CONNECT WITH VICTORIA

Email: TopHen@VictoriaTwead.com (emails welcome)

Website: www.VictoriaTwead.com

Old Fools' Updates Signup: www.VictoriaTwead.com

This includes the latest Old Fools' news, free books, book recommendations, and recipe. Guaranteed spam-free and sent out every few months.

Free Stuff: http://www.victoriatwead.com/Free-Stuff/

Facebook: https://www.facebook.com/VictoriaTwead (friend requests welcome)

Instagram: @victoria.twead

Twitter: @VictoriaTwead

Publish with Ant Press: www.antpress.org

We Love Memoirs

Join me and other memoir authors and readers in the We Love Memoirs Facebook group, the friendliest group on Facebook.

www.facebook.com/groups/welovememoirs/

ACKNOWLEDGEMENTS

Gayle and **Iain Macdonald** for their constant support along the way. I have shamelessly plundered their knowledge of Spanish cuisine and recipes.

Carrie Compton from Missouri, who was one of my very first 'fans' and whose loyalty and generosity helped me enormously through the launching of *Chickens* and the writing of *Olé!*

Justin Aldridge and the members of *EyeOnSpain.com*, who gave me so much encouragement when *'Chickens'* was launched.

Our amazing friends, the Gin Twins, **Sue and Juliet**. May they long continue to visit us in El Hoyo. The gin bottle will always await their arrival, along with chilled tonic and ice-cubes.

My son **Shealan** (my computer guru) who has always taken an interest in my small successes.

My daughter **Karly** for allowing her stories and photographs to be used, (yet again), and for her constant encouragement. And thanks to **Cam, Di** and **Barry** for embracing Karly into their family, allowing me to stop worrying about her being so far away.

My wonderful friends **Tweek** and **Al** and their daughters **Emma, Beth** and **Meg** for always being in the background rooting for me.

Hanna Uehre, one of the sweetest, most

thoughtful people I have ever met on the Internet. Twitter name @Travelmaus.

If I have made mistakes in any of the recipes, please forgive me. I am no chef or mathematician. Similarly, please overlook any Spanish language errors; I still have much to learn.

This memoir reflects my recollections of experiences over a period of time. In order to preserve the anonymity of the wonderful people I write about, some names have been changed, including the name of the village. Certain individuals are composites and dialogue and events have been drawn from memory and, in some cases, compressed to facilitate a natural narrative. —VT

MORE ANT PRESS BOOKS
AWESOME AUTHORS ~ AWESOME BOOKS

If you enjoyed this book, you may also enjoy these other Ant Press memoir authors. All titles are available in ebook, paperback, hardback and large print editions from **Amazon**.

These two booksellers offer FREE delivery worldwide.
Blackwells.co.uk and **Wordery.com**

More Stores
Waterstones (Europe delivery), **Booktopia** (Australia), **Barnes & Noble** (USA), and all good bookstores.

VICTORIA TWEAD
New York Times bestselling author
The Old Fools series

1. Chickens, Mules and Two Old Fools
2. Two Old Fools ~ Olé!
3. Two Old Fools on a Camel
4. Two Old Fools in Spain Again
5. Two Old Fools in Turmoil

6. Two Old Fools Down Under
7. Two Old Fools Fair Dinkum
8. One Young Fool in Dorset (Prequel)
9. One Young Fool in South Africa (Prequel)

Dear Fran, Love Dulcie: Life and Death in the Hills and Hollows of Bygone Australia

PETER BARBER
**Award-winning bestselling author
The Parthenon series**

1. A Parthenon on our Roof
2. A Parthenon in Pefki
3. A Parthenon on our Roof Rack

Musings from a Greek Village

BETH HASLAM
The Fat Dogs series

Fat Dogs and French Estates ~ Part I
Fat Dogs and French Estates ~ Part II
Fat Dogs and French Estates ~ Part III
Fat Dogs and French Estates ~ Part IV
Fat Dogs and French Estates ~ Part V
Fat Dogs and Welsh Estates ~ The Prequel

DIANE ELLIOTT
Lady Goatherder series

Butting Heads in Spain: Lady Goatherder 1
El Maestro: Lady Goatherder 2 (to follow)

EJ BAUER
The Someday Travels series

1. From Moulin Rouge to Gaudi's City
2. From Gaudi's City to Granada's Red Palace
3. From an Umbrian Farmhouse to Como's Quiet Shores

NICK ALBERT
Fresh Eggs and Dog Beds series

Fresh Eggs and Dog Beds: Living the Dream in Rural Ireland
Fresh Eggs and Dog Beds 2: Still Living the Dream in Rural Ireland
Fresh Eggs and Dog Beds 3: More Living the Dream in Rural Ireland
Fresh Eggs and Dog Beds 4: More Living the Dream in Rural Ireland

For more information about stockists, Ant Press titles or how to publish with Ant Press, please visit our website or contact us by email.

WEBSITE: www.antpress.org

EMAIL: admin@antpress.org

FACEBOOK: https://www.facebook.com/AntPress/

INSTAGRAM: https://instagram.com/publishwithantpress

PUBLISH WITH ANT PRESS
AWESOME AUTHORS - AWESOME BOOKS

This book was formatted, produced and published by Ant Press.

Can we help you publish your book?

Website: www.antpress.org
Email: admin@antpress.com

Facebook: www.facebook.com/AntPress
Instagram: www.instagram.com/publishwithantpress
Twitter: www.twitter.com/Ant_Press

We publish beautiful, bestselling books.

www.ingramcontent.com/pod-product-compliance
Lightning Source LLC
Chambersburg PA
CBHW021137080526
44588CB00008B/101